HOUSES IN GRAECO-ROMAN EGYPT

ARENAS FOR RITUAL ACTIVITY

Youssri Ezzat Hussein Abdelwahed

ARCHAEOPRESS ARCHAEOLOGY

Archaeopress Publishing Ltd
Gordon House
276 Banbury Road
Oxford OX2 7ED

www.archaeopress.com

ISBN 978 1 78491 437 0
ISBN 978 1 78491 438 7 (e-Pdf)

© Archaeopress and Y E H Abdelwahed 2016

Cover: Serenos and his family at a meal, accompanied by a flautist, and the domestic shrine with holes for holding lamps in House C119 at Karanis, Kelsey Museum Archives 812.

Printed and bound in Great Britain by
Marston Book Services Ltd, Oxfordshire

All rights reserved. No part of this book may be reproduced, in any form or by any means, electronic, mechanical, photocopying or otherwise, without the prior written permission of the copyright owners.

This book is available direct from Archaeopress or from our website www.archaeopress.com

Contents

List of Figures iii
Acknowledgement v
Note to the Reader vii

Chapter I: The Internal Division of Houses 1
    I.1. The *aithrion*-house 1
    I.2. The *oikia dipurgia* (two-towered house) 3
    I.3. Rural Houses 5
    I.4. Conclusion 6

Chapter II: The Domestic Pylon 7
    II.1. Representations of Domestic Pylons in the Pharaonic Period 7
    II.2. Entranceways in Greek Papyri 10
    II.3. Other Domestic Entranceways 11
    II.4. The Architectural Layout of the Domestic Pylon 13
    II.5. The Use of the Domestic Pylon 14
    II.6. Conclusion 15

Chapter III: Ritual Activities Enacted Before the Front Door of Houses 16
    III.1. The Front Door of Houses 16
    III.2. The Sacrifice of Fish on 9 Thoth (Julian: 7/8 September) 17
    III.3. The Sacrifice of Pigs on 15 Pachon (Julian: 10 May) 21
    III.4. Conclusion 25

Chapter IV: The Illumination of Lamps (*Lychnocaia*) for Athena-Neith on 13 Epeiph (Julian: 24 June) 26
    IV.1. The Festival of Lamps in Herodotus' *Histories* 26
    IV.2. Lamps in Ancient Egyptian Religion and Magic 27
    IV.3. Evidence for the Illumination of Lamps for Athena-Neith in Graeco-Roman Egypt 30
    IV.4. The Goddess Athena-Neith 31
    IV.5. The Symbolism of the Illumination of Lamps 34
    IV.6. The Illumination of Lamps: An Ethnic Perspective 35
    IV.7. Conclusion: 38

Chapter V: The House as Social Space 39
    V.1. Dining in the House 39
    V.2. Birthdays 40
    V.3. The Mallokouria 42
    V.4. The Epikrisis 43
    V.5. Marriage 44
    V.6. Conclusion 45

Chapter VI: The House as Religious Space 46
    VI.1. Domestic shrines 46
    VI.2. Wall Paintings and Figurines 47
    VI.3. Conclusion 56

Chapter VII: The House as Funerary Space 57
    VII.1. Mourning rituals for Dead Animals: the Case of Dogs 57
        VII.1.1. Animal Cult in Ancient Egypt 57
        VII.1.2. The Dog in the Myth of Isis and Osiris 59
        VII.1.3. Other Capabilities of Dogs 61
        VII.1.4. Dogs in the Dynastic Period 63
        VII.1.5. Dogs in the Graeco-Roman Period 64
            VII.1.5.1. Anubis/Hermes (Hermanubis) 64
            VII.1.5.2. The "Dog-headed One" in Greek Papyri 64
            VII.1.5.3. Anubis and the Lunar Disc of Osiris in Birth-houses (*mammises*) of Egyptian Temples 66

- VII.1.5.4. Mourning Rituals for Dead Dogs in Houses 67
- VII.1.6. Mummification and Burial in Sacred Hypogea 67
- VII.2. Mourning Rituals for Dead Humans 70
  - VII.2.1. The Osirian Myth and Burial Rituals 70
  - VII.2.2. Burial as Necessity and Obligation 71
  - VII.2.3. The Egyptian Mode of Burial 72
    - VII.2.3.1. The Ekphora 72
    - VII.2.3.2. The Peristolē 75
    - VII.2.3.3. The Kēdeia 77
    - VII.2.3.4. The Apostolē and Beyond 81
    - VII.2.3.5. The Tribunal 82
    - VII.2.3.6. The Opening of the Mouth Ritual 82
    - VII.2.3.7. The Funerary Banquet 82
- VII.3. Conclusion 84

General conclusion 85

Appendix 1: Catalogue of Roman-period Houses 86
- 1. Houses in the Fayum, the Arsinoite: 86
  - 1.1. A sample of houses at Karanis (Kom Aushim): 86
    - 1.1.1. House C42 86
    - 1.1.2. House C43 86
    - 1.1.3. House C45 86
    - 1.1.4. House C50/51 86
    - 1.1.5. House C56 87
    - 1.1.6. House C57 87
    - 1.1.7. House C59 87
    - 1.1.8. House C60 87
    - 1.1.9. House C62 87
    - 1.1.10. House C68 87
    - 1.1.11. House C71 88
    - 1.1.12. House C119 88
  - 1.2. Houses at Soknopaiou Nesos (Dimê): 88
    - 1.2.1. House II 201 88
    - 1.2.2. Houses II 202, II 203 and II 204 88
    - 1.2.3. Houses on the West Area 89
  - 1.3. Houses at Bacchias (Kom Umm el-Atl): 89
  - 1.4. Houses at Philadelphia (Kom el-Kharab el-Kebir): 89
  - 1.5. Houses at Tebtunis (Kom Umm el-Boreigat): 89
    - 1.5.1. House No. 1100 89
    - 1.5.2. House No. 3000 89
    - 1.5.3. House No. 3200 89
  - 1.6. Houses at Kom Medinet Ghoran: 90
  - 1.7. Houses at Narmuthis (Kom Medinet Maadi): 90
  - 1.8. Houses at Theadelphia (Kharabit Ihrit): 90
  - 1.9. Houses at Euhemeria (Qasr el-Banat): 90
  - 1.10. Houses at Dionysias (Qasr Qarun): 90
- 2. Houses in the Dakhla Oasis, the Thebaid: 91
  - 2.1. Houses at Kellis (Ismant El-Kharab): 91
    - 2.1.1. Houses Nos. 1, 2, and 3 91
    - 2.1.2. House No. B/3/1 91
  - 2.2. Houses at Trimithis (Amheida): 91
    - 2.2.1. The House of Serenos 91
    - 2.2.2. The House of Area 1 92

Bibliography 93

List of Figures

Figure 1. The ground plan of the house drawn in *P.Oxy*. XXIII.2406, the second century AD. 2

Figure 2. Model of a house, Graeco-Roman period, British Museum, No. 2462. 3

Figure 3. Model of a house, Graeco-Roman period, Cairo Museum. 4

Figure 4. Tower-houses at Karanis. 5

Figure 5. Alston's Reconstruction of a Pharaonic house with two towers attached to the frontage. 5

Figure 6. An oven in the courtyard of a house at Karanis. 6

Figure 7. An olive press in the courtyard of a house at Karanis. 6

Figure 8. The pylon of the Ptolemaic temple of Horus at Edfu. 8

Figure 9. The two-towered pylon of the royal palace in the tomb of Meryra at Tell El-Amarna. 8

Figure 10. The double-towered pylon of a palace in the Tomb of Meryra at Tell El-Amarna. 9

Figure 11. Representation of an Egyptian villa in the tomb of Sennefer (TT 96). 9

Figure 12. Reconstruction of an Egyptian villa in the tomb of Sennefer (TT 96). 9

Figure 13. The propylon of the theatre at Antinoopolis in 1799. 10

Figure 14. The Triumphal Arch at Antinoopolis in 1799. 10

Figure 15. The propylon of the gymnasium at Cyrene. 11

Figure 16. The front door of House C68 at Karanis. 16

Figure 17. The front door of House C50 in Karanis. 16

Figure 18. The bolt-case of the front door of House C50 in Karanis. 17

Figure 19. The entry and exit of a house at Karanis. 19

Figure 20. A street in Karanis. 20

Figure 21. The sacrifice of a hippopotamus on the inner ambulatory of Edfu temple. 23

Figure 22. Gardiner's sign R7. 27

Figure 23. An Egyptian floating wick saucer lamp found at Kom Hadid locus 7613. 27

Figure 24. Petosiris accompanied by a hieroglyphic inscription alluding to the Khoiak mysteries of Osiris. 29

Figure 25. A terracotta Osiriform lamp found in House 11 at Karanis, Kelsey Museum 6478. 29

Figure 26. An Osiriform bronze lamp at the Museum of Hatay. 30

Figure 27. Neith with her martial emblems, the bow and the arrows. 31

Figure 28. The ensign of the Saite nome. 31

Figure 29. Fully armed Athena on a third century AD Roman lamp. 32

Figure 30. Lantern of helmeted Athena inside a Greek temple in the Museum of Alexandria. 33

Figure 31. Lantern of Athena-Neith inside an Egyptian temple in the Louvre Museum. 33

Figure 32. The domestic shrine with holes for holding lamps in House C119 at Karanis, Kelsey Museum Archives 812. 37

Figure 33. The Thracian Heron and Isis suckling Harpocrates in House B50 at Karanis, Kelsey Museum Archive 5.2159. 37

Figure 34. A cupboard niche in a house at Karanis. 46

Figure 35. The domestic shrine in room B of House C60 at Karanis. 46

Figure 36. The domestic shrine in house C71 at Karanis. 47

Figure 37. Harpokrates and Tithoes on the south wall of alcove CF4 of House C65 at Karanis. 48

Figure 38. Polis and Olympian deities watch the adultery of Aphrodite and Ares. 50

Figure 39. Serenos and his family at a meal, accompanied by a flautist. 50

Figure 40. Swaddled doll-figurine, 8 × 3 cm, Kelsey Museum, 26413. 51

Figure 41. Terracotta figure of Isis-Hathor or Isis-Aphrodite, c. 300-100 BC, British Museum, 1888, 0601.110. 53

Figure 42. Terracotta figure of female tambour player, c. AD 1-200. 53

Figure 43. Pottery vessel marked 'eulogia', c. AD 100-300, British Museum, OA.9431. 55

Figure 44. A dog beneath its master's chair on a Ptolemaic situla in the Cleveland Museum of Art. 60

Figure 45. A relief of the 5th Dynasty shows a dog catching a gazelle by the leg, while another attacks a hyena from the neck, the Metropolitan Museum of New York. 61

Figure 46. A sketch of the 20th Dynasty shows a Pharaoh spearing a lion with the help of his dog, the Metropolitan Museum of New York. 62

Figure 47. A Ptolemaic canine-headed anthropomorphic statuette of Anubis in the Metropolitan Museum of New York. 65

Figure 48. A canine terracotta mask of Anubis. 65

Figure 49. Dogs buried with children at Qasr Allam in the Bahariya oasis. 66

Figure 50. The falcon/Horus and the dog/Anubis on a funerary stelea from Terenouthis (Kom Abu Bellou). 69

Figure 51. An *ḥ* | *Ḳr n=Rq* stela. 79

Figure 52. An anthropomorphic bust belonging to a domestic cult of the dead. 79

Figure 53. A stela from Abydos showing a woman involved in worshipping an ancestral bust. 79

Figure 54. The first century AD mummy-cupboard of Padikhons from Abusir el-Melek. 80

Figure 55. The Opening of the Mouth ritual on the papyrus of Nesitanebisheru, the daughter of Pinedjem II, who died around 930 BC. 83

Acknowledgement

The idea of this book comes from the third chapter of my doctoral dissertation at the Department of Classics & Ancient History, the University of Durham, which is already published as Abdelwahed, Y. 2015. *Egyptian Cultural Identity in the Architecture of Roman Egypt (30 BC-AD 325)*, Archaeopress Roman Archaeology 6, Oxford. In the third chapter of my published dissertation, I have considered the relationship between layers of identity assertion and ritual practices in the domestic space. The research on rituals performed within the domestic property revealed that further research on the ritual side of houses is preferable. A separate monograph on the topic will be welcomed by scholars working on the archaeology and rituals of post-Pharaonic Egypt. This monograph is the outcome of a post-doctoral fellowship funded by the Mission Sector, Ministry of Higher Education, Egypt, for which I like to express my utmost gratitude. Special word of thanks must go to Prof. Annalisa Marzano, Head of Classics Department, University of Reading, and Dr. Rachel Mairs, Lecturer in Classics of the same institution for accepting my request to conduct the research at their respected university.

Note to the Reader

For citation of Greek papyri, I adhere to the *Checklist of Editions of Greek, Latin, Demotic and Coptic Papyri, Ostraca and Tablets*, which is available at http://scriptorium.lib.duke.edu/papyrus/texts/clist.html. For ancient classical works, I follow the conventions of the Oxford Classical Dictionary, 4th edition, which is available at http://classics.oxfordre.com/staticfiles/images/ORECLA/OCD.ABBREVIATIONS.pdf. For citation of periodicals, I follow *The Egyptian Journal of Archaeology*, available at http://www.ees.ac.uk/publications/journal-egyptian-archaeology.html and *The American Journal of Archaeology*, available at http://www.ajaonline.org/editorial/175.

Chapter I
The Internal Division of Houses

Any consideration of houses in the Graeco-Roman period should start with the question of architectural layout and internal organization. Before attempting to reconstruct the architectural and spatial elements of houses in Graeco-Roman Egypt, we should first consider the materials from which they were built. In contrast with temples and tombs which were enormous and constructed out of stone,[1] houses were often built in smaller scale and from mud-brick.[2] However, wooden beams, posts, frames, windows, and doors as well as stone lintels were also used.[3] As representations of houses in tombs suggest, it was common in the Pharaonic period for wealthy Egyptians to inscribe their names and titles in prominent positions on or by the main doorway of their houses, advertising the owner's social status.[4] In Herodotus's time, the Egyptians used to sleep on the roofs of their tower houses (*purgoi*), a practice which the historian ascribes to their desire to escape mosquitoes that were unable to fly so high in the wind.[5] In ancient Egyptian literature, the house was regarded as a place of peace and rest as well as safety for the entire family,[6] and this notion continued into the Graeco-Roman period.[7] Not infrequently, travellers asked the general of the night guards to keep an eye on their households and houses.[8]

Diodorus provides an insight into the Egyptian conception of domestic space:

> While they [the Egyptians] give the name of lodgings (καταλύσεις) to the houses (οἰκήσεις), thus intimating that we dwell in them but a brief time, they call the tombs of the dead eternal homes (ἀιδίους οἴκους), since the dead spend endless eternity in Hades (the underworld). Consequently, they give less thought to the furnishings of their houses, but on the manner of their burials they do not abstain from any excess of zeal.[9]

At first glance, the passage reveals a remarkable similarity to Roman funerary inscriptions which refer to the earthly house (*aedes*) as an ephemeral lodging (*hospitium*) and to the tomb (*monumentum* or *sepulchrum*) as an eternal home (*aeterna domus*).[10] As in many other cultures, the Roman living house was considered to have less permanence than the house of the dead.[11] The Roman tomb, on the other hand, was regarded as an eternal abode, a function confirmed by its monumental structure, imperial Latin literature, and formulaic inscriptions.[12]

The custom reported by Diodorus may to some extent reflect Graeco-Roman conceptions of domestic and funerary space. But funerary papyri of Graeco-Roman Egypt, written mostly in demotic, confirm that tombs continued to be used and conceived as homes of the dead.[13] By serving as an ephemeral resting-place of mummies, houses appear to have shared this funerary function, even if temporary.[14] Being a place of impermanent stay for occupants does not mean that inhabitants in Graeco-Roman Egypt always gave less attention to either the construction or adornment of houses, which were sometimes equipped with good furniture that might reflect an extravagant life.[15] In most cases, however, houses were equipped with furnishings that provided the inhabitants with the basic necessities of life.

The lack of archaeological evidence for urban housing makes it hard to form a clear picture of the architectural layout and internal organisation and thus to understand their inhabitants. Papyri from urban and rural sites and archaeological remains of village houses together partly compensate for these deficiencies.

I.1. The *aithrion*-house

P.Oxy. XXIII.2406 sheds light on the αἴθριον or court-house, which is frequently attested in urban and rural contexts (Figure 1), and helps to reconstruct the internal arrangement of domestic space in Graeco-Roman Egypt.[16]

According to Eric Turner, the papyrus dates to the second century and shows the ground plan of a house. The architectural layout of the house, in Turner's view, consists of a single entrance door (on the left), giving access to three successive courtyards, rather than rooms. The first of them was called πυλ(ών), the second as ἀτρεῖον and the third was left undesignated. In the second courtyard there is a door named θύρα καταγ(αίου) leading down

---

[1] For temples: Arnold 1999. For tombs: Venit 2002a.
[2] Luckhard 1914, 46-7; Hobson 1985, 214.
[3] Husselman 1979, 33-48.
[4] Perrot and Chipiez 1882, 457.
[5] Hdt. 2.95. But the real reason may have been a wish to enjoy the fresher air, as in Egypt today.
[6] On a review of this literature: Parlebas 1977.
[7] Alston 2001, 85.
[8] *P.Oxy.* VI.933.24-26.
[9] Diod. Sic. 1.51.2.
[10] On a particular, explicit example of Roman funerary inscriptions: *CIL* VI.27788 = *CLE* 1488 = Borg et al 2005, 144, no. 91.
[11] Wallace-Hadrill 2008, 39-78.
[12] For a discussion of Latin funerary texts: Thomas 2007, 183-4.
[13] E.g. Smith 2009.
[14] Willeitner 2004.
[15] On the furnishings of houses in Roman Egypt: Gazda 1983, 24-30.
[16] Parsons 2007, 18. *P.Oxy.* XXIII.2406 contains only a drawing of the ground plan of a house. See also, Husson 1983, 29-36.

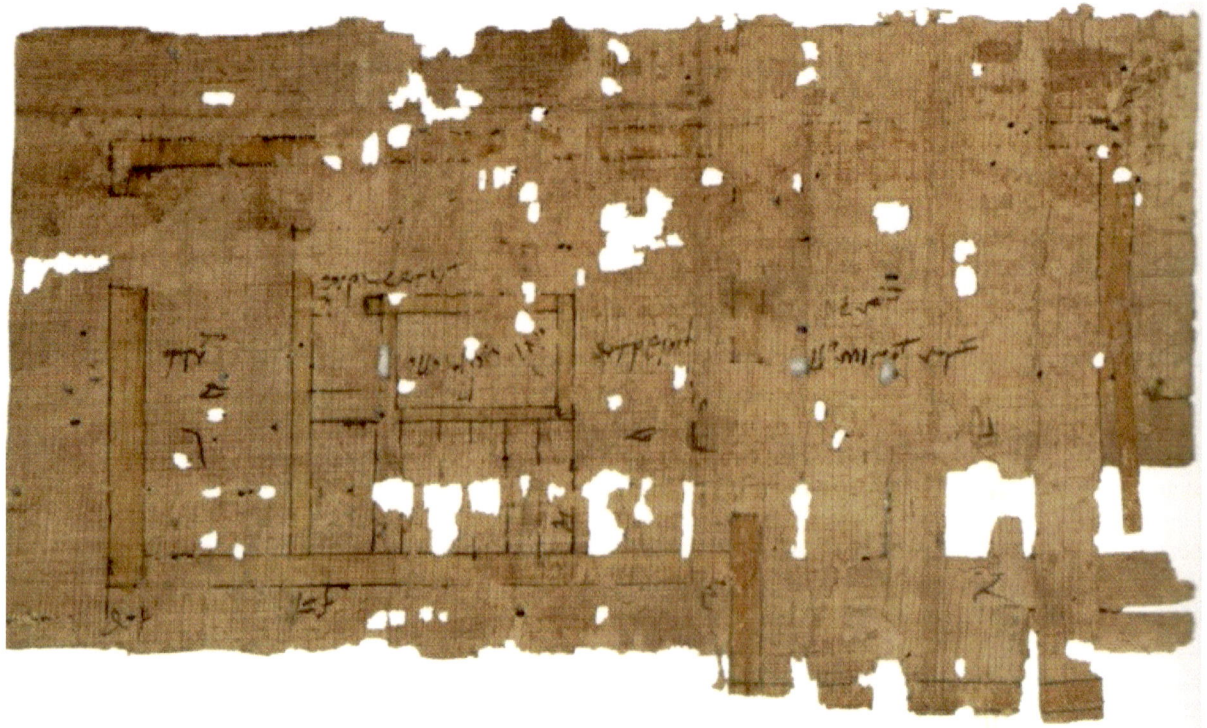

FIGURE 1. THE GROUND PLAN OF THE HOUSE DRAWN IN *P.OXY*. XXIII.2406, THE SECOND CENTURY AD.

to a cellar.[17] Since pylon has never been attested in papyri to mean a courtyard, Turner's interpretation of the pylon as a court is untenable.[18]

Herwig Maehler, on the other hand, argued that the house consists of a tower-like gateway (πυλών), giving access to a central courtyard open to the sky in the form of an *aithrion* (αἴθριον), rather than an *atrium*. In the middle of the *atreion* there is a structure named *obolisk(os)* and a flight of steps leading up to the upper stories and a door leading down to a cellar. Finally, the central courtyard leads directly to an unnamed court or yard, probably an *aule*.[19] The plan of this house is similar to that of House 3 at Kellis, which consists of an entrance hall leading to two successive courts acting respectively as an *aithrion* and an *aule* (Appendix 1).

As for the size of the house, Turner noticed that the 'measurements given on the plan, if they are measurements, cannot be reconciled with each other or interpreted in absolute terms as dimensions of the house'.[20] For example, δ = 4 under πυλ(ών) could be applied to the distance between its parallel walls, β = 2 under ὀβολίσκ(ος) could be applied to the distance between the two horizontal limits, and δ = 4 upside down under ἀτρεῖον could be taken to be the same unit and applied to the distance from the wall to the exit door leading to the undesignated court. However, it is not a unit that will fit the figure εγ´ = 5⅓ of the horizontal measurements of the undesignated room, or the two γ's (one in the πυλ(ών) and one by the exit door from the ἀτρεῖον). Although the Egyptian cubit (52.5 cm) was still in use in the Roman period as a unit of measurement for traditional monuments,[21] the figures are not meant to be measured against the Egyptian cubit, or the Roman cubit (44.4 cm), particularly when compared to house measurements in other papyri.[22]

Despite the incompatibility of measurements and the inadequacy of the plan, which is clear from the absence of room-divisions, the plan throws light on the internal organization of domestic space in Graeco-Roman Egypt. The πυλ(ών) is the first architectural structure in the house.[23] The annotated drawing in *P.Oxy.* XXIII.2406 refers to the central spatial feature next to the *obolisk(os)* as ἀτρεῖον. However, since the ἀτρεῖον has never been attested elsewhere in Egyptian domestic architecture,[24] and only occurs in papyri in connection with public and religious buildings,[25] it is probable that the central court of the house took the form of an *aithrion* (αἴθριον), rather than an *atrium*. The absence of the *impluvium*, which is

---

[17] For the edition of *P.Oxy.* XXIV.2406: Turner 1957.
[18] Husson 1983, 243-46.
[19] Maehler 1983, 136.
[20] Turner 1957, 145.
[21] Arnold 1999, 229.
[22] Cf. *P.Lond.* I.50.7 in which a house measures 21 × 13 cubits and its *aule* measures 4 × 13 cubits.
[23] For a full discussion of the domestic pylon, see chapter two.
[24] The ἀτρεῖον is not included in Husson's monograph on domestic vocabulary in Egypt.
[25] *P.Fouad* I.21.4 (63): ἐν τῷ μεγάλῳ ἀτρίωι, ἐπὶ βήματος; *SB* V.8247.15-16 (63-4); *P.Yale Inv.* 1528; *IGR* I.1048, 1175 (the representation of Isis known as the Ἶσις ἐν ἀτρίωι).

a characteristic feature of *atria* in Roman houses, may support the assumption that this was an *aithrion* house-type.[26] In fact, there is no need for the presence of the *impluvium* as it is rainless in the *chora*.[27] Houses in Graeco-Roman Egypt had instead a draw-well (φρέαρ) in their courtyards.[28] Since the house is not architecturally recognisably as an *atrium*-house, it is widely accepted that the *atreion* corresponds to the *aithrion*.[29] The two words are even etymologically related.[30] The *aithrion* is the central, internal court of the house; it is the open courtyard which provides light to the interior of the house. Since it could not be sold separately, the *aithrion* was an integral part of the house.[31]

The *aithrion* should be distinguished from the αὐλή (*aule*), which could be sold separately or even shared with another house. In that sense, the *aule* was not integral to the house. The expressions αὐλήν περὶ τετιχισμένην[32] and τῆς προσούσης αὐλῆς[33] indicate that the *aule* was a small yard 'surrounded by walls' and 'annexed to the house'. It was probably used for agricultural or household works.[34] Houses may have had an *aithrion* and an *aule*, as in a papyrus of 164 from Oxyrhynchus, attesting the lease of a house with its appurtenances for 18 months at a rent of 200 drachmas per year. The tenant, Ptolema, daughter of Theon, is bound to deliver the buildings in good condition at the end of the lease, and the landlord, Dionysia, daughter of Chairemon, is responsible for the police-tax and brick-tax. The house contained 'a courtyard (αὐλήν) and two yards (αἴθρια δύο), in one of which there is a well (φρέαρ)'.[35] An unclear structure, the ὀβολίσκ(ος), appears in the middle of the courtyard in *P.Oxy.* XXIII.2406. Unfortunately, nothing is known about the structure and function of the *obolisk(os)*.[36] Turner hesitantly suggested that it was used to designate 'water-pipe' or 'conduit'.[37] In a late papyrus from Herakleopolis, the *oboliskos* is mentioned in association with a domestic pylon, suggesting that it was an important element of the house with certain unknown functions.[38] Nothing can be said about the undesignated part of the house behind the *aithrion*. However, it was perhaps another court or a backyard.

I.2. The *oikia dipurgia* (two-towered house)

Another house-type that is more often connected with urban rather than rural sites is the οἰκία διπυργία.[39] Strictly speaking, the *purgos* or tower is a distinctive structure that is frequently mentioned in Greek papyri uncovered from Graeco-Roman Egypt.[40] In Greek military architecture, however, the *purgos* refers to a defensive tower as well as a place of habitation for soldiers.[41] In contrast, it is mentioned in domestic contexts in Egypt to designate a distinct form of tower used for certain purposes, possibly for storage of agricultural products.[42] A papyrus of AD 79 from Oxyrhynchus registers the mortgage of a house in which there are 'a two-storied tower (πύργος δίστεγος), a propylon, an exedra, an *aithrion*, and a vaulted room'.[43] The *purgos*

FIGURE 2. MODEL OF A HOUSE, GRAECO-ROMAN PERIOD, BRITISH MUSEUM, NO. 2462.

---

[26] Maehler 1983, 137.
[27] Diod. Sic. 1.10.4.
[28] *P.Oxy.* III.502.18 (179) = *SB* XX.14199.
[29] Alston 1997b, 25-39.
[30] Chantraine 1964, 7-15.
[31] Husson 1983, 29-36.
[32] *P.Oxy.* III.505.7 (179) = *SB* XX.14199.
[33] *P.Oxy.* III.482.11-13 (109).
[34] Husson 1983, 45-54.
[35] *P.Oxy.* III.502.17-18.
[36] The ὀβολίσκος is not included in Husson's monograph on the vocabulary of houses.
[37] Tuner 1957, 145.
[38] *P.Lond.* II.391.2.

[39] Alston 1997a.
[40] Husson 1983, 248-51.
[41] Hellmann 1992, 361-4.
[42] Preisigke 1919; Nowicka 1972.
[43] *P.Oxy.* II.243.15-17.

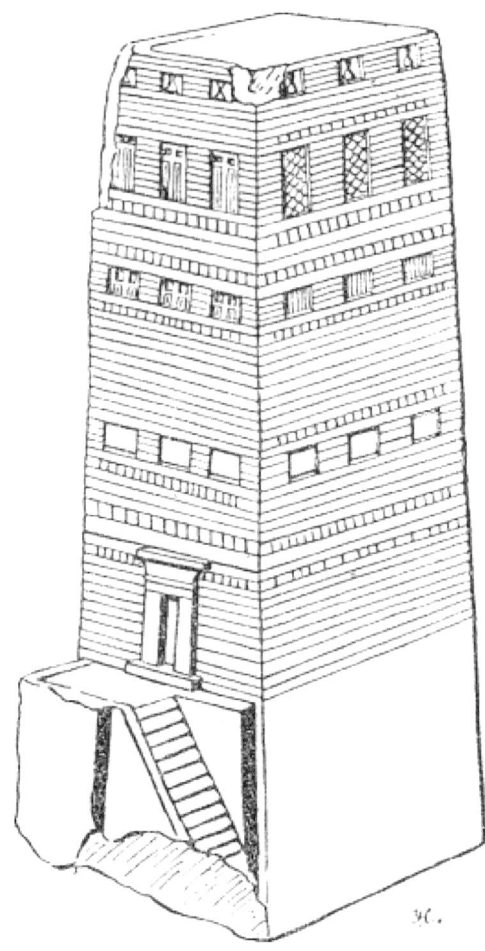

FIGURE 3. MODEL OF A HOUSE, GRAECO-ROMAN PERIOD, CAIRO MUSEUM.

is also used in Egypt as a form of tower-house used for habitation.[44] Multi-storied tower-houses were known since the Pharaonic period.[45] Together models of houses in the form of towers (figures 2-3) and excavations at Karanis (figure 4) confirm that tower-houses continued to be a common feature of housing in Graeco-Roman Egypt.[46]

The oikia dipurgia was a distinctive house-type related in some cases to wealthy families. A papyrus of AD 90 mentions 'a two-towered house in the middle of which there is a court'; the house also contained an annexed aule.[47] A papyrus of AD 261 concerns the cession of a two-towered house, which belonged to magistrates and was located in an Oxyrhynchite village.[48] P.Oxy. LXIV.4438 of AD 252 is the only surviving reference to a three-towered house (οἰκία τριπυργία), which contained an aithrion and two aule. The house was bought by the wife of a former magistrate of Oxyrhynchus

from a gymnasiarch of the same city, suggesting that it was a residence for the elites.[49] The aithrion and aule were distinctive features of the oikia dipurgia and oikia tripurgia. Unfortunately, nothing is known about the physical appearance of these towered houses and little is known about their internal arrangement. However, it seems safe to say that the towers were integral and prominent architectural features of the houses, as their names imply. Alston suggests a reconstruction of the physical appearance of the oikia dipurgia on the basis of ancient Egyptian representations which show large houses with two slanting towers attached to the frontage (figure 5).[50]

The façade of the oikia dipurgia may have been flanked by two towers, which were perhaps used for habitation.[51] According to Alston, the construction of two huge towers was meant to create a more imposing frontage. Impressive house frontages might have the potential not only to 'assert the status of the occupants of the house in the public space of the street', but also to 'demarcate the boundary between public and private'.[52]

The occupants of such houses probably exploited the two towers as an architectural means to assert their social status on the public space of streets. Representations of houses in Pharaonic tombs show that wealthy Egyptians inscribed their names and titles on the main doorway of their houses, advertising their social status. Prominent and externally visible towers served to identify the house in the Roman period, as did the names of neighbours in sale and lease contracts.[53] The identification of a house by the name of its owner continued into the Roman period.[54] Houses of named individuals were used as landmarks in directions to couriers.[55] Similarly, the use of houses of named residents as topographical points in surveys unrelated to taxation confirms this assumption of a close relationship between the occupant and his or her house.[56]

There is no archaeological evidence for two-towered houses, three-towered houses, bath-houses, and gate-houses in the well-excavated sites of the Fayum and the Dakhla oasis. Although they have not been identified in urban sites, it is possible that they are closely associated with cities, given their frequency in urban contexts. The court-house, however, has been identified in surviving houses at Karanis and Kellis. In urban and rural sites,

---

[44] Hdt. 2.95; P.Tebt. I.47.15-16 (113 BC).
[45] Davies 1929, 236-9.
[46] Engelbach 1931, 129-30; Gazda 1983, 19, fig. 30.
[47] P.Oxy. II.247.23: οἰκίας διπυργίας ἐν ᾗ κατὰ μέσον αἴθριον.
[48] P.Oxy. XIV.1703.

[49] P.Oxy. LXIV.4438.14-5.
[50] Alston 1997c, 31, fig. 2. For an illustration of a two-towered pylon in a Pharaonic house: Davies 1929, pl. xxxii.
[51] Nowicka 1973, 175-8.
[52] Alston 1997a, 30-7.
[53] P.Mich. V.294.
[54] E.g. P.Oxy. XVII.2145 (building measurements for a bath in the house of [---] Severus, AD 185); Husson 1983, 58-60. Cf. P.Theon. 15 (the mid-second century).
[55] Llewellyn 1994.
[56] Alston 1997a, 36.

FIGURE 4. TOWER-HOUSES AT KARANIS.

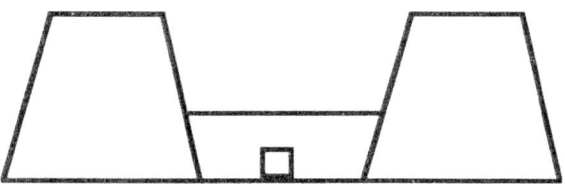

FIGURE 5. ALSTON'S RECONSTRUCTION OF A PHARAONIC HOUSE WITH TWO TOWERS ATTACHED TO THE FRONTAGE.

some of the houses comprised just one storey;[57] however, two-storey houses seem to have been standard,[58] as was the case in the Pharaonic period.[59] Three- and four-storey houses were not uncommon, as papyri and rural archaeological material confirm.[60] The construction of multi-storied houses in the Roman period is a tradition preserved from the Pharaonic period and confirms the persistence of traditional structures and techniques.[61]

I.3. Rural Houses

A clearer picture of the internal divisions of rural houses can be formed from the archaeological remains at Karanis.[62] The topographical study of the site suggests that it was occupied from the late Ptolemaic period to the early fourth century.[63] However, papyri and coins suggest a lengthier occupation from c. 270 BC to c. AD 500, and possibly later.[64] In the Roman period, the villages of Egypt had substantial houses that were used over longer periods of time. More than 106 houses were excavated in Karanis by the University of Michigan between 1924 and 1935; however, the excavations were never completely published (for a sample, see Appendix 1).[65] The villages were also dominated by modest houses constructed of mud-brick with a floor space measuring about sixty square meters.[66] These houses were smaller than those at Pompeii, which have mean areas of 266 square meters (Region I) and 289 square meters (Region VI), and Herculaneum, which have a mean area of 241 square meters.[67]

Although many houses in Karanis reveal a pattern in their internal arrangement, other houses of the same village do not. Houses in Karanis usually had an underground basement with vaulted ceilings, serving as storage bins for keeping the family's cereal stock and other foodstuffs.[68] The dominant feature of the houses is the central courtyard, which occupies about a quarter of the total floor space. It was usually situated at one end or at the side of the house, where there was direct access to a street or a passageway. It sometimes occupied the centre of the house with a number of adjoining rooms. The courtyard was open to the sky and enclosed with walls. It was around these courtyards that household

---

[57] P.Oxy. VII.1027.3 (the first century): οἰκ[ίας] μονοστέγου.
[58] P.Oxy. IV.719.15 (193): οἰκιῶν δύο διστέγου.
[59] Badawy 1966, 15-8.
[60] P.Oxy. XLVII.3365.ii.77 (241): οἰκία τρίστεγος; Gazda 1983, 19 (fig. 30).
[61] Husson 1981; Gros 1996, 216.
[62] Boak and Peterson 1931.
[63] Husselman 1979.
[64] Haatvedt and Peterson 1964.
[65] Husselman 1979.
[66] Luckhard 1914, 16-23.
[67] These figures are taken from Wallace-Hadrill 1994, 76.
[68] Bowman 1986, 149.

FIGURE 6. AN OVEN IN THE COURTYARD OF A HOUSE AT KARANIS.

FIGURE 7. AN OLIVE PRESS IN THE COURTYARD OF A HOUSE AT KARANIS.

activities generally revolved. The presence of fireplaces, ovens (figure 6), grain bins, Theban millstones (small hand-mills of a traditional design) and other cooking pots and jars in the courtyards of many houses at Karanis indicates that the courtyard was the kitchen.

Given that pigs, sheep, goats, geese, and other domesticated animals and birds were reared in the courtyards of houses, the inhabitants looked upon the interiors of their houses, particularly courtyards, as an important source of income. Storage bins, animal pens, feeding troughs, and mangers were largely located in the courtyards of houses at Karanis.[69] In addition to helping the inhabitants in field works by transporting seeds and hoeing the earth, domesticated animals supplied the inhabitants with their dietary needs from milk, butter, and meat, not to mention the economic value obtained from selling them.[70] The presence of bases of olive presses in many courtyards (figure 7) also suggests that the courtyard functioned also as a small factory producing highly economic products.[71]

Leaving the courtyard aside, the internal stairway is another important feature of multi-storied houses at Karanis. It is a continuous staircase connecting all the floors of the house. The living accommodation on the floors of houses consisted of two or three rooms of relatively considerable size with plastered walls and wall-niches.[72] Excavations revealed that houses at the nearby village of Soknopaiou Nesos (Dimê) (Appendix 2) bore a remarkable resemblance to those of Karanis in both layout and material. Yet much less pottery and household furniture were found in houses at Dimê. Similarly, houses at Dimê consisted of an entrance-doorway leading directly to a courtyard or to a short passage and a courtyard, around which a number of rooms were arranged. Houses also had a stair unit, which led down to the underground rooms and up to the upper floors.[73] Like other houses in the Dakhleh oasis, houses at Kellis typically consist of a single storey with vaulted roofs. A staircase provided access to the roof, which was often used as a storage space. Within the house, there was a central courtyard surrounded by living and work spaces. Walls were mud-plastered and often contained strips of white wash along the rear walls and around doorways and wall niches (Appendix 1).[74]

I.4. Conclusion

Together, archaeology and papyri help to reconstruct the internal arrangement of Egyptian houses in the Graeco-Roman period. There was a variety in house type in both urban and rural sites. House types included the aithrion-house, the oikia dipurgia, the oikia tripurgia, and the bath-house. Multi-storied houses were also common in poleis, metropoleis, and komai. Some domestic facilities such as oil-presses and household activities such as animal breeding provided the occupants with nutritional necessities and revenues. The house was a marker of social status as the occupants emphasised their position within the local community by such externally features of the house as the two-towers, the three-towers, and the domestic pylon.

---

[69] Husselman 1979, 49-54.
[70] Bowman 1986, 149-50.
[71] Husselman 1979, 38-9.
[72] Bowman 1986, 149.
[73] Boak 1935.
[74] Hope 1988; Gardner and Lieu 1996; Knudstad and Frey 1999.

Chapter II
The Domestic Pylon

This chapter attempts to reconstruct the internal arrangement and functions of the domestic pylon in the light of Greek papyri uncovered from Egypt. It first deals with representations of domestic pylons in the Pharaonic period to visualize the structure. It then considers domestic entranceways attested in Greek papyri and it finally addresses the architectural layout and use of the domestic pylon. In 1973, Pierre Chantraine addressed the origin of the Greek term pylon.[1] In 1983, Husson published her *Oikia* where she alphabetically collected the vocabulary of domestic architecture of Egypt, including the pylon, attested in papyri from the Ptolemaic to the Byzantine period.[2] In 2001, Alston mentioned the domestic pylon in passing in his considerations of social life and ritual activities in Roman Egypt.[3] None of these scholars has dealt in depth with the architectural layout and use of the domestic pylon.

II.1. Representations of Domestic Pylons in the Pharaonic Period

Unfortunately, there is no surviving example of a domestic pylon in Egypt, indicating that the structure was probably built out of mud-brick. The absence of archaeological parallels makes it hard to form a clear picture of the physical appearance of the structure and, as we shall see, the papyri offer only limited evidence for this. However, Pharaonic representations of what seem to be domestic pylons help to visualize the pylon mentioned in papyri of Graeco-Roman period, given the remarkable continuity of native techniques used in domestic architecture.[4] This section therefore visualizes the physical appearance of the domestic pylon on the basis of representations of similar domestic structures in the Pharaonic period.

The ancient Egyptians used the word *bẖnt* to refer to the pylon (figure 8).[5] It is derived etymologically from a verbal stem, which means 'be vigilant'.[6] *Bẖnt* refers to the whole structure and is sometimes followed by the determinative for a pylon, consisting of two towers and a central doorway in between. In other cases, however, it is followed by a single tower or without a determinative.[7] From the Eighteenth Dynasty and down to the Roman period, the word *sbꜣ* is sometimes used to designate the pylon.[8] The term *sbꜣ* is first used during the Fifth Dynasty to mean a normal 'doorway',[9] and often refers to 'the doors of houses as well as temples'.[10] *Sbꜣ* also occurred in demotic, and survived into Coptic to mean 'door'.[11] The central gate of the pylon was called *mꜣht*,[12] while the balcony above it was called *mꜣrw* (the viewing place) or *ssd-n-ḥꜥ* (the window of appearance).[13] 'Pylon' is the English for the Greek πυλών (monumental gateway),[14] which is used in Egyptian religious contexts to designate the double-towered gateway of traditional temples.[15] Most classical authors used the word 'propylon' to designate the two-towered entrance of Egyptian temples.[16] Diodorus was the first and perhaps the sole classical writer to use the word 'pylon' in his reference to the Egyptian monument.[17]

The earliest prototype of the pylon is a series of temple gateways, which date back to the Middle Kingdom and are built out of mud-brick, except for the frames of the doorways, which aremade of stone.[18] This tradition was maintained in mortuary temples of the Nineteenth Dynasty (1307-1196 BC) built on the west bank of Thebes.[19] The entrance to the Chapel of King Sankhkare Montuhotep III (1998-1991 BC) at Qurna is often referred to as the 'earliest known pylon'.[20] The earliest appearance of the term *bẖnt* is found in Ineni's statement, inscribed in his tomb at Thebes (TT 81), concerning his supervision of the construction of the fourth and fifth pylons of the Temple of Karnak under Tuthmosis I (1504-1492 BC). The 'superintendent of the royal buildings' records that 'I have supervised the great monuments which he (Tuthmosis I) made at Karnak. A noble hall with columns was erected; great pylons (*bẖntw*) in fine Tura limestone were erected on either side of it (the hall)'.[21] The use of monumental pylons as the facade-entranceways to traditional temples continued from the Pharaonic and down to the Roman period.[22]

Turning now to the appearance of the domestic pylon. Although the physical appearance of the domestic pylon cannot be ascertained, I would argue that the domestic

---

[1] Chantraine 1973.
[2] Husson 1983.
[3] Alston 2001, 60-1.
[4] Husson 1981.
[5] Faulkner 1962, 84; Wilson 1997, 326-7.
[6] Sethe 1933, 903.
[7] Erman and Grapow 1926, 471.
[8] Shubert 1981, 137-8; Blackman 1915, 4.
[9] Spencer 1984, 207.
[10] Wilson 1997, 815-6.
[11] Erichsen 1954, 419; Crum 1930, 321b.
[12] On the orthography of the word *mꜣht*: Wilson 1997, 405.
[13] Junker 1912, 58-9. On other uses of the word *mꜣrw*: Wilson 1997, 404-5.
[14] Jaros-Deckert 1982, 1202.
[15] Hellmann 1992, 353.
[16] Hdt. 2.121; Strabo 17.1.28; Plut. *De Is. et Os.* 32.8-10;
[17] Diod. Sic. 1.47.2.
[18] Badawy 1966, 177-8.
[19] Spencer 1984, 193.
[20] Nims 1965, 70.
[21] Shubert 1981, 136-7.
[22] Abdelwahed 2015, chapter two.

Figure 8. The pylon of the Ptolemaic temple of Horus at Edfu.

pylon had similar physical features to the entrance-pylon of Egyptian temples (figure 8). The first indication for this is the Tomb of the High Priest Meryra at Tell el-Amarna. In the tomb, the front view of the royal palace of King Akhenaton is represented on the upper half of the east wall as a series of elevations of successive, superimposed sections (figure 9).[23] The lowest level shows the façade of the palace, which has a two-towered pylon as its main entrance with a broken lintel doorway, flanked by two side entrances, probably for the servants. The second level represents the actual front of the palace with the Window of Appearance, which is flanked by a colonnade on each side. Above the façade there is the interior part of the palace, which still preserves the triple division. In the middle lies the Hall of Appearance, serving as the royal banquet and being flanked by a corridor. Finally, the upper level contains store-rooms and apparently the bed room, which appears to have a ventilator.[24] The appearance of the domestic pylon can be visualized on the basis of the pylon of this royal palace and other wealthy houses, because the pylon is used in religious, funerary, and domestic architecture alike, perhaps due to its distinctive form and symbolism.[25]

The representation of the estates of Aten at el-Amarna, which are depicted on the eastern side of the northern wall in the Tomb of Meryra, shows a domestic structure

Figure 9. The two-towered pylon of the royal palace in the tomb of Meryra at Tell El-Amarna.

which is often interpreted as a palace (figure 10).[26] In the drawing the whole structure is preceded by a water-tank with steps, probably used for irrigation. The palace

---

[23] Davies 1903, pl. xxvi.
[24] Smith 1968, 209, 235.
[25] E.g. the tomb of Ankh-hor, a wealthy chief administrator in the estates of the Gods Wives of Amun under Psamtik II and Apries of the Twenty-sixth Dynasty, at El-Assasif necropolis on the Western Bank of Thebes (TT 414) has a huge mud-brick pylon as its facade-entranceway.

[26] Davies 1903, 40-1, pl. xxvii.

Chapter II The Domestic Pylon

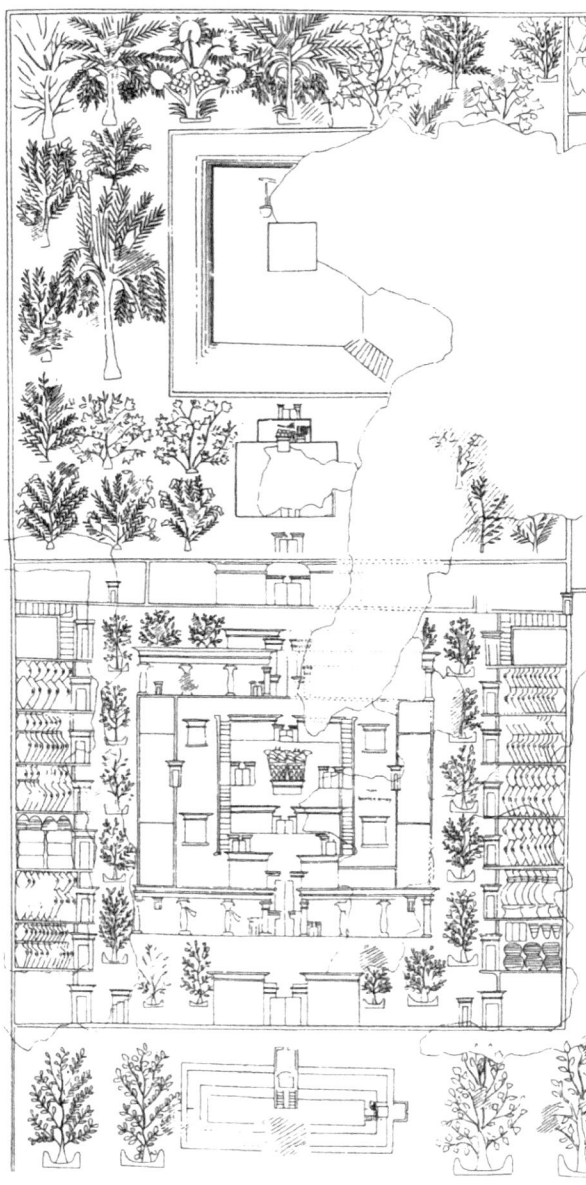

Figure 10. The double-towered pylon of a palace in the Tomb of Meryra at Tell el-Amarna.

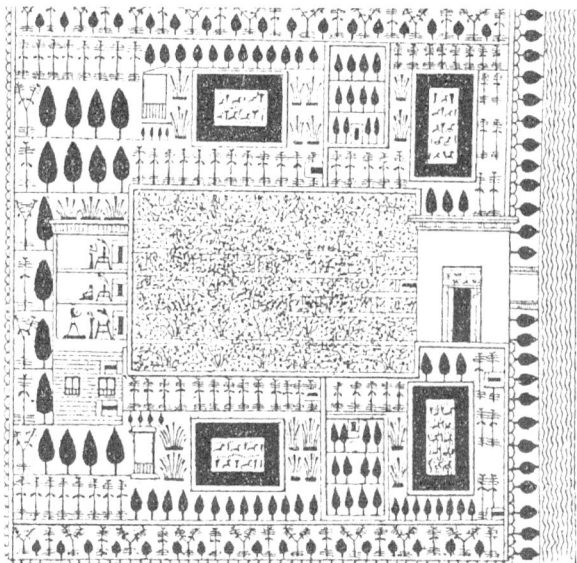

Figure 11. Representation of an Egyptian villa in the tomb of Sennefer (TT 96).

Figure 12. Reconstruction of an Egyptian villa in the tomb of Sennefer (TT 96).

is entered through a double-towered pylon, which is flanked by two small entrances, again possibly for the servants. This pylon entrance leads to the main structure, which is symmetrically arranged with further pylon-gateways at both ends. These have a central doorway and two small side-entrances on the façade of its towers. The interior of the central structure has lines of trees and a series of store-rooms, eight on each side. At the back, the two end spaces have turning stairs, leading to the roof of the store-rooms. Along the front and back there is a portico. On both sides of the central structure there is a flight of steps, leading up to a platform. Thus multiple pylon gateways were used to access the interior of this domestic, possibly palatial, space.

Based on the representation of an Egyptian villa in the Tomb of Sennefer (TT 96) (figure 11), Georges Perrot and Charles Chipiez showed that the villa is entered through a domestic pylon, the top of which is decorated with a cavetto cornice like the pylon of traditional Egyptian temples (figure 12).[27] A hieroglyphic inscription is carved on the lintel of the doorway, possibly recording the name and title of the owner. Like those of the palaces at el-Amarna, the pylon-entrance is flanked by two side-entrances, possibly used by the servants. The villa overlooked the Nile and was approached by a harbour with steps. The pylon gave access to the interior of the

---

[27] Perrot and Chipiez 1882, 457, fig. 258, 483, fig. 267.

villa, which contained a garden, trees, flowers, and the main dwelling-structure.

Taking these various instances of non-religious pylons into account, we would argue that the domestic pylon of the papyri looked like the domestic pylons portrayed in tombs of the Pharaonic period, which themselves resemble the pylons of Pharaonic temple architecture. Such a similarity in forms between domestic, funerary and temple architecture is not unlikely, given that architectural forms and motifs can easily transfer between domestic, religious, and funerary architecture. The broken-lintel doorway is a case in point. It is used, for example, in the pronaos of the Ptolemaic temple at Deir el-Medina,[28] and also appears in funerary architecture at Alexandria, occurring in Fort Saleh Tomb 1. Architecturally, the tomb consists of a rock-cut stairway, giving access to an open court, from which rooms cut with *loculi* extend on a north-south axis. At the north end of the complex there is a painted room with a burial niche. The façade of the burial chamber combines traditional and Greek motifs, where a Greek *kline* is flanked by columns with Egyptian composite capitals. The inner faces of the columns are attached to an Egyptian broken-lintel doorway.[29]

II.2. Entranceways in Greek Papyri

The word pylon occurs in Greek papyri from the Ptolemaic to the Byzantine period.[30] The earliest surviving attestation of the Greek term pylon occurs in *P.Lon.* VII.1974 of 254 BC, while the latest surviving occurrence is in *SB* VI.8988 of AD 647. It is associated with different forms of architecture; it is used to designate the main entrance to granaries, temples, theatres, gymnasia, and, most notably, houses. It seems that the physical appearance and use of the pylon depended largely upon the context in which the term is used. Since the temple pylon has been sufficiently covered in the previous section, and given that there is no information about the pylon associated with granaries,[31] we will only focus in this section on the appearance and architectural layout of pylons associated with theatres and gymnasia.

In a second century AD papyrus from the Fayum, the monumental gateway of a theatre is described as 'a double-valve pylon',[32] thus forming the façade-entrance to one of the most important structures of entertainment in Roman Egypt. Since it is associated with a distinctively classical-style structure and given the presence of

FIGURE 13. THE PROPYLON OF THE THEATRE AT ANTINOOPOLIS IN 1799.

FIGURE 14. THE TRIUMPHAL ARCH AT ANTINOOPOLIS IN 1799.

archaeological parallels of such theatrical gateways,[33] I would suggest that this pylon took the shape of a Greek propylon rather than an Egyptian pylon. One can compare this gateway with the propylon of the theatre at Antinoopolis, which consisted of a monumental gateway with three entrances, where the middle entrance is double in height and three times wider than the two lateral ones (figure 13).[34] Thus, the architecture of the Greek propylon did resemble that of triumphal arches like the one at Antinoopolis (figure 14).[35]

The pylon is also mentioned as the entrance to gymnasia. In AD 283 a papyrus mentions two joiners, who were responsible for joining the wooden beams of a colonnade at Oxyrhynchus, asking Aurelius Apollonius, a holder of numerous municipal officers, for the payment of 4 talents, 4.000 drachmas for their labour in the construction

---

[28] Bagnall and Rathbone 2004, 199-200.
[29] Venit 2002, 93.
[30] *P.Münch.* XI.19-20. The papyrus dates to the reign of Maurice.
[31] *P.Mich.* V.226. deals with the rent of the granary of the temple of Kronos/Sobek at Tebtunis to the deceased granary guard Thenapynchis and her living son Apynchis, son of Harmiysis, and his wife Thaesis. According to the papyrus, the granary contains "a tower (*purgos*) and another tower (*purgos*) adjacent to it and a gateway (*pulwn*)".
[32] *BGU* IV.1024.9-10.

[33] Kühn 1913, 63-4.
[34] McKenzie 2007, 158, fig. 265.
[35] McKenzie 2007, 157, fig. 263a.

FIGURE 15. THE PROPYLON OF THE GYMNASIUM AT CYRENE.

of a street, which ran 'from the principal gateway (pylon) of the gymnasium as far south as the Hierakion Lane'.[36] The pylon also occurs in connection with the gymnasium at Alexandria: 'Take notice at Alexandria before the principal gateway (pylon) of the gymnasium'.[37] According to Jean Delorme, the gymnasium at Alexandria took a classical appearance and had two entrances; a principal gateway that gave access to a secondary one.[38] The pylon of the gymnasium at Alexandria can be compared with the propylon of the gymnasium at Cyrene (figure 15).[39] The appearance of domestic pylons differed from the appearance of the pylons associated with theatres and gymnasia, when the latter clearly had Classical, Greek, appearance. The Greek propylon refers to the front gateway, which precedes the enclosure wall of sanctuaries, like propylon A of the Serapeion C at Delos and the Inner Propylaea at Eleusis.[40] It also designates a separate structure within the temple's precinct, where it is approached by a stairway, like the propylaea on the Acropolis of Athens. The physical appearance of the Greek propylon can be seen in the gymnasia at Epidaurus, Olympia, and Cyrene. The latter was associated with Ptolemaic ruler-cult, and was remodelled as a Caesareion dedicated to Augustus (figure 15).[41] The pylons of theatres and gymnasia therefore had different forms to the pylons of traditional Egyptian temples and palaces, and, in the author's view, domestic pylons.

II.3. Other Domestic Entranceways

Having explored the appearance of the pylons of such public structures as theatres and gymnasia, let us now consider other domestic entranceways. The domestic pylon must be distinguished from other physical and spatial elements connected with houses, including θύρα, πρόθυρον, προπυλών, and πύργος. The occurrence of these terms together in papyri suggest that they differ from each other in architectural terms. In papyri and classical literature on Egypt θύρα is the normal word for 'doorway', including the front door of the house.[42] In a petition of AD 110-112, Heraclas son of Pausirion accused Apollos son of Heraclides, both from Oxyrhynchus, of attacking his wife, Taamois, while she was standing 'before the front door' of the house.[43] However, there were different ways of referring to the front door. One is the πάροδιος θύρα, i.e. the traversing or passing door.[44] The πάροδιος θύρα is mentioned in two petitions from Tebtunis, where a number of villagers complained about a gang of intruders who 'crushed the front door' of their house.[45] Another word for the front door is ἡ ἐξωτέρα θύρα, i.e. the exterior or outer door,[46] which is also mentioned in a papyrus from Oxyrhynchus, testifying a lease of a workshop with its front door.[47] The third phrase used to designate the front door is ἡ αὐλεία θύρα.[48] Whether followed by θύρα or not, the αὔλειος or αὐλεία can refer to the main entrance.[49]

Unfortunately, not much information is given by papyri about the design and function of the πρόθυρον and προπυλών. However, both were undoubtedly associated with the house frontage, as their combined names imply. The πρόθυρον was probably a 'vestibule',

---

[36] P.Oxy. I.55.9.
[37] P.Flor. III.382.15-16.
[38] Delorme 1960, 358.
[39] Burkhalter 1992, 308, fig. 5.
[40] Hellmann 1992, 350-3.
[41] On those at Epidaurus and Olympia, see Lauter 1986, 202-3. On that at Cyrene, see Ward-Perkins et al 1958.
[42] P.Oxy. XXXVI.2758.10; Hdt. 2.48; Plut. De Is. et Os. 7. See also Husson 1983, 93-107.
[43] P.Oxy. XXXVI.2758.10: πρὸ τῆς θύρας.
[44] Husson 1983, 98-99.
[45] P.Tebt. I.45.21-22; P.Tebt. I.47.13-14: συντρίψαντες τὴν παρόδιον θύραν.
[46] Husson 1983, 99. In P.Oxy. VI.903.20, it occurs as τὰς ἔξω θύρας.
[47] P.Oxy. XVI.1966.14-15. AD 505.
[48] P.Tebt. III.795.7: τῆς αὐλείς θύρας τῆς οἰκίας.
[49] Husson 1983, 99-100.

which preceded the main entrance to the house. It could also mean the entrance to the *aule*.⁵⁰ A papyrus of AD 586 testifies that Aurelia Tapia has sold half a house to Flavius Kriakos at Syene (Aswan). The house consisted of 'an outer vestibule, a pylon, a terrace, a court, and a baking-oven (τε προθύρον καὶ πυλῶνος καὶ τεσσοῦ καὶ αἰθρίων καὶ κλιβάνου)'.⁵¹ Yet in a papyrus from Oxyrhynchus a πρόθυρον of a landlord's house is exceptionally mentioned to have a small room within it.⁵² In religious contexts, however, the πρόθυρον could also mean the space in front of the main entrance of a temple.⁵³ Thus, a Greek metrical inscription on the pylon of the temple of Isis and Serapis at Qysis (QasrDouch) records a collection of money by the high priest of Isis on behalf of the reconstruction of the temple, including 'the πρόθυρον which was built up within the enclosure wall'.⁵⁴

The propylon, on the other hand, has several meanings in connection with different forms of architecture. It was probably used in connection with domestic architecture to mean a 'porch' of the entrance. In that case, it was an essential part of the house, that is, it could not be rented or sold separately.⁵⁵ It may have projected from the façade of the house and preceded the pylon, as its combined name implies.⁵⁶ It is also mentioned in connection with a temple at Busiris, yet the papyrus does not indicate anything about its appearance or function, although it is likely that it simply refers to a monumental gateway.⁵⁷

A papyrus of AD 79 certifies the mortgage of a house by Dionysius, son of Phanias in favour of Didymus, son of Sarapion. The house was located in the Quarter of Hermaeus near the Serapeion at Oxyrhynchus, and consisted of 'two-storied tower and propylon and passage and court and a vaulted chamber (πύργος δίστεγος καὶ προπυλῶν καὶ ἐζώδιον καὶ ἔθριον καὶ καμάρα)'.⁵⁸ The occurrence of the tower (purgos) and the propylon in this papyrus indicates that the two structures were architecturally distinguished from each other. The purgos is a distinctive structure that is frequently mentioned in papyri.⁵⁹ In Greek military architecture, it refers to a defensive tower as well as a place of habitation for soldiers.⁶⁰ In contrast, the purgos in Egyptian domestic contexts designates a distinctive form of tower used for certain purposes, including storage of agricultural products,⁶¹ and habitation (Cf. figures 2-4).⁶² A papyrus of AD 79 mentions 'a two-storied tower-house in which there are a propylon, an exedra, an aithrion and a vaulted room'.⁶³ Multi-storied tower-houses were known since the Pharaonic period.⁶⁴ Models of houses in the form of towers (figures 2-3) and excavations at Karanis (figure 4) confirm that tower-houses continued to be common in Graeco-Roman Egypt.⁶⁵

The oikia dipurgia was a distinctive house-type related in some cases to families of considerable wealth.⁶⁶ Unfortunately, nothing is known about the physical appearance of this house-type, and little about its internal arrangement. However, on the basis of ancient Egyptian representations, which show large houses with two slanting towers attached to the frontage,⁶⁷ Alston has suggested a reconstruction of its physical appearance (figure 5).⁶⁸

The frontage of the oikia dipurgia was probably flanked by two towers, which were mainly used for habitation.⁶⁹ According to Alston, the construction of two huge towers was perhaps meant to create a more imposing frontage. As elsewhere in the Roman Empire, there was an architectural emphasis on the house frontage in Roman Egypt. Impressive house frontages had the potential not only to 'assert the status of the occupants of the house in the public space of the street', but also to 'demarcate the boundary between public and private'.⁷⁰

The use of the house frontage for communicating social statuses and identities is known also in the Pharaonic period, when representations of houses in tombs show that some wealthy Egyptians used to inscribe their names and titles in prominent positions on or by the main doorway of their houses.⁷¹ A good example is the house of the chief builder Hatiay (T34.1 & 4) at el-Amarna, which is notable for its complete and brightly painted door lintel that carries his name and positions (now in the Egyptian Museum, Cairo).⁷² Such major architectural and externally visible features as the pylon and dipurgia served to identify the house in the Roman period, as the names of neighbours in sale and lease contracts had done.⁷³ Thus, a variety of other entranceways and house façades were known in Graeco-Roman Egypt; those

---

⁵⁰ Husson 1983, 237-8.
⁵¹ *P.Münch.* 11.19-20. The papyrus dates to the reign of Maurice.
⁵² *P.Oxy.* XVI.2044.16:εἰς τὸ κελλ(ίον) τὸ εἰς τὰ πρόθυρ(α) τῆς γεουχ(ικῆς) οἰκ(ίας).
⁵³ Hellmann 1992, 348-9.
⁵⁴ *SEG* XXXVIII.1796 = *SEG* LIV.1738 = Bernand 1969, 471-5, no. 118: Ἐν[θ]ά[δε] τὸ πρόθυρον δωμήσατο τεῖχος ἐντὸς ὑψηλοῦ ζαθέης Ἰσιδος ἀρχιερεύς.
⁵⁵ *P.Oxy.* II.243.15.
⁵⁶ Husson 1983, 238.
⁵⁷ *P.Oxy.* XX.2272.5-6, 10.
⁵⁸ *P.Oxy.* II.243.15-16.
⁵⁹ Husson 1983, 248-51.
⁶⁰ Hellmann 1992, 361-4.
⁶¹ *P.Mich.* V.226.20-21. Preisigke 1919; Nowicka 1972.
⁶² Hdt. 2.95; *P.Tebt.*I.47.15-16.
⁶³ *P.Oxy.* II.243.15-17.
⁶⁴ Davies 1929, 236-9.
⁶⁵ Engelbach 1931, 129-31; Gazda 1983, 19.
⁶⁶ *P.Oxy.* XIV.1703.
⁶⁷ For illustrations of a two-towered pylon in an ancient Egyptian house, see Davies 1929, pl. xxxii.
⁶⁸ Alston 2001, 62.
⁶⁹ Nowicka 1973.
⁷⁰ Alston 1997c, 30-7.
⁷¹ Perrot and Chipiez 1882, 457.
⁷² Frankfort and Pendlebury 1933.
⁷³ *P.Mich.* V.294.

associated with the larger houses of wealthier families tend to take monumental forms in order to assert status. Such entranceways can be architecturally distinguished from the domestic pylon, which has other distinctive architectural features that will be discussed below.

II.4. The Architectural Layout of the Domestic Pylon

Having explored the general appearance of the domestic pylon with regards to its likely similarity to the pylons of Egyptian temples, and discussed the other forms of domestic entranceways, let us now turn to the architectural layout of the domestic pylon. The domestic pylon appears in papyri as an architectural unit.[74] The first question that should be raised is the location of the pylon in relation to the house. *P.Oxy.* XXIII.2406 seems to provide the answer. The papyrus depicts the internal arrangement of the aithrion-house, which is frequently attested in urban and rural contexts (fig. 1).[75]

The pylon is the first architectural structure in the house. Since the word πυλ(ών) is never used to designate the front door of the house,[76] it follows that it is written on a court-shaped space in order to show that it was not a simple doorway, but a huge tower-gateway, which had an extension in depth. The pylon itself then had an entrance-door (thura).[77] This position recalls the already discussed pylon of Egyptian-style temples and the two-towered gateway of houses and palaces which appear on representations of Pharaonic tombs.[78] *P.Oxy.* XXIII.2406 therefore confirms that the pylon formed its façade-entrance.

References to pylons in papyrus documents, related in particular to the rent, sale, or confiscation of domestic properties, provide various hints as to their possible appearance. The pylon could be a free-standing[79] or an attached structure (εἰς τὸν προσπαρακείμενον πυλῶνα).[80] Like other architectural elements of the house, the pylon could be refurbished, as occurred at the house of Diotimos in third-century BC Philadelphia,[81] or repaired, if damaged.[82] Papyri also confirm that the domestic pylon could be rented,[83] confiscated,[84] or even sold whether in whole or part.[85] Thus, in a papyrus only the triclinium-chamber within the pylon was sold.[86] It seems that there is no pattern as for the orientation of the pylon. The orientation of the pylon simply followed that of the main house, the directions of which must have been dictated by its location in relation to the street and other houses. According to surviving papyri, the pylon could be oriented east (νε[ύο]ντα εἰς ἀπηλιώτην),[87] west (νεύοντος εἰς λίβα),[88] or north (νεῦον εἰς βορρᾶ).[89] Although there is no surviving papyrus in which the pylon is oriented towards south, it is likely that pylons were oriented to the south as well.[90] The domestic pylon appears in papyri as a multi-storied structure.[91] *P.Oxy.* III.495 refers to the presence of 'an exedra and a room in the upper (*sc.* storey) of the pylon'.[92] A papyrus of AD 96 confirms that a domestic pylon consisted of at least two stories with different rooms, some of which served as living suites.[93]

Papyri seem to suggest that bath-houses such as the house of [---] Severus at Oxyrhynchus lacked such pylons.[94] The same holds true of the oikia dipurgia (two-towered house) and the oikia tripurgia (three-towered house). Papyri indicate that domestic pylons were associated with gate-houses and aithrion houses.[95] The high cost of constructing multi-storied pylons suggests that pylon-gateways were closely associated with wealthy houses such as the family of Soeris mentioned below.[96] The occupants perhaps used the pylon to create an imposing frontage and probably to assert their social status and position within their local community.

The pylon could also be associated with communal structures.[97] Thus in AD 240 the estate centre of Sphex in the Fayum contained a number of workshops, rooms, and a pylon in which there is a porter's lodge used by Saprion.[98] It is unclear whether this structure had the same architectural form as the gate-houses. There is no other attestation of a pylon in a rural estate context in Roman Egypt. However, one might compare tower-houses illustrated in late Roman mosaics and the fortified farms in North Africa such as the castellum at Nador, which an inscription carved over the entrance identifies as the estate of M. Cincius Hilarianus. The façade of its entrance is characterized by the presence of an impressive central arched gate, which is framed by two monumental rectangular towers.[99] This simply means that the pylons of rural estates did resemble those of other houses.

---

[74] Luckhard 1914, 55-6; Husson 1983, 243-6.
[75] *P.Oxy.* XXIII.2406. This papyrus only contains a drawing of the ground plan of a house.
[76] Husson 1983, 243-46.
[77] *P.Princ.* III.153.5-6.
[78] Dombart 1933; Shubert 1981; Jaros-Deckert 1982; Graefe 1983.
[79] *P.Lond.* III.1023.19. *This is inferred from the papyrus where the pylon is not attached to any other building.*
[80] *P.Lond.* V.1722.18-19.
[81] *P.Cair.Zen.* IV.59764, verso, 27.
[82] *PSI* V.546, recto, 13-14.
[83] *Stud.Pal.* XX.53.19-20.
[84] *BGU* VI.1222.23.
[85] *P.Mich.* V.295.4.
[86] *P.Mich.* V.295.4.

[87] *P.Lond.* III.978.8, 10, 13.
[88] *SB* VI.9586.14.
[89] *P.Lond.* V.1724.25.
[90] *BGU* VI.1222.23.
[91] *BGU* VI.1222.23: πυλῶνος διστέγου.
[92] *P.Oxy.* III.495.8: τε ἐξέδρα καὶ κέλλη τῇ ἐπάνω τοῦ πυλῶνος.
[93] *P.Oxy.* I.104.25-26: ἐν οἴκῳ ἑνὶ ἐν ἐπιπέδῳ ἐν τῷ πυλῶνι.
[94] *P.Oxy.* XVII.2145.
[95] *P.Oxy.* XXIII.2406;
[96] *P.Oxy.* I.104.25-26.
[97] *P.Mich.* XI.620.i.9-10.
[98] *P.Mich.* XI.620.9 from Theadelphia: πυλὼν ἐν ᾧ θυροουρικόν.
[99] Anselmino et al 1989, 46-52, fig. 13.

II.5. The Use of the Domestic Pylon

Having considered the architectural layout of the domestic pylon, let us now turn to its use. Like other types of the above mentioned entranceways, the domestic pylon shaped the house frontage, making it a potential arena for harassment, normally caused by settlers. Thus in 221 BC one person complained that Antigonus, a Persian of the Epigone and a settler in Berenikis Thesmophoru in the Arsinoite, 'hit him before the pylon of the house (ἑστῶτός μου πρὸς τῶι πυλῶνι [τῆς] οἰκίας)'.[100] Similarly, in AD 126-132 Akous son of Herakleos from Tebtunis petitions the strategos and complains about a gang of intruders, who 'made a bold attack upon my house in the village ... in the gateway (ἐπῆλθον αὐθάδως εἰς ἣν ἔχω ἐν τῇ κώμῃ οἰκίαν [...]φασαριων ἐν τῷ πυλῶνι)'.[101]

Papyri indicate that the ground floor of the pylon contained a number of rooms, some of which served as living-suites for the house owners.[102] *P.Oxy.* I.104, written in AD 96, is a will of Soeris in which she bequeaths her house to her son, Areotes. Her husband has the right to live in it, with a yearly payment of 48 drachmas till the husband has received 300 drachmas, which is the amount she had borrowed from him. If the father dies, the son has to pay the sum to his sister, Tnepheros. Soeris allocated 'one room on the ground floor in the pylon' as the dwelling-place of her daughter, Tnepheros, if she becomes separated from her husband.[103]

Storehouses were also located in the ground floor of the pylon (ἐπὶ τοῦ ταμείου ἐπιπέδου ἐντὸς τοῦ πυλῶνος ἐστίν),[104] in which were stored various items and supplies, including wine jars.[105] Although storehouses are not confirmed on the ground floor of the pylon of the house of Soeris, there is no reason for assuming that storehouses were absent from the pylons that had dwelling areas on the ground floors. Presumably there were different rooms and spaces located on the ground floor of pylons, as was the case on the upper floors, and some of these could be used as storehouses or living suites or perhaps for both ends. Perhaps because of its possible commercial use, there was a tax levied on the pylon in the Ptolemaic period. Thus in a papyrus of 239 BC Sokrates acknowledged that Therous daughter of Nektathumis, an Arsinoite, with her guardian Herakleides son of Apollonios, 'has paid to the Crown at the Bank of Python at Krokodilon polis the tax on a house and a pylon and a bath-room'.[106] Furthermore, the domestic pylon mentioned in a papyrus of AD 189-190 from Philadelphia had a 'vaulted chamber' (καμάρα), which was possibly used for storage,[107] as were the καμάραι located ἐν τῷ καταγαίῳ of the main house.[108]

Being located at the house frontage, certain rooms within the pylon were appropriate spaces for hosting social events and thus for communicating the family's social status through the furnishings of its rooms. A papyrus of AD 333 from Hermopolis Magna confirms an *andron* in the first floor of the pylon.[109] As late as AD 647 a *symposion* is located in an upper storey of a domestic pylon of a house located in Oxyrhynchus.[110] Similarly, at Tebtunis in the first century AD Thasos, daughter of Konnos, sold to Paches, son of Peteeus, 'a dining room with three couches (*sc.* located) in the pylon, in which there are a storehouse and a silo (τρίκλινον ἐπὶ τοῦ πυρῶνος, ἐν ᾧ ταμῖον καὶ σιρὸς)'.[111] Given the common λ–ρ shift in Greek papyri uncovered from Egypt, the meaning of the word πυρών should not be puzzling.[112] It is almost certain that πυρών occurs in Egyptian domestic contexts to designate the πυλών.[113] In contrast with Roman houses elsewhere, as at Pompeii and Ephesus, where triclinia were located deep within the house;[114] triclinia are normally located in Graeco-Roman Egypt near the house frontage, although they could also be located in courts.[115] The construction of triclinia in houses in Egypt might have been a Graeco-Roman influence; however, banquets in domestic space are attested since the Pharaonic period. Simon Ellis stressed the capacity of western Roman triclinia, which were usually fitted out with fine mosaic floors and wall-paintings, to articulate social relations and communicate the social status of the owner.[116] In its use as a space for dining, the domestic pylon therefore provided an arena for ritual activities, which reinforced the social and cultural identity of the participants.

Symposia are also associated with the upper storey of the pylon, particularly in the Byzantine period.[117] A papyrus of AD 331 from Hermopolis locates a small chamber (μικρὰν κέλλαν), an oven ([κά]μινον), and an *andron* (ἀνδρεῶνα) in the first floor of the pylon (ἐπὶ τῆς πωρ´ τῆς στέγης ἐπάνω τοῦ πυλῶνος).[118] The andron refers to men's apartment in a house. It also designates a banqueting-hall, where men meet for feasting or the

---

[100] *P.Enteux.* 74.3-4.
[101] *P.Tebt.* II.331.7-9.
[102] *P.Oxy.* I.104.25-26.
[103] *P.Oxy.* I.104.25-6: ἐν οἴκῳ ἑνὶ ἐν ἐπιπέδῳ ἐν τῷ πυλῶνι. See also Lindsay 1963, 206.
[104] *PSI* VIII.913.3-5.
[105] *P.Princ.* III.153.5-6.
[106] *P.Tebt.* III.1.814.30-5.
[107] *BGU* VII.1575.9.
[108] *P.Lond.* III.978.8, 10, 12, 13-14. This house has four cellars in which there are vaulted chambers.
[109] *P.Lond.* III.978.13.
[110] *SB* VI.8988.57-8: συμποσίου ἐπάνω τῆς πυλῶνος τῆς αὐτῆς οἰκίας.
[111] *P.Mich.* V.295.4.
[112] The word πυρών also occurs in a second-century BC inscription from Delos (*Inscr.Délos* 444 B 107: καὶ πυρῶνα παρ' Ἀγάθωνος).
[113] The word is absent from the monographs of Husson (Husson 1983) and Hellmann (Hellmann 1992).
[114] Wallace-Hadrill 1988.
[115] Husson 1983, 279-81.
[116] Ellis 1991, 1997.
[117] *P.Lond.* V.1724.24-26.AD 578-582; *SB* VI.8988.57-58 (AD 647).
[118] *P.Lond.* III.978.8, 10, 13.

guests of the master of the house were received.[119] It is unclear whether men and women dined together in Roman Egypt. Dinner invitations were normally held by men;[120] however, some invitations were issued by women.[121] The existence of a male dining area (andron), which is infrequently mentioned in late papyri, is insufficient in itself to suggest that the internal arrangement of houses or pylons reflected any gender differentiation.[122] The presence of an andron in the second floor of a pylon also does not indicate that women dined separately.[123] In Greek houses like those at Olynthos, dinner parties were presumably held in the andron and were probably limited to males.[124] The andron was sometimes so separated that it could be entered without approaching the main house (oikos).[125] In Roman society, women participated in private dinner parties, and this practice is taken for granted as a major distinctive feature of Roman social life.[126] Dining rooms were a major feature of Roman houses, and were important space for the display of wealth and luxury.[127] In addition to public structures and temples,[128] the domestic pylons in Graeco-Roman Egypt provided dining facilities for a variety of important social occasions, including the birthday of a son.[129] Given the location of the pylon at the house frontage, the positioning of the triclinium, symposion and andron within it may also indicate that the residents wanted to limit access and maintain the privacy of the internal areas of the house.

The upper floors of the pylon would have other kinds of rooms, which served numerous functions. A papyrus of AD 181/4 locates 'an exedra and a chamber in the upper (sc. storey) of the pylon (ἔν τε ἐξέδρᾳ καὶ κέλλῃ τῇ ἐπάνω τοῦ πυλῶνος),[130] which might have been used as parlours or saloons as is the exedra attested in a private house in Roman Oxyrhynchus.[131] The reference to a silo (a place for storing grain) in the pylon sold by Thasos, daughter of Konnos, to Paches, son of Peteeus, at Tebtunis, suggests that it was located in the upper floor, because an oven has been confirmed in the upper storey of the pylon elsewhere.[132] While the ground floor of the pylon contained living suites for house owners, a small bedroom is also confirmed in the second floor of a pylon (μικροῦ κοιτῶνος...ἐν τῇ δευτέρᾳ σ[τέγ]ῃ ἐπάνω τοῦ πυλῶνος).[133]

II.6. Conclusion

The domestic pylon of the Pharaonic and post-Pharaonic periods appears to have been influenced by the pylon of traditional Egyptian temples in its physical appearance. The domestic and religious pylons were huge structures, which contained multiple stories and rooms that were approached by an internal stairway. Both structures served as the façade of, and entrance to, the construction in which they are embedded. Yet the function of each architectural form depended on the context in which it was used. The domestic pylon appears in papyri as a huge, self-contained structure, forming the centrepiece of the house frontage. It consisted of multi-stories and contained numerous rooms. The rooms in the upper stories served as bed-rooms, magazines, store-rooms, silos, andreia, triclinia, and symposia, whereas those in the ground floor were used as dwelling-places for the house occupants, but also for storage. Therefore, the rooms in the ground floor mainly served living and storage purposes, while those located in the upper stories were allocated for sleeping, storage, and different social occasions. The rooms in the upper floor of the pylon were reached by an internal stairway, which connected all the stories of the structure. The pylon was used as an indicator of social status as it was associated with houses of wealthy families.

---

[119] For papyrological attestations of the ἀνδρών, see Husson 1983, 37-40.
[120] P.Oxy. XIV.1755.
[121] P.Oxy. XII.1579; P.Coll.Youtie I.52 (the second or third century AD).
[122] On attestations of the ἀνδρών in papyri: Husson 1983, 37-40.
[123] P.Flor. III.285.12: ἐν τῇ δευτέρᾳ στέγῃ.
[124] Robinson and Graham 1938, 75-80.
[125] Nevett 1994, 1995. For the architecture of Greek houses in general: Nevett 2005.
[126] Vitr. De arch. 6.4.
[127] Clarke 1991; Salter 1991.
[128] E.g. the first birthday of a daughter in the Serapeion at Oxyrhynchus (P.Oxy. XXXVI.2791); a dinner invitation issued by the exegetes 'in the temple of Demeter' (P.Oxy. XII.1485); a feast 'in the Thoereion' in relation to a coming-of-age ceremony (P.Oxy. I.110; P.Oxy. XII.1484; P.Oxy.XXXI.2592; P.Oxy.XXXVI.2791; P.Oxy.LII.3693; PSI XV.1543; SB XVIII.13875); a dinner party in the birth house (P.Köln I.57.3; P.Oxy.VI.927; P.Oxy.XII.1484); and a banquet 'in the gymnasium' in relation to the crowning of a son (as a magistrate?) (P.Oxy. XVII.2147).
[129] P.Oxy. IX.1214 (the fifth century AD).
[130] P.Oxy. III.495.8-10.
[131] P.Oxy. VI.912.12-13. Cf. P.Oxy. VIII.1128.15.
[132] P.Lond. III.978.8, 10, 13.
[133] SB VI.9586.14.

Chapter III
Ritual Activities Enacted Before the Front Door of Houses

III.1. The Front Door of Houses

The relation of houses to the public arena was important in the ancient world.[1] As in many other cultures, the front door of houses was integrated with the public space of streets in Graeco-Roman Egypt, where the front door of the house was a suitable place for social interaction, particularly involving women. Women used to stand at the front door of the house to chat with neighbours and watch what was going on in the street. However, they were sometimes subject to harassment by drunken pedestrians.[2] Papyri suggest that the residents of the house placed a particular emphasis on the material of the front door. Generally made out of wood (θύραν ξυλίνην),[3] doors of high-quality material such as tamarisk (θύρας μυρικίνας) and acacia (θύρας ἀκακίας), which are attested both papyrologically and archaeologically and were cultivated in the Western Desert and the Nile Valley, maximised their ability to assert the social status of their owners.[4]

Archaeology in particular has revealed that the front doors of houses were often well designed and constructed in the Roman period.[5] The entrance-door of House C68 in Karanis (figure 16), which is made of acacia wood, is a case in point.[6]

The lintel consists of four superimposed parts: a strip of wood projects slightly across the top of the lintel. Beneath this strip of wood is a heavy beam, which is curved to match the concave courses of bricks in the wall in which it was set and is held in place by means of tenons. Below this beam and supporting it on either side of the doorway is a series of smaller binding blocks with short facing strips of wood between them. Under these binding blocks, again on either side of the entrance doorway, is a long strip of wood supported by four blocks set horizontally into the wall. The doorway was locked by a wooden bolt, still *in situ*, set in a heavy case on the left side of the doorway.

This common method of fastening the lintel to the jambs is also used in the front door of House C50 in Karanis (figure 17), which is also made of acacia. The width of the doorway between the jambs is 75 cm; the length of the lintel is 2 m and its height is 30 cm. Within the door jamb on the right side there is a large bolt case, which is framed by a common type of carving in the form of a doorway of traditional temples, the lintel of which is curved outward in imitation of a cavetto cornice and rests on jambs like square pilasters with a supporting threshold at the bottom (figure 18).[7]

FIGURE 16. THE FRONT DOOR OF HOUSE C68 AT KARANIS.
(HUSSELMAN 1979)

FIGURE 17. THE FRONT DOOR OF HOUSE C50 IN KARANIS.
(HUSSELMAN 1979)

---

[1] Laurence 2007, 102-16.
[2] *P.Oxy.* XXXVI.2758.10 (110/12).
[3] *BGU* III.731.11-12 (180).
[4] *P.Tebt.* I.45.22, 37; *P.Tebt.* I.47.14. 35 (113 BC); Husselman 1979, 40-4. Cf. Hdt. 2.96. Later papyri indicate that doorways within houses were sometimes made out of iron (σιδηρᾶ θύρα) (Bell et al 1933, verso A, I. 12.).
[5] Gazda 1983, 24.
[6] On the construction of doors in Pharaonic Egypt: Koenigsberger 1936.

[7] Husselman 1979, 40-1.

FIGURE 18. THE BOLT-CASE OF THE FRONT DOOR OF HOUSE C50 IN KARANIS. (HUSSELMAN 1979)

Such examples illustrate the common and longstanding tendency to secure the house from the street.[8] It is likely that the inhabitants of some houses in Graeco-Roman Egypt looked upon the front door of their houses as a sacred entrance with religious connotations. In Pharaonic Egypt, the front gate of houses had some religious significance. In the Eleventh Dynasty, the front door of the two models of a house from the Tomb of Maket-Re carries a decoration consisting of the Djed pillar of Osiris surmounted by two bunches of lotus flowers.[9] Equally, the house depicted on the Papyrus of Nakht of the Eighteenth Dynasty is textually described as 'the house from the [front] door of which he pays adoration to the gods'. This gate is bordered with a torus moulding and topped with a cavetto cornice, recalling the monumental doors of traditional temples.[10] The front door is neither inside nor outside the house. Rather, it is a sacred boundary and a liminal zone between the private and public spaces associated respectively with the house and the street.[11] For this reason, it is unsurprising that traditional Egyptian ritual activities were performed before the front door of houses. It is these privileges that paved the way for the space before the front door to integrate their houses with the public space, strengthening social relations, and to communicate aspects of personal and social identity in times of social and religious gatherings.

III.2. The Sacrifice of Fish on 9 Thoth (Julian: 7/8 September)

At certain times of year, the space before the front door of some houses in ancient Egypt played a fundamental role as a religious place and a social focus. One of these times was the 9th of Thoth. In his treatise *De Iside et Osiride*, Plutarch reports an important ritual associated with the front door of houses, when he states:

Οἱ δ' ἱερεῖς ἀπέχονται πάντων· Πρώτου δὲ μηνὸς ἐνάτῃ τῶν ἄλλων Αἰγυπτίων ἑκάστου πρὸ τῆς αὐλείου θύρας ὀπτὸν ἰχθὺν κατεσθίοντος οἱ ἱερεῖς οὐ γεύονται μὲν κατακαίουσι δὲ πρὸ τῶν θυρῶν τοὺς ἰχθῦς.

The [Egyptian] priests, on the other hand, abstain from all fish, and on the ninth day of Thoth, when all the other Egyptians eat roast fish before the front doors of their houses, the priests do not taste the fish, but burn them before their front doors.[12]

Scholars often consider Plutarch's monograph a philosophical text, reflecting middle-Platonic metaphysical ideas about the genesis of the soul and the structure of the universe.[13] For Scott-Moncrieff, the treatise reflected Plutarch's narrow interest in the Hellenised Alexandrian cult.[14] However, Daniel Richter has recently argued that the *De Iside et Osiride* is a metaphysical discourse, demonstrating the superiority of Greek philosophy over Egyptian cult.[15] As the treatise provides a wide range of information about τὴν Αἰγυπτίων θεολογίαν in general, and expresses deep knowledge of the cult of Isis and Osiris in particular, the Egyptian material in the *De Iside et Osiride* cannot be dismissed as worthless.[16] In fact, Plutarch's accounts of Egyptian myths and rites, 'showed, on the whole, a remarkable reliability when compared with the evidence of the Egyptian sources'.[17] Although the sources of Plutarch's composition cannot be identified with certainty, it is not impossible that some Egyptian texts were at his disposal during his visits to Alexandria,[18] Athens or Delphi. At Athens, Plutarch pursued his studies under the Platonist Ammonius, who had an Egyptian name and came to Athens from Egypt.[19] For evidence on the contemporary cult of Egyptian deities, Plutarch also partly relied on his friend Clea, to whom the book

---

[8] Alston 2001, 85.
[9] Kemp 1989, 151-2 (fig. 54).
[10] Davies 1929, 248; Endruweit 2004, 392, fig. 107, British Museum, EA 10471/72.
[11] Bourdieu 1977, 130-2.
[12] Plut. *De Is. et Os.* 7.
[13] E.g. Froidefond 1972, 1987; Dillon 1989. Christopher Jones gives 115 as the date of this composition (Jones 1966b, 73), but Gwyn Griffiths suggests 120 (Griffiths 1970, 16-18).
[14] Scott-Moncrieff 1909.
[15] Richter 2001.
[16] Hani 1976; Froidefond 1978, 1979.
[17] Griffiths 2001, 54.
[18] Plut. *Symp.* 5.5.1. Plutarch voyaged to Alexandria, but whether he travelled further into Egypt is doubtful. On Plutarch's life: Trench 1873; Griffiths 1970.
[19] Jones 1966a. Many Greek philosophers and scholars visited Egypt. Cf. Dio. Sic. 1.69.2-3.

is dedicated. Clea was a priest of Isis and of Dionysus at Delphi and was thus acquainted with Egyptian cults.[20] Plutarch himself, according to an inscription, was still priest at Delphi and epimelete of the Amphictyons in 117.[21]

Plutarch's passage does not make it clear whether the ritual was performed in urban or rural sites. The statement comes in his account of the taboos which the Egyptian priests observed in metropoleis like Memphis, Heliopolis, Oxyrhynchus and Syene, establishing an urban context for the ritual. Yet the possible association of the ritual with inundation and the river Nile seems to suggest a widespread festival. Be that as it may, the passage indicates that the space before the front door of Egyptian houses served as the arena for an important festival, during which the front door acted as its physical setting. The αὐλεία θύρα is one of the Greek designations used to refer to the front door of the house.[22] Since the passage does not speak of a ritual enacted 'in the houses (ἐν τοῖσι οἴκοισι)' or 'in the streets (ἔξω ἐν τῇσι ὁδοῖσι)', but rather 'before the front door (πρὸ τῆς αὐλείου θύρας or πρὸ τῶν θυρῶν)', it is clear that this ritual was performed before the main entrance to the house. While 'ἔξω ἐν τῇσι ὁδοῖσι' only referred to public space,[23] 'πρὸ τῆς αὐλείου θύρας' or 'πρὸ τῶν θυρῶν' meant in private or semi-public space.[24]

Since the Pharaonic period, the living space extended beyond the limits of houses to include the streets.[25] Several domestic activities like spinning and weaving were enacted before the front door of the house in the street. In Herodotus's time, the Egyptians used to 'eat out of doors in the streets (ἐσθίουσι δὲ ἔξω ἐν τῇσι ὁδοῖσι)'.[26] In Pharaonic Egypt, the front door of houses served as a focus of religious domestic practice, and Plutarch's passage seems to suggest the persistence of religious domestic activities in the Roman period.[27] Classical literature and Greek papyri refer to a number of festivities held in honour of both Graeco-Roman and Egyptian deities all the year around in post-Pharaonic Egypt.[28] Equally, demotic papyri confirm a number of traditional festivals celebrated in the month of Thoth, including the Festival of Drunkenness and the W3g festival.[29]

There is no doubt that the festival in question, which was celebrated on 9 Thoth, the first month of inundation (Akhet) and of the year, was associated with inundation and the river Nile, which symbolized the discharge and effusion of Osiris.[30] In Graeco-Roman Egypt, the month of Thoth represented the commencement of the inundation season, which in turn symbolized the victory of Osiris over Seth.[31] Yet this festival must be distinguished from 'the sacrifice to the most sacred Nile' on 30 Pauni.[32] From the Pharaonic to the Roman period, Egypt owed its fertility to the river's annual flood, which brought a new soil adding to the fertility of the land and resulting in an increase in agricultural produce.[33] Successive prefects continued to sacrifice to the god of the Nile in the Roman period.[34]

Given that levels of identity in the past were expressed through a variety of different media,[35] festivals, as times of social gatherings, were important media for articulating identity. In the festival of 9 Thoth, the front doorway of houses was integrated with the public space of the street in solidifying social relations and articulating the social status of the occupants within the community. The front door was an important physical feature of the house frontage, leading from and to the house as well as from and to the street. The front door is a frontier of crossing from one place/space to another. In other words, it is a place of passage, but also of meeting between the two spaces.[36] Since the front door of the house was sometimes called ἡ παρόδιος θύρα, it was envisaged as a liminal space between the domestic and public space.[37]

Domestic properties in Graeco-Roman Egypt extended to include certain spatial and physical features located before the front door of the house in the street, including the πρόθυρον, προπυλών, and εἴσοδος καὶ ἔξοδος. The εἴσοδος καὶ ἔξοδος, i.e. entry and exit, took the form of a paved passage giving access directly to the main entrance of the house (figure 19).[38] They were legally considered the outer physical limits of the house.[39] Such physical features were practically located in the public space of the street. However, they were considered essential parts of the house since they could be sold or leased with it.[40] Equally, windbreaks were sometimes constructed before houses at Karanis to protect doorways from dust and keep

---

[20] Jones 1966b, 73.
[21] SIG II.829.A: ἐπιμελητεύοντος ἀπὸ Δελφῶν Μεστρίου Πλουτάρχου τοῦ ἱερέως; Swain 1991, 320.
[22] P.Tebt. III.1.795.7 (200/176 BC); Husson 1983, 99-100.
[23] Hdt. 2.35.
[24] P.Oxy. XXXVI.2758.10 (110/12). It is noteworthy that in contemporary Egypt, Muslim Egyptians usually slaughter their cows or goats at Eid el-Adha (Feast of Sacrifice) before the front door of their houses. They also soak their hands in the blood of the sacrifice and stamped them on the front side of the front door. This custom has nothing to do with Islam, but it seems that it passed over generations through social tradition and enculturation.
[25] Alston 1997a, 38.
[26] Hdt. 2.35.
[27] Davies 1929, 248; Endruweit 2004, 392.
[28] E.g. P.Oxy. IV.731 (8/9) in which the festivals of Isis and Hera are mentioned. For public and religious festivals in Roman Egypt: Vandoni 1964; Perpillou-Thomas 1993.

[29] Smith 2009, 412.
[30] Plut. De Is. et Os. 33; Assmann 2005, 355-63; Abbas 2010, 4-13.
[31] Perpillou-Thomas 1993, 144.
[32] P.Oxy. IX.1211 (the second century); Lewis 1983, 95.
[33] Strauss-Seeber 2004, 376-85.
[34] Bowman 1986, 183.
[35] Millett 2007.
[36] Bourdieu 1973.
[37] Husson 1983, 98-9.
[38] Husson 1983, 65-72.
[39] Taubenschlag 1927.
[40] P.Oxy. III.502.20-21 (164).

Figure 19. The entry and exit of a house at Karanis.

the privacy of the interiors by preventing pedestrians from watching the inside. Although the windbreak was actually located in the public space of the street, it was considered a physical part of the house.[41] In times of Egyptian religious activities, the front door of houses integrated between two types of spaces, one inside the house and the other outside in the street. Indeed, this festival was an important ritual activity and a suitable time of social interaction in front of the house. In this festival, the front door of houses did not divide, but rather integrated private and public space. It was expected that the front door was kept open during the whole period of celebration. Thus it marked the meeting point of space and the interplay between public and private.[42]

It is unknown whether Roman and Greek citizens participated in such rites. Whether Plutarch means the Hellenised metropolitan elites when he mentions 'the other Egyptians' is unclear. In Roman Egypt, aiguptios designated any inhabitant who was neither a Roman nor a citizen of Greek poleis or Jew. Metropolites and villagers alike were classed as "Egyptian". Although Plutarch visited Alexandria, it is doubtful whether he travelled further into the *chora*. Whether Plutarch was familiar with such a legal hierarchy when he visited Alexandria in the early second century is a matter of guess. It is difficult to argue from Plutarch's text alone that only those legally-defined as Egyptian performed the rite before the gate of their houses. That Egyptian priests and other participants used the rite to solidify their group identity as opposed to non-Egyptians seems historically unlikely. Romans, Alexandrians, and the Hellenized metropolites equally patronized traditional cults and temples. The metropolitan magistrates called Graeco-Roman and Egyptian festivities and sacrifices in the theatre and hippodrome. It is likely that any resident who was interested in such rituals could partake of them without difficulty.

Plutarch's passage mentions that the Egyptians, including priests, took part in this festival. However, their actions were quite different from each other. While priests burnt the fish, other inhabitants would eat the fish before the front gate of their house. The priests could not only mark the high position of their profession, but also emphasized the superior status of their houses within the community.[43] According to the Gnomon of the Idioslogos, priests were required to dress in linen rather than wool and were forbidden to wear long hair.[44] This legislation made a long-standing ritual dress compulsory, visibly and legally marking the priests apart from other residents of Egypt. Some Egyptian priests were even exempted from the poll-tax.[45] By burning fish rather than eating it, the priests probably marked their high status as opposed to non-priestly residents of other houses. Thus, the priests might have used the ritual to assert their personal and social identities. In that sense, the ritual might have served to define the house in relation to other houses. Identity could thus be multi-layered.

---

[41] Windbreaks are still used in contemporary Egypt, especially in villages.
[42] Wallace-Hadrill 1988.
[43] Alston 2001, 85.
[44] Riccobono 1950, 58.
[45] *P.Tebt.* II.294.

Fish was a favourite diet in Graeco-Roman Egypt.[46] The probable connection of this festival with inundation and the river Nile explains the reason for which fish was particularly associated with this celebration. Some of the proceedings of this festival might have occurred within the house, including the preparation of food, whereas others took place before the front door in the street, including eating the food. In such a celebration, it was expected that the participants saluted and congratulated each other, and possibly exchange fish as well. It is through participation in the ritual that the social identity of the house occupants was articulated before the front gate. I suggest that the domestic pylon was influenced in some features by that of traditional temples. Both were huge structures acting as façade-entrances to the structures with which there are associated. The domestic pylon contained a *triclinium*, *symposion*, and *andron*, which could be easily used in times of ritual and social gatherings.[47] The occupants of houses might have invited their neighbours to join them in the meal in the dining-rooms of such domestic pyla. Due to its religious significance and architectural and spatial abilities to address all inhabitants, the front door of houses and the space before it was an appropriate arena for ritual activities associated with personal, social, and cultural identity in the Roman period. It is argued that rituals enacted in the street are important features of any culture. Such practices often enhance cultural and social communications.[48] Thus, culture is widely regarded as 'the outcome of the processes by which values and beliefs pattern social and individual identity, which, in turn, are influenced by them'.[49] The front door of houses and the space before it in the street together became a place for shared religious activities and a focus of personal and social identities. Ritual times often provide opportunities for social interaction between individuals. Experiences of the street shape social practices and identities.[50]

Apart from the main thoroughfares of cities and villages, streets were generally narrow in Roman Egypt, measuring 1.5 m in Karanis (figure 20).[51] Karanis has two main thoroughfares running from south to north, CS210 on the east and CS400 on the west, with a possible third main street connecting the North Temple and South Temple. Apparently, no main east-west thoroughfare ran across the village. The blocks of houses were arranged along main streets, minor streets, and passageways. Although the front doorways of many houses were easily accessible from streets, others were obstructed by steps leading to doorways or by the windbreaks, as House C68 from Street CS95, C56 from CS52, C151 from CS160, and to C146 from CS160.[52] As the average size of families of

FIGURE 20. A STREET IN KARANIS.

---

[46] On fish trade in the Roman Empire: Jones 1974, 140-50. On papyrological references to fish and salted fish in Roman Egypt: *P.Oxy.* VI.928 (the second century); *P.Oxy.* VI.937 (the third century); *P.Oxy.* VII.1067 (the third century).
[47] *P.Mich.* V.295.4 (the first century); *P.Lond.* III.978.13 (331); *SB* VI.8988.57-8 (647).
[48] Fyfe 1998.
[49] Davies 2008, 9.
[50] Fyfe 1998, 1.
[51] Hobson 1985, 214.
[52] Husselman 1979, 29-31.

all household types was higher in villages (4.46 people) than in cities (4.04),[53] it could be suggested that social interaction between the inhabitants was stronger in villages than in cities. Narrow streets and more family members meant more social interaction, particularly since 'extended families and multiple family households were more common in villages'.[54] In any case, a dynamic interplay occurred in this celebration between the front door of the house and the street, forming together a joint space of action and solidarity. The front door of houses was thus an important site of ritual practices, which are part of the image of the streets.[55] As a ritual practice, the festival held on 9 Thoth constituted engagement, communication, interaction, contact, enjoyment and articulation of personal and social identity. It also possessed the capacity to foster social and cultural interaction among its participants. Ritual behaviour is often regarded as both a 'social act' and a 'form of communication'.[56] Equally, there is a general consensus that ritual act is 'a special mode of social intercourse'.[57] In this ceremony, the participants engaged in a shared practice, the 'habitus' in Bourdieu's terms, whereby they engaged in a repeatedly renewed familiarity with and commitment to their cultural values and ideas.[58]

The American anthropologists Eliot Chapple and Carleton Coon called the ritual moments in which members of communities gather to re-engage with their basic values and ideas 'rites of intensification'. The Christians' participation in the Eucharist and the Muslims' daily prayers are good examples of 'rites of intensification'.[59] The annual inundation of the river Nile, with which this festival was associated, was an important event in the life of inhabitants in Graeco-Roman Egypt. The fundamental role that the Nile played in the life of the population, with the prosperity and fertility it guaranteed, necessitated its veneration and probably provided a reason for such a ceremony. Festivals and rituals contribute to the inclusion and integration of individuals within their local communities.[60] Festal and ritual times often involve the inculcation of cultural values and ideas that become second nature to the individuals concerned, whose sense of identity is partly composed of these values and ideas. Ritual is a process in which individuals bring their basic ideas to mind and engage with them in and through the acts performed, the objects used, and the place of performance. The participation of the Egyptians renders the ritual a collective character, but the participants could articulate layers of identity assertion. This celebration was performed at a prescribed time (9 Thoth) and at a certain space (before the front door of houses) and in the special manners in which its participants acted (eating and burning fish) to communicate their personal and social identities.

The role of a particular place is of fundamental significance in 'the rites of intensification', when the cultural ideas and values of individuals, according to Douglas Davies, are brought to a spatial and behavioural focus.[61] As the arena for and the physical focus of the ritual held on 9 Thoth, the front door of the house and the space before it together were important for remembering the ritual, particularly since architectural and spatial features were used in ancient cultures as environments of memory.[62] It is argued that a sense of identity emerges in domestic space through a variety of cultural practices.[63] The annual integration of the house and the street on 9 Thoth seems to have set the scene for emphasizing the occupants' familial identity. Repetition and fixity of time and place have been consistently cited as central features of the communicative function of rituals, which play a major part in the formation of social identity.[64]

III.3. The Sacrifice of Pigs on 15 Pachon (Julian: 10 May)

The ritual on 9 Thoth was not the only celebration held before the front door of the house for Herodotus reports another festival when he states that:

> Τῷ δὲ Διονύσῳ τῆς ἑορτῆς τῇ δορπίῃ χοῖρον πρὸ τῶν θυρῶν σφάξας ἕκαστος διδοῖ ἀποφέρεθαι τὸν χοῖρον αὐτῷ τῷ ἀποδομένῳ τῶν συβωτέων.

> To Dionysus, on the evening of his festival [15 Pachon] every [Egyptian] sacrifices a pig which he kills before his front door and then gives it to the swineherd himself who has sold it, for him to take away.[65]

This passage refers to another ceremony performed at the front door of houses. As it stands, the sacrifice of pigs before the gate of the house was the most important feature of this ritual.

First, I would suggest that the festival in question was associated for the most part with the god Osiris, his wife, the goddess Isis, and their son, the god Horus. As far as we can tell, the frenzied rites associated with the festivals of Dionysus lacked such a ritual.[66] It is highly likely that Herodotus had the god Osiris in mind when he wrote this passage. It is a common feature in Herodotus' writings on Egypt to give the names of Greek gods to the Egyptian

---

[53] Bagnall and Frier 1994, 66-71.
[54] Alston and Alston 1997, 207.
[55] Crouch 1998, 160.
[56] Bell 1992, 54-89.
[57] Platvoet 1995, 36.
[58] Bourdieu 1990.
[59] Chapple and Coon 1942, 507-28.
[60] Platvoet 1995, 36.
[61] Davies 2008, 13.
[62] Crouch 1998, 166.
[63] Davies 2008, 13.
[64] Platvoet 1995, 28; Bell 1992, 91-2.
[65] Hdt. 2.48.
[66] On the cult, myth, and frenzied festivals of Dionysus: Otto 1965.

deities. Hence for Herodotus Ptah was Hephaestus,[67] Neith was Athena,[68] Osiris was Dionysus,[69] and Isis was Demeter.[70] Equally, classical writers of the Roman period used to equate Egyptian and Greek deities. For example, Plutarch mentioned that 'Amun is the proper name of Zeus among the Egyptians'.[71] I would argue that this celebration persisted into the Roman period. Before considering the evidence for the continuity of this ritual and the role it played in expressing Egyptian religious traditions and aspects of the participants' social and local identities under Roman rule, a brief digression is necessary to discuss the role and status of pigs in ancient Egyptian religion and culture.

Throughout the successive periods of ancient Egyptian history, pigs were among the most common domesticated animals.[72] In Ptolemaic and Roman Egypt, pig-breeding continued to be a relatively important economic activity. Pigs were reared alongside other domesticated animals in the courtyards of houses in both towns and villages.[73] This activity led to the emergence of a 'pig tax' levied from those breeding and trading on pigs[74] and even from those sacrificing pigs.[75] Pigs played a role in the diet of the inhabitants,[76] and were consumed at least by the lower classes.[77] Pigs were closely associated in ancient Egyptian religion and mythology with the god Seth, lord of chaos.[78] Together with hippopotami and donkeys, pigs were considered the evil animals of the god Seth.[79] No Egyptian god took the form of a pig, however.[80] Due to their connection with Seth, pigs had an ambiguous status in ancient Egyptian religion and culture.[81] Pork was never used in traditional temple offerings. However, pigs were included in lists of temple properties.[82] The association of pigs with dirt and filth may explain their lowly status in ancient Egyptian culture.[83] However, the taboo on pigs was reinforced due to the connection of pigs with Seth.[84]

In ancient Egyptian religion, it was believed that Seth transformed himself into a black boar when he attacked the god Horus. Chapter 112 of the Book of the Dead, which is entitled 'Spell for Knowing the Souls of Pe', reads:

Now the black pig was Suti [Seth] who had transformed himself into a black pig. It was he who had aimed the blow of fire [the thunderbolt] which struck the eye of Horus. Then said Re unto those gods: 'The pig is an abominable thing to Horus; but he shall be well, although the big is an abomination to him'.[85]

Having looked at the boar, a serious injury occurred to the left eye of Horus associated with the moon.[86] Plutarch indirectly referred to this spell when he mentioned that 'according to the belief and account of the Egyptians, Typhon (Seth) at one time smites the eye of Horus, and at another time snatches it out and swallows it, and then later gives it back to the Sun'.[87] The pig was associated with Seth, because Seth took the shape of a pig, whereby it became a symbol of chaos. Pigs continued to be regarded as 'unclean animals' in the Roman Period.[88]

Although the first passage of Herodotus does not indicate the date or time of this festival, another passage seems to clarify the time in which the sacrifice of pigs was performed:

Τοῖσι μέν νυν ἄλλοισι θεοῖσι θύειν ὗς οὐ δικαιεῦσι Αἰγύπτιοι, Σελήνῃ δὲ καὶ Διονύσῳ μούνοισι τοῦ αὐτοῦ χρόνου, τῇ αὐτῇ πανσελήνῳ, τοὺς ὗς θύσαντες πατέονται τῶν κρεῶν.

Nor do the Egyptians think it right to sacrifice swine to any god but the Moon and Dionysus. To these they sacrifice swine at the same time, in the same season of full moon, and then they eat of the flesh.[89]

Herodotus emphasised the religious context of the festival by twice using the verb 'to sacrifice', θύειν and θύσαντες. Since it is widely accepted that Selene is used in Herodotus' writing on Egypt to refer to Isis and Dionysus to Osiris, it follows that sacrificing pigs was associated with a festival held in honour of Osiris and Isis.[90] This religious festivity was recurrently held on the evening of a full moon night of a certain month. Since sacrificing pigs was primarily associated with the Osirian cult, it is tempting to suggest that pigs were also sacrificed for the god Horus.[91]

Egyptian textual and visual evidence, papyri, and classical literature argue for a remarkable continuity of this festival into the Roman period. Before studying this evidence in detail, we should first consider the evidence for the Ptolemaic period. In the calendar of the Ptolemaic

---

[67] Hdt. 2.121.
[68] Hdt. 2.59.
[69] Hdt. 2.47-48.
[70] Hdt. 2.59, 122.
[71] Plut. *De Is. et Os.* 9.
[72] Shaw and Nicholson 1995, 35. On textual, pictorial and zooarchaeological evidence for pigs in ancient Egypt: Hdt. 2.14; Newberry 1928, 211; Houlihan 1996, 25-8.
[73] Bowman 1986, 102.
[74] *P.Oxy.* IV.733 (171).
[75] *P.Giss.Bibl.* 1.2 (the second century BC).
[76] Pedding 1991, 25.
[77] Hecker 1982, 62.
[78] Bonnet 1952, 112.
[79] Dieleman 2005, 130-8.
[80] Houlihan 1996, 26.
[81] Helck 1984, 764.
[82] Newberry 1928, 211.
[83] Houlihan 2001, 47.
[84] Lloyd 2007, 271.

[85] Faulkner 1972, 85.
[86] Plut. *De Is. et Os.* 52; Budge 1909, 159.
[87] Plut. *De Is. et Os.* 55.
[88] Plut. *De Is. et Os.* 8; Ael. *NA* 10.16. On the low status of swineherds in Pharaonic Egypt: Hdt. 2.47.
[89] Hdt. 2.47.
[90] Bonnet 1952, 691.
[91] Lloyd 2007, 271.

Chapter III Ritual Activities Enacted Before the Front Door of Houses

FIGURE 21. THE SACRIFICE OF A HIPPOPOTAMUS ON THE INNER AMBULATORY OF EDFU TEMPLE.

temple of Edfu, which is approximated to 88-80 BC and continues to function in the Roman period, a text reads:

> The festival of the 15 day of the month [of Pachon], the day of full moon: it is a big festival all over the country (ḥb ꜥꜣ m tꜣ) when a pig is being sacrificed (snḳ=tw ipḥ).[92]

The inscription indicates that the sacrifice of pigs on 15 Pachon continued in the Ptolemaic period. A distinctive feature of this event was to sacrifice a pig on the full moon night of 15 Pachon, the first month of harvest (*Shemu*) and the ninth of the year. Although Herodotus' passage does not explicitly refer to the date of the festival, there is no room for doubt that the ritual mentioned by Herodotus was the one held in the month of Pachon.

The presence of a ritual during which a pig is being sacrificed at the front door of the house raises a number of questions, the most important of which is concerned with its religious significance and symbolism. Visual evidence from the temple of Edfu, which records the struggle between Horus and Seth, may provide an answer to this question.[93] On the western wall of the inner ambulatory there is a relief representing the sacrifice of a hippopotamus (figure 21).[94]

Ptolemy X Alexander is depicted to the left feeding a goose, which symbolizes the king's triumph over his enemies. In the middle a priest representing the deified Imhotep is reading from the book of rituals. The slaughterer is shown to the right cutting a hippopotamus (*nš* in the accompanying inscription) with a knife, although no blood is spilled.[95] The sacred drama in which the triumph of Horus, heir of Osiris, over Seth, Horus' coronation as King of Upper and Lower Egypt, and his marriage with the goddess Hathor of Tentyris were annually performed at Edfu.[96] The triumph of Horus is frequently represented in terms of Horus' harpooning a hippopotamus,[97] which, according to an inscription at Edfu, occurs on 15 Pachon,[98] as the sacrifice of pigs, but in this relief in terms of slaughtering the hippopotamus. Since Seth is shown here in the form of a hippopotamus, and given that the sacrifice of a pig, another evil animal identified with Seth/Typhon, is also confirmed from the Edfu calendar on 15 Pachon, the sacrifice of pigs at the front door of houses may have been similarly meant to

---
[92] Alliot 1949, 331 = Bonneau 1991, 334.
[93] Bonnet 1952, 691.
[94] Contrary to Newberry's assumption that the animal is a pig (Newberry 1928, 214).
[95] Chassinat 1934, XIII, pls.441-2; Blackman and Fairman 1943, 30. This hieroglyphic word for a hippopotamus comes from a verb, *nš*, which means 'to drive away' (Wilson 1997, 549). It is interesting to know that this verb is still used in modern Egypt to give the same meaning especially in contexts such as 'drive away flies or mosquitoes'.
[96] Blackman and Fairman 1942, 1943.
[97] Chassinat 1934, XIII, pls. 508, 510, 512-13. Cf. Mettinger 1988, 196, fig. 15.
[98] Blackman and Fairman 1943, 5.

commemorate the triumph of Horus over Seth and, by extension, Osiris over Seth and order over chaos. The festival also commemorated the time when Seth turned into a black boar and destroyed the left eye of Horus associated with the moon, and this is why the festival was held on the full moon night.[99] As Seth transformed himself into a black pig and injured the left eye of Horus, the participants probably wished to prevent the recurrence of this incident by sacrificing a pig annually on the night of the full moon in the month of Pachon. The full moon was the most suitable moment for this rite because of the moon's association with the left eye of Horus which Seth destroyed. Pigs were mainly offered to the god Horus, Lord of the Moon Eye, at Edfu,[100] and the festival was undoubtedly one of the most splendid all over the country, as the inscription indicates.

Classical authors confirm the continuity of this ritual into the Roman period.[101] Although the space where the ritual is celebrated is not mentioned, the circumstantial evidence of later sources would suggest that we are dealing with the same ritual. Writing in the early second century, Plutarch unmistakably refers to his festival when he states that:

ὁμοίως δὲ καὶ τὴν ὗν ἀνίερον ζῷον ἡγοῦνται· τὸν δὲ λόγον, ὃν θύοντες ἅπαξ [τοῦ ἔτους] ὗν ἐν πανσελήνῳ καὶ κατεσθίοντες ἐπιλέγουσιν, ὡς ὁ Τυφῶν ὗν διώκων πρὸς τὴν πανσέληνον εὗρε τὴν ξυλίνην σορόν, ἐν ᾗ τὸ σῶμα τοῦ Ὀσίριδος ἔκειτο, καὶ διέρριψεν.

In the same way they [the Egyptians] consider the pig to be an unclean animal; when they sacrifice a pig once every year in full moon and eat it, they narrate a story that Typhon, as he was pursuing a pig in full moon, found the wooden coffin, in which the body of Osiris lay, and tore it up.[102]

Plutarch agrees with other classical writers that pigs continued to be regarded as 'unclean animals'. However, he referred to another reason for associating them with the god Seth. In Plutarch's passage, Seth was chasing a pig in full moon when he came across the wooden coffin of Osiris, which he promptly destroyed into pieces. In contrast, Egyptian sources confirm that Seth himself took the form of a pig and injured the moon eye of Horus. Of special interest in Plutarch's passage is his statement that a religious festival was celebrated once a year in full moon time, during which pigs were sacrificed and their flesh would be eaten.

Based on Manetho of Sebennyte, Aelian, who lived in the late second and early third century, refers to this festival when he states that:

Πεπιστεύκασι δὲ Αἰγύπτιοι τὴν ὗν καὶ ἡλίωι καὶ σελήνηι ἐχθίστην εἶναι· ὅταν δὲ [Αἰγύπτιοι] πανηγυρίζωσιν τῆι Σελήνηι, θύουσιν αὐτῆι ἅπαξ τοῦ ἔτους ὗς, ἄλλοτε δὲ οὔτε ἐκείνηι οὔτε ἄλλωι τῶν θεῶν τόδε τὸ ζῷον ἐθέλουσι θύειν [ὡς μυσαρόν].

The Egyptians believe that swine are particularly abhorrent to the sun and moon: they sacrifice these animals once a year when they held the annual lunar festival, but on no other occasion do they offer them either to the moon or to any other gods.[103]

Aelian's passage makes clear that swine continued to be regarded as hateful animals to the sun (Horus) and moon (Isis). The reason for regarding pigs as detestable animals to the sun and moon is traced back to Chapter 112 of the Book of the Dead. The passage also confirms that a religious festival was annually held on a full moon night. Although sacrificing pigs was the most distinctive feature of this celebration, sacrificing pigs on other occasions appears to have been prohibited. Although the passages mentioned above state that the participants in this ritual were Egyptians, one should not overestimate the validity of such literary texts since the reality on the ground was more complex. The fact that the ritual is typically traditional does not necessarily mean that only those legally-defined as Egyptian sacrificed pigs. It is also unclear whether the house occupants would slaughter the animal by themselves or butchers were required to slaughter on their behalf.

It is unclear whether the pig sacrifice on 15 Pachon was part of the famous Pachon festival, which lasted, according to a papyrus of AD 253, from 13 to 19 Pachon which were granted public holidays,[104] and to which a *mimus*, a musician, a dancer, and a Homericist were invited to conduct their performances in the theatre at Oxyrhynchus.[105] Investigations of the archaeology of poleis and metropoleis have confirmed that urban centres were multicultural sites, where Graeco-Roman and Egyptian cultural traditions were closely integrated. It is even argued that Egyptian religious traditions were preserved in the Roman period through their incorporation into the dominant Hellenic milieu.[106] The sacrifice to the 'most sacred Nile' occurred in the hippodrome at Oxyrhynchus and the festival of Kronos/Souchos was held in the temple of Jupiter Capitolinus at Ptolemais Euergetes. Like the ritual on 9 Thoth, it is unclear whether Romans and Greeks participated in

---

[99] On the sacrifice of pigs in the ancient Near East: de Vaux 1966, 252-69.
[100] Newberry 1928, 214; Bonnet 1952, 691.
[101] On Christian sacrifices of pigs in the sixth century: *P.Oxy.* XLVI.3866.3.
[102] Plut. *De Is. et Os.* 8.
[103] Ael. *NA* 10.16.
[104] *P.Oxy.* XXXI.2586.39-42; Perpillou-Thomas 1993, 110-12.
[105] *P.Oxy.* XVII.2127 (171).
[106] Alston 1997c, 89.

this ritual. If the ritual of 15 Pachon was part of the long Pachon festival of papyri then we have another example of the integration of a traditional ritual into a classical structure. Given the lack of evidence, this connection between the two Pachon festivals cannot be proven.

Unlike the festival on 9 Thoth where the role of Egyptian priests is stated, nothing is known about their behaviour during the ritual on 15 Pachon in the Roman period. The participants in this ritual sacrificed pigs and ate their flesh at the front door of their houses. Even the poor who could not afford a pig were perhaps not precluded from sharing this cult activity with other individuals. It is plausible that the poor continued to 'mould swine of dough, which they then bake and sacrifice'.[107] The symbolism of sacrificing pigs at the front door of houses was probably so simple and clear that it needed no explanation and was apparent to the participants. By killing pigs, the animals of Seth/Typhon, the participants might have symbolically wanted to kill Seth and thus took part in the triumph of Horus and his father Osiris over their arch-enemy.

III.4. Conclusion

Through the performance of ritual activities, the 'space' before the front door of the house becomes a 'place' of festivity.[108] In addition to the ritual held on 9 Thoth, the celebration of a second ceremony before the front door of the house on 15 Pachon indicates that the front door was used as a sacred place and social focus at certain times of year. The first ritual was performed in the first month of the year, while the second was held in the ninth. In the festival of Thoth, the participants ate and burnt fish at the front door of houses, whereas pigs were sacrificed in the festival of Pachon. Although it is stated that the Egyptians partook of both festivities, their actions differed according to their social status and position. In the first ritual, the priests burnt the fish to mark their superior status as well as that of their houses, whereas the rest of the inhabitants ate roast fish. In the second ritual, the priests might have sacrificed pigs within the temples, although they never tasted it.[109] Other inhabitants sacrificed and eat pigs at the front door of houses, whereas the poor perhaps moulded pigs of dough, which they baked and ate.

Such collective celebrations also had the potential to bring members of the local community together. Being at the house frontage, it is no wonder that these rituals were performed before the gate of the house, linking the private with the public. The space before the front gate was the arena for such 'rites of intensification', during which the participants not only emphasised their social identity, but they might have also constructed a sense of belonging to their local community. It is noteworthy that the two rituals were performed in the first month of two of the three seasons of the Egyptian year. 'Rites of intensification' are often performed in correspondence with environmental change, such as the alternation of day and night, the phases of the moon, and the progression of the seasons in their annual cycle.[110] As a liminal threshold between two spaces, the area before the front door of the house was unsurprisingly an appropriate place for performing the rites connected with such transitional periods as the change of seasons.[111]

---

[107] Hdt. 2.47.
[108] On the distinction between 'space' and 'place': Larmour and Spencer 2007, 11.
[109] Sext. Emp. *Pyr.* 2.223: 'the Egyptian and Jewish priests would prefer to die rather than to eat pigs'.
[110] Chapple and Coon 1942, 507-8.
[111] Bourdieu 1990, 228-33.

Chapter IV
The Illumination of Lamps (*Lychnocaia*) for Athena-Neith on 13 Epeiph (Julian: 24 June)

Egyptologists and classicists have considered ancient Egyptian religion from different perspectives.[1] The creator and warrior goddess Neith and her northern cult centre Sais (Sa el-Haggar) were points of scholarly interest.[2] Light has been shed on the assimilation of Neith with the Greek warrior goddess Athena[3] and on lanterns and lamps associated through their figurative details with Athena-Neith.[4] Among the festivals confirmed in Greek papyri for Athena-Neith at Sais is the festival of lamps (*Lychnokaia*).[5] This chapter deals with the illumination of lamps for Neith-Athena from the Pharaonic to the Roman period, which was performed within and outside houses. The *Lychnocaia* was a nocturnal ceremony of a spectacular festival for Neith-Athena in Sais, Esna, and countrywide, and I argue that it also symbolised a ceremony in the Osirian myth. The chapter first addresses the nature of this ceremony in Pharaonic Egypt and evidence for its maintenance in Graeco-Roman times. Then, the identification of Athena and Neith and the symbolism of the *Lychnocaia* are addressed. Finally, the *Lychnocaia* is considered from an ethnic perspective, highlighting the complexity of associating ritual activities with ethnic or legal groups in Graeco-Roman Egypt.

IV.1. The Festival of Lamps in Herodotus' *Histories*

The performance of ritual activities around or within the domestic space was an important feature of religious and social life of the Egyptian society since the Pharaonic period. The house was the locus of domestic and religious practices.[6] Certain ceremonies were celebrated at the main gate of the house. The house depicted on the funerary papyrus of Nakht, now kept in the British Museum (EA 1047/72), for example, has been described as 'the home from the door of which he (Nakht) pays adoration to the gods'.[7] Similarly, 'on the ninth day of the first month (Thoth), when every one of the other Egyptians eats a broiled fish in front of the outer door of his house, the priests do not even taste the fish, but burn them up in front of their doors'.[8] Equally, the sacrifice of pigs to Osiris on 15 Pachon, the first month of harvest (Shemu) and the ninth of the year, was performed at the front door of the house.[9]

Writing in the fifth century BC, Herodotus was the first classical author to mention, although in passing, a festival of lamps for Athena-Neith in Sais:

> At the times when they [the Egyptians] gather together at Sais for their sacrifices, on a certain night they all kindle many lamps many round about the houses. They use lamps in the shape of flat dishes filled with a mixture of salt and oil, on the top of which a wick floats and keeps burning all night. This is called the Festival of Lamps. The Egyptians who do not come to this solemn assembly observe the night of sacrifice by burning their own lamps at home, so that on that night lamps are burning not only at Sais but throughout Egypt. And there is a religious reason assigned for the special honour paid to this night, as well as for the illumination which accompanies it.[10]

Drawing on the description of Herodotus, Themistius (AD 317-390) indicates that during the *panegyris* of Athena, 'Sais is illuminated by the sacred fire during that night'.[11] The illumination of lamps took place at night before a certain sacrifice, presumably for Athena-Neith. Judging from a Trajanic inscription in Esna Temple, discussed later, lamps were illuminated for Neith on 13 Epeiph (Julian: 24th June), the third month of harvest and the eleventh of the year.[12] According to Herodotus, it was a representative occasion, in which all Egyptians participated not only at Sais, but also countrywide. In his commentary on the second book of Herodotus, Alan Lloyd identified the flat dish lamp as Alan Gardiner's sign R7 (figure 22),[13] however, the sign does not represent a dish and Gardiner himself interpreted it as 'an incense bowl with smoke rising from it', suggesting that it was an incense burner rather than a lamp.[14] The Egyptian floating wick saucer lamp found at Kom Hadid locus 7613 (figure 23) definitely visualises Herodotus' description of the lamps used at Sais.[15] As lamps were a defining feature of the *Lychnocaia*, let us first consider the role of lamps in ancient Egyptian religion and magic

---

[1] E.g. Assmann 1995, 2005; Alston 1997a; Finnestad 1997; Borg 1997; Frankfurter 1998; Venit 2002; Assmann 2005; Hart 2005; Riggs 2005; Smith 2009.
[2] El-Sayed 1982; Wilson 2001.
[3] Quaegebeur et al 1985.
[4] Dunand 1976.
[5] Perpillou-Thomas 1993, 121-22.
[6] Cf. Abbas and Abdelwahed 2014.
[7] Davies 1929, 248.
[8] Plut. *De Is. et Os.* 7.
[9] Hdt. 2.48; Plut. *De Is. et Os.* 7-8; Ael. *NA* 10.16; Abdelwahed 2015, 84-91.
[10] Hdt. 2.62.1-2. Translation: Godley 1920.
[11] Them. *Or.* 6.49.a-c.
[12] *P.Hib.* I.27.165 = Grenfell and Hunt 1906, 144; Sauneron 1962, 302.
[13] Lloyd 1976, 280-3.
[14] Gardiner 1957, 501.
[15] Thomas 2015a, 2, fig. 1.

FIGURE 22. GARDINER'S SIGN R7.

FIGURE 23. AN EGYPTIAN FLOATING WICK SAUCER LAMP FOUND AT KOM HADID LOCUS 7613. (LEONARD 2001)

and their close association with the god Osiris before dealing with the identification of Neith and Athena.[16]

IV.2. Lamps in Ancient Egyptian Religion and Magic

A huge number of lamps (in Egyptian, Greek, Graeco-Egyptian, and Roman-style) were uncovered from Egypt.[17] Lamps were simply used for providing light in temples, tombs, and houses,[18] but they carried additional meaning in certain circumstances and contexts. They were used as votive gifts to the gods and during temple ritual practices and nocturnal festivals.[19] Lamps also played a major role in ancient Egyptian religion and magic because they were closely associated with the god Osiris.

During the Middle Kingdom, the rite of the illumination of lamp (*jrt tk3*) is closely connected with the god Osiris, as the inscriptions of Middle Kingdom tombs at Hatnub and El-Bersheh (in modern Minia) confirm.[20] This connection between lamp-lighting and Osiris continued throughout the successive periods of ancient Egyptian history. In the festival calendar of the Tomb of Neferhotep (TT 50), the divine father of Amun under King Horemheb at Thebes, the illumination of lamps is associated with the Osirian festivals of Khoiak and Mesore.[21] A vignette from the tomb, known as the Bankes fragment, shows the son of the deceased presenting a jar of ointment and two lamps. Although the first column of text is damaged, the remaining six columns read as:

... *tk3 pn nfr n Wsjr jt ntr Nfr-htp m mᶜndt m msktt n skj=f nn htm=f n dt jn s3=f wᶜb Jmn-m-jnt m3ᶜ=hrw*

... this beautiful lamp for Osiris, the divine father Neferhotep, in the day bark and in the night bark. It [the lamp] shall not be destroyed. It shall not ever perish. Says his son, the purification priest Ameneminet, justified.[22]

It was necessary to provide light for the deceased in his passage into the darkness of the underworld, and this is why a lamp is placed in the day and night barks of Osiris, king of the hereafter. During the New Kingdom, priests performed the rite of affording light to the dead in the dark necropolis, but, on celebrations, relatives and friends could present them in pairs along with fat for their replenishment.[23] One, two, or three wicks standing in a cup are shown on the west walls of Tomb 51 at Deir el-Medina, where the god of flame, Sejti, presents them to Osiris as the sun sets in the western hills. In the same tomb, the rite of lamp-lighting is accompanied by the censing and libation of offerings and by women mourning for the dead. In the court of Tomb 23 at Deir el-Medina there is a long inscription, emphasising the identification of lamps with Osiris and the Eye of Horus associated with the moon: 'Hail to you good candle of Osiris N! Hail to you, Eye of Horus, who guides the gods in darkness and guides Osiris N from any resting-place of his to the place wherein his spirit desires to be'.[24]

During the Twenty-sixth Dynasty (664-525 BC), also called the Saite Period after Sais, individuals continued to donate portions of land to maintain lamps in Egyptian temples for Horus, Isis, and Neith. A stele of Amasis records the donation of ten arourae of land to support the illumination of lamps for the temple of Horus, the son of Osiris, at Hutnesu (modern Sharuna).[25] Another stele

---

[16] Egyptian texts use the terms *tk3* and *st3* synonymously with the same determinative ( ) to designate lamps, torches, or tapers (Faulkner 1988, 253, 301).
[17] Robins 1939; Dunand 1976.
[18] Bailey 2001.
[19] Cf. *P.Stras.* IV.300.27 (Apollonopolis Magna, AD 100-200); *BGU* II.362 (Arsinoe, AD 215).
[20] Anthes 1928, 22.4; Newberry and Griffith 1893, 13, 25.
[21] Making the Osiris bed on 18 Khoiak and making the Osiris bed and other rites on 23 Mesore.
[22] Manniche 1985, 105-8.
[23] Griffiths 1958.
[24] Davies 1924, 13.
[25] Leahy 1988.

of Amasis offers land to illuminate lamps for the temple of Isis, the consort of Osiris, at Buto (modern Tell el-Farain).[26] Similarly, a number of stelea, mostly from the Saite Dynasty, record the dedication of lands to provide lamps for the temple of Neith at Sais.[27]

In the fifth century BC, Herodotus visited Egypt and recounted the *Lychnocaia* for Athena in Sais: 'the Egyptians do not hold a single solemn assembly, but several in the course of the year. The principal one of these and the most enthusiastically celebrated is that in honour of Artemis [the cat-goddess Bastet] at the town of Bubastis, and the next is that in honour of Isis at Busiris…The third greatest festival [*Lychnocaia*] is at Sais in honour of Athena [Neith]'.[28] The reason for associating the illumination of lamps with Sais on 13 Epeiph can also be found in Herodotus' *Histories*:

> Here too, in this same precinct of Athena at Sais, is the grave of one whom I think it not right to mention in such a connection [i.e. Osiris]. It stands behind the temple, against the back wall, which it entirely covers. There are also some large stone obelisks in the enclosure, and there is a lake near them ... On this lake, the Egyptians represent by night his sufferings whose name I refrain from mentioning and this representation they call their Mysteries.[29]

Sais was the main venue for the performance of the illumination of lamps on 13 Epeiph for another claim to fame of the city was the 'grave of Osiris' and the passion-play of Osiris' mysteries enacted on the lake. Sais was one of the mythological destinations of funerary rituals for the deceased. The evil god Seth dismembered the body of his brother Osiris into fourteen or twenty-six pieces.[30] Aided by Anubis, however, Isis collected and buried the dispersed body of Osiris in different parts of Egypt, notably Abydos, Busiris, and Sais. In their studies on Middle Kingdom coffins and the outer coffin of King Merenptah, Harco Willems and Jan Assmann concluded that burial rites included a ceremonial passage of divine tribunal at Sais. According to the inscriptions of Merenptah, after mummification Osiris was justified and crowned as king in the presence of the Enneads and the Two State Chapels. When Osiris reached Sais, his enemies were destroyed. Thus, the journey to Sais incorporated Osiris' victory over his enemies and his coronation as a king in the netherworld.[31] In Coffin Text spell 15, the judgment of the dead is pronounced by the goddess Neith, which is evidence that the trial of the deceased takes place near Sais.[32] The tragedy of Osiris was performed by priests assuming the roles of gods at night on the sacred lake of the burial place of Osiris at Sais.[33] The connection between Sais and Osiris could be seen as a reason for the illumination of lamps on 13 Epeiph.

Together, Egyptian funerary literature, Osiriform lamps, and Greek and Demotic Magical Spells confirm that lamps continued to be closely associated with Osiris in the Graeco-Roman period. Egyptian funerary texts connected the illumination of lamps with Osiris' mysteries of Khoiak, where lamps are lighted for the benefit of the deceased. For instance, Bodl. MS. Egypt. A. 3 (P) of the second half of the first century BC reads:

> A lamp will be elevated in [the tomb] on account of darkness in [...]. The goddess will pro[tect you]. The *djed*-pillar will be raised at the front.[34]

Lamps are also kindled for the deceased on the New Year's Eve as P. Leiden T 32, which records a long version of the Book of Traversing Eternity and dates to the first half of the first century AD, confirms:

> A lamp will be lit for you before him of the embalming chamber on the eve of the opening of the year festival (4/28) ... The task of kindling a lamp will be performed for you each evening when the god's path is illuminated at nightfall (5/17).[35]

Lamps were thus illuminated for the deceased on different occasions and festivities. Darkness represented a deep concern for the ancient Egyptians, because it signified the forces of chaos. The god Osiris had to overcome an underworld passage during the twelve hours of night, where he fought an endless battle against Apophis, the iconic symbol of darkness and chaos, who gave his name to the month of Epeiph. Lamps are also depicted at the prow of the night boat of Osiris, illuminating his way in darkness. This is why a particular emphasis was placed in Egyptian texts of the afterlife to provide lamps for the deceased. Lamps provided illumination, which in turn permitted movement in the underworld. In Coffin Text Spell 22, the deceased is told: 'You will have control over your legs at dawn, you will have control over your legs at the lighting of the torch'.[36]

On 13 Epeiph, lamps were equally illuminated for Neith, who, by the Pyramid Era, was regarded as the consort of Seth, the archenemy of Osiris.[37] Among other things, it seems that lamps were illuminated for Neith to gain her favour as the provider of light and to avoid her husband's

---

[26] Meeks 1979.
[27] Leahy 1981.
[28] Hdt. 2.59.1-3.
[29] Hdt. 2.170-71.
[30] Plut. *De Is. et Os.* 87; Dio. Sic. 1.21.2.
[31] Willems 1988, 150-5; Assmann 2002, 52-60.
[32] Willems 1988, 149.

[33] Hdt. 2.170-71.
[34] Bodl. MS. Egypt. A. 3(P), 1/1-1/4 = Smith 2009, 655. The erection of the *djed*-pillar of Osiris occurs in Khoiak; the goddess here is Isis. The raising of the *djed*-pillar accompanies the lighting of torches in Spell 137A of the Book of the Dead (Budge 1898: 195-6).
[35] Smith 2009, 418, 420.
[36] De Buck 1935, 66e-67d.
[37] Hart 2005, 110.

power of darkness in the hereafter. The festival also probably reflected the participants' will to assist Isis in her search for the body of Osiris and to illuminate the way of Osiris into the underworld. In contrast to Osiris, the goddess Neith has a limited role in the afterlife and, therefore, she is rarely mentioned in Egyptian funerary texts of the Graeco-Roman period. For instance, P. Harkness of a woman named Tanaweruow, who held the priestly title of 'bringer of the distant one' (Greek *isionomos*) and lived under Nero in the tenth Upper Egyptian nome, reads as:

> You will go on board. It is Isis who has rescued [you]. It is Neith who has given you a bark. It is the great gods of your town who have freed your brick. They will give a bark [...] your prison and regard you beneath the sails of Osiris, while this bright red band and dark red cloth are placed upon your body and the [am]ulets of all the gods are affixed to your arms. A good mummification is favourable.[38]

As a goddess of crafts, Neith here provides a bark for the female deceased, probably to be used in her Nile journey to the necropolis or in her travel up-and-downstream to attend the mysteries of Osiris in Khoiak, which frequently occur in funerary papyri and tomb inscriptions of the Graeco-Roman period, such as the second-century AD Tomb of Petosiris in the Dakhla Oasis (figure 24).[39]

FIGURE 24. PETOSIRIS ACCOMPANIED BY A HIEROGLYPHIC INSCRIPTION ALLUDING TO THE KHOIAK MYSTERIES OF OSIRIS.

A huge number of lanterns and lamps with figurative decoration of full deities or their busts were uncovered from Graeco-Roman Egypt.[40] Iconographically, many lamps are connected with Athena, Athena-Neith, Aphrodite, Isis, Isis-Thermouthis, Harpocrates, and Osiris. The latter usually take the shape of mummiform lamps. Osiriform lamps come from houses at Karanis and elsewhere in Egypt and abroad. For example, a terracotta lamp found in House C11 at Karanis shows Osiris as a bust-length mummy (figure 25).[41]

The Museum of Hatay (Antakya, Turkey) also preserves an Osiriform bronze lamp (Inv. No. 7587) of the second or third centuries AD (figure 26). It measures 38 cm long and 8 cm wide and takes the shape of an individual entirely wrapped in a funerary bandage, which leaves only the face uncovered. The comparatively large size of the lamp, the material, and the Greek magical

FIGURE 25. A TERRACOTTA OSIRIFORM LAMP FOUND IN HOUSE 11 AT KARANIS, KELSEY MUSEUM 6478.

---

[38] Smith 2009, 278.
[39] Osing et al 1982, 92-3, pl. 71: O Osiris-Petosiris, may you be great, strong, and powerful. May you follow Osiris; may your *ba* follow Sokar; may you follow Osiris everyday; may you enter and leave the Necropolis [the tomb] freely, may your *ka* travel to heaven to join the gods and goddesses living there, may you receive a wreath during the day of the twenty-fifth and on the morning of the twenty-sixth [the mysteries of Osiris and the festival of Sokar held in Khoiak], may this [your] body reach Osiris, may you take wing like an ibis, may you alight as the alighting hawk without your *ba* coming across any obstacle in the underworld, forever.
[40] Dunand 1976.
[41] Gazda 1983, 40, fig. 70.

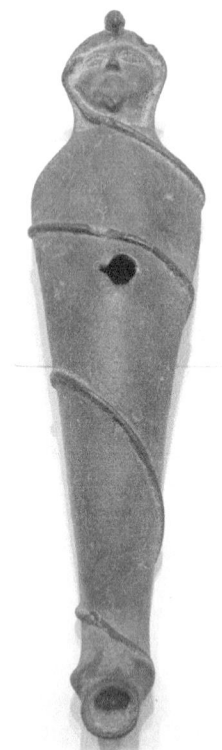

FIGURE 26. AN OSIRIFORM BRONZE LAMP AT THE MUSEUM OF HATAY.

inscription on it suggested that it was not used simply to light a private house, but was used in a place of worship.[42] Osiriform lamps were probably used in the ceremony of searching for and discovering Osiris' corpse.[43]

Lamps also appear in Greek and Demotic magical spells in close association with Osiris.[44] *PDM* XIV.174a-176a: 'The writings which you should write on the lamp: BAXYXSIXYX (and hieroglyphs) ... you should recite this other invocation to the lamp also. *Formula*: 'O Osiris, o lamp, it will cause [me] to see those above'.[45] The god Osiris and the lamp were identified with each other, and so it is possible that the lamp allowed a manifestation by him, and perhaps was shaped in the form of this god.[46] Similarly, *PGM* XXIIb.27-31 is a 'request for a dream oracle to a lamp, which lights the way to Osiris'.[47] Also, *PDM* XIV.150-160 is a recipe in which a lamp is addressed as 'Osiris', and is prescribed to be put into a cavity of a wall.[48] This seems to be the archaeological context of the Osiriform lamps uncovered from houses at Karanis and elsewhere. The Osiriform lamps were probably used for performing mantic séances and other rituals, in which Osiris was supposed to be in some way forced to do what he was asked.[49]

Lamp-lighting was associated with many festivals in Graeco-Roman Egypt, notably those celebrated on the five epagomenal days of the year, following Mesore, the fourth month of harvest and the last of the year. The birthday of Horus on the second epagomenal day was characterised with lamp-lighting. The birthday of Isis was similarly celebrated on the fourth intercalary day (Julian: 12th August) with a lamp-lighting ceremony (*Lychnapsia*) in Egypt;[50] it is also confirmed in the calendar of Philocalus.[51] Major ceremonies of lights occurred for the sacred rites of Osiris on 22 Khoiak, when 365 lamps were lit up. The lights of the Egyptian epagomenal days were placed for the dead in tombs.[52] The practice of lamp-lighting was part of rites for the care of the dead, in which context lamps could illuminate the darkness of the underworld and perpetuated the soul of the deceased.[53] Given their connection with Osiris, lamps played an important role in funerary rituals and became a significant part of the furniture of burials, such as those found in the Roman-period cemetery at Terenouthis (modern Kom Abou Bellou).[54]

IV.3. Evidence for the Illumination of Lamps for Athena-Neith in Graeco-Roman Egypt

Two festivals of Athena-Neith at Sais are mentioned in the religious calendar for the Saite nome.[55] *P.Hib.* I.27 is a religious calendar dating to 300 BC, whose author explains in the preface that he learned the matter of his treatise in Sais from a very wise man, probably an Egyptian priest, who 'demonstrated the entire truth in practice using the stone dial, which is in Greek called the gnomon'.[56] The papyrus lists the lengths of the day and the night, astronomical and meteorological events, and the Graeco-Egyptian religious festivals held at Sais. It confirms that the Illumination of Lamps for Athena-Neith survived into the Ptolemaic period. Col. xii, l.165-8 reads as:

ἐν Σάι πανήγυρις Ἀθηνᾶς καὶ λύχνους καιουσι κατὰ τὴν χώραν, καὶ ὁ ποταμὸς ἐπισημαίνει πρὸς τὴν ἀνάβασιν.

[There is] a festival in Sais in honour of Athena [Neith], when lamps are illuminated in the *chora* and the river gives indications of rising.[57]

The term *chora* here designates the countryside apart from Alexandria rather than the countryside of Sais, because lamps were also illuminated for Neith in Esna and Herodotus recounted that it was celebrated ἀνὰ πᾶσαν Αἴγυπτον.[58]

A text in the festival calendar of the Temple of Khnum at Esna confirms that lamps were kindled for Neith on 13 Epeiph under Trajan (AD 98-117):

---

[42] Laflı et al 2012, 422, fig. 1.
[43] Gallo 1997, 500, no. V.183, 1998.
[44] Betz 1986.
[45] *PGM* XIV.174a-176a.
[46] Laflı et al 2012, 434-5.
[47] *PGM* XXIIb.27-31.
[48] *PGM* XIV.150-160.
[49] Cf. Mastrocinque 2008.
[50] *P.Hib.* I.27.76 (Mecheir), *P.Hib.* I.27.166-9 (Epeiph).

[51] Salem 1937, 166.
[52] Griffiths 1975, 183-8.
[53] Georgiadou and Larmour 1998, 150.
[54] El-Sawy and Bouzek 1979.
[55] *P.Hib.* I.27.76-7 (16 Mecheir), *P.Hib.* I.27.165-7 (13 Epeiph).
[56] *P.Hib.* I.27.19-28; Moyer 2011a, 238-9.
[57] *P.Hib* I.27.166-9 = Grenfell and Hunt 1906, 149. See also Perpillou-Thomas 1993, 121-2, Rutherford 2005, 132.
[58] Cf. Moyer 2011b.

[hieroglyphic text]

wḏꜣ r pꜣ pr.s m ḥtp ḏd mdw jn ḥm=nṯrw hy sp-sn js jj(t) m nḏm-ib Nt jḥt wrt jj(t) m ḥtp hy sp-sn n jwy.s Nt wrt nbt tꜣ=sny Mnḥt-Nbtw nbt ḥmt-tꜣ ḥnꜥ ntrt tn ḥnꜥ psḏt.s ḥtp ḥr st.s wrt stj tkꜣ ꜥšꜣw m-ẖnw pr pn sw hrw nfr jn hꜣyw ḥmwt sw jhy in njwt tn r ḏr.s rn ꜥwy jrt.n s-nbw r ḥḏ=tꜣ dj tꜣ=snty m ḥb.

Going to this her house (i.e. temple) in peace. Words spoken by the servants of the gods, 'Hail, hail, coming in sweetness of heart, Neith, the great cow! Come in peace! Hail, hail at her coming, Neith, the great, god's mother, lady of Esna! Menheyet-Nebtu, Lady of Khent-Ta. Appearance of this goddess together with her Ennead, resting in her great place. Lighting many lamps inside this house. It is a happy day for (lit. by) men and women. It is joy for (lit. by) this entire city, so that the eye of no-one sleeps/closes until dawn. Putting Esna in festival![59]

This passage is part of a long text, recording the departure of Neith and her retinue from Esna and her arrival at Sais on 13 Epeiph. Like Esna, on the evening of 13 Epeiph, lamps were illuminated at Sais in the presence of Neith and the participants celebrated until dawn.[60] The lighting of lamps was a notorious ceremony of this nocturnal festival for Neith, the patron goddess of Sais.[61] Yet Sais had no monopoly of the illumination of lamps.

IV.4. The Goddess Athena-Neith

At Sais, Neith and Athena were assimilated to one another. The identification of Neith and Athena is confirmed by classical literature and Greek papyri uncovered from Egypt. In my opinion, there are five reasons, which fostered the assimilation of Neith and Athena in Egypt in the Graeco-Roman period, if not earlier. First, the martial character of the two goddesses; Neith and Athena were associated with war and are usually portrayed in warrior imagery. As a goddess of war, Neith was said to make the weapons of warriors. Iconographically, she is represented as a lady wearing the Red Crown of Lower Egypt and her martial symbols, the shield and arrows (figure 27).[62] This warlike emblem is reflected in her titles 'the mistress of the bow' and 'the ruler of the arrows' and shaped the ensign of the fifth Lower Egyptian nome, with Sais as its capital (figure 28).[63] Similarly, the goddess Athena usually appears fully armed (figure 29),[64] fitting the description of her in Homeric Hymn XI: 'Dread is she, and with Ares she loves deeds of war, the sack of cities and the shouting and the battle'.[65]

Secondly, Neith and Athena were patron goddesses of crafts, especially weaving. Neith is said to weave the bandages and shrouds worn by the dead warriors. She was also the patron of domestic weaving.[66] At Athens, Athena shared the great temple overlooking the market square with Hephaistos, also a patron of crafts. A special robe (*peplos*) was woven and decorated as a gift for Athena, the patron goddess of weaving, by working maidens (*ergastinai*) carefully chosen from Athenian aristocratic families.[67] Thirdly, the association of Neith and Athena with wisdom facilitated the identification of the two goddesses. In a papyrus of the Twenty Dynasty giving an account of the struggle between Horus and Seth, a brief passage brings Neith into the struggle over the throne of Egypt as a wise counselor of the gods:

FIGURE 27. NEITH WITH HER MARTIAL EMBLEMS, THE BOW AND THE ARROWS.

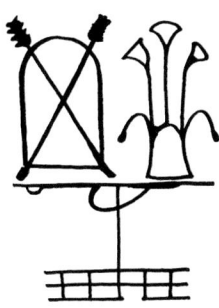

FIGURE 28. THE ENSIGN OF THE SAITE NOME.

Banebjedet urges Re to seek the advice of Neith the Great to solve the eighty-year dispute. Neith's advice, which is the court eventually but not immediately adopted, is to award the throne to Horus (also to compensate Seth by giving his the goddesses Astarte and Anat as his wives). Aggressively Neith threatens in her letter the court that if Horus does not win she will grow angry and the sky will crash to the earth.[68]

Similarly, Athena, as a goddess of wisdom, often appears in Greek myths as a counselor of gods and heroes. She

---

[59] Sauneron 1962, 302. Transliteration: author.
[60] Sauneron 1962, 28-34.
[61] Hdt. 2.59.3; Wilson 2001.
[62] Erman 1907, 13, fig. 12.
[63] Hart 2005, 103.
[64] Camp 1980, 8, fig. 7.
[65] *Homeric Hymns* XI.2-3 = Shelmerdine 2000.
[66] El-Sayed 1982.
[67] Neils 1992.
[68] Hart 2005, 101.

FIGURE 29. FULLY ARMED ATHENA ON A THIRD CENTURY AD ROMAN LAMP.

helped Heracles with his Twelve Labours, Odysseus with his home-coming, and Perseus with the killing of Medusa. She was also associated with philosophy and was thought to guide the typical Greek *poleis*. Her cult titles included Boulaia 'goddess of the council' and Polias 'goddess of the city'.[69]

Fourthly, the primordial link between Sais and Athens, which were often portrayed by classical authors as sister cities, augmented the identification between Neith and Athena. Diodorus recounts that the Athenians built Sais before the great flood, which supposedly destroyed Athens and Atlantis. While all Greek cities were destroyed during that catastrophe, Egyptian cities, including Sais, survived.[70] The identification of Athena and Neith received assurances of Plato and Proclus. In the Socratic dialogue *Timaeus*, written by Plato, one reads:

> There is in Egypt, said Kritias, in the Delta, at the apex of which the river Nile divides, a certain district called the Saitic, and the great city of this district is also called Sais, the birthplace of Amasis the king. The founder of their city is a goddess, whose name in the Egyptian tongue is Neith, and in Greek, they assert, Athena; the people are great lovers of the Athenians, and say that they are in some way related to them.[71]

For Proclus (AD 412-485), the adytum of the temple of Athena at Sais carried the following inscription: 'I am the things that are, that will be, and that have been, and no one has ever laid open the garment by which I am concealed. The fruit which I brought forth was the sun'.[72] Classical literature and Greek papyri also confirm that Athena was identified with the Egyptian goddess Isis. In the early second century AD, Plutarch states that 'they [the Egyptians] often call Isis by the name of Athena, which in their language expresses this sentence, 'I came from myself,' and is indicative of a motion proceeding from herself'.[73] He also records that 'in Sais the statue of Athena, whom they believe to be Isis, bore the inscription: 'I am all that has been, and is, and shall be, and my robe no mortal has yet uncovered'.[74] These passages refer to the identification of Isis with Athena, but at Sais Athena-Isis is of course Neith.[75] The creative powers of Neith can also be inferred from these texts. According to the Esna cosmology, Neith emerged from the primeval waters to create the world. She then follows the flow of the Nile northward to found Sais in company with the subsequently venerated lates-fish.[76] Greek papyri similarly confirm Athena's assimilation with the local hippopotamus goddess Thoeris at Oxyrhynchus.[77]

Finally, the connection between Neith and Athena with lamps also provided a reason for their identification with each other. On an account of the struggle between Horus and Seth, Neith is said to have 'illuminated the first face'.[78] She is also associated with lamp-lighting in Herodotus's passage, *P.Hib*. I.27, and in the Trajanic inscription of Esna Temple. In the Greek world, large quantities of lamps were uncovered from religious precincts and public structures like the Athenian agora.[79] Lamps were closely associated with Athena in Greek religion and mythology.[80] When Odysseus and Telemachus working at night to remove the helmets, shields, and spears out of their enemies' reach, Homer informs that 'Pallas Athene went in front of them with a golden lamp, casting a brilliant light'.[81] Like Hephaistos and Prometheus, many

---

[69] Sacks 2005, 56-7.
[70] Dio. Sic. 5.57.
[71] *Pl. Ti.* 21e = Taylor 1820, 82.
[72] Lesko 1999, 60-3; Taylor 1820, 82.
[73] Plut. *De Is. et Os.* 62.
[74] Plut. *De Is. et Os.* 9.
[75] *P.Oxy.* XI.1380.30 (the early second century AD); Quaegebeur et al 1985, 219.
[76] Sauneron 1962, 30.
[77] Quaegebeur et al 1985, 224-30. Thoeris had at least four temples in the city (*PSI* III.215, 6; *P.Mert.* I.26, 4-5; *P.Mert.*I.26.5; *P.Oxy.* IX.1188.3). The main temple of Thoeris remained a topographical point and religious landmark in the early fourth century AD (*P.Oxy.* I.43, verso).
[78] Hart 2005, 101.
[79] Camp 1980.
[80] In the mock epic *The Battle of Frogs and Mice*, the mice used the *mesomphaloi* of lamps as shields. After the mice had armed, Zeus called a council of the gods to take sides. When he asked Athena if she would like to help the mice, she answered that she would never do that because the mice had done her much mischief, ruining her lamps in their efforts to get at the oil. Athena's unlucky enemies occasionally appear on lids provided to keep mice out of lamps (Perlzweig 1963, 6; Chapman 2001).
[81] Hom. *Od.* 19.30-34.

Greek rituals in honour of Athena involved torches used at night.[82] Except for slaves, all Greek inhabitants could participate in the Great Panathenaea, which was believed to be an observance of Athena's birthday and a celebration of her honour as the city's patron deity, Athena Polias. This festival was held every four years over a number of days, with many public events, including an evening torch race (*lampadephoria*) and nocturnal ritual with dancing and singing (*pannychos*).[83]

Since Herodotus, the identification of Athena and Neith is a fact for the Greeks, and probably also for the Egyptians. In a metrical inscription, the goddess of Sais was entitled Tritogenes, an allusion to her Greek birth-myth.[84] From Esna, the southern cult centre of Neith, two Greek supplications attest to divine justice rendered by Athena-Neith among the townspeople, including Roman soldiers, one addressed to *kyria Athena* or 'lady Athena', the other to the *eidola Athenas* or 'the images of

FIGURE 31. LANTERN OF ATHENA-NEITH INSIDE AN EGYPTIAN TEMPLE IN THE LOUVRE MUSEUM.

Athena'.[85] These 'images of Athena' undoubtedly refer to the local holy fishes as the ostraca were found in the necropolis of mummified Nile perch (*Lates niloticus*), sacred to the goddess Neith.[86]

In the Museum of Alexandria, two lanterns with a rooftop cupola represent a bust of helmeted Athena, wearing a Greek tunic stitched on shoulders; another in the shape of a vertical triangular pediment Greek temple, within which appears the bust of the goddess (figure 30).[87] These Hellenic details represent the characteristic attributes of the Greek goddess. Other lanterns or lamps show the goddess within an Egyptian-style temple with a frieze of uraeus (figure 31).[88] These have been interpreted as representing Athena more or less identified with the warrior Egyptian goddess Neith.[89] The assimilation of Athena and Neith, let alone Athena-Isis and Athena-

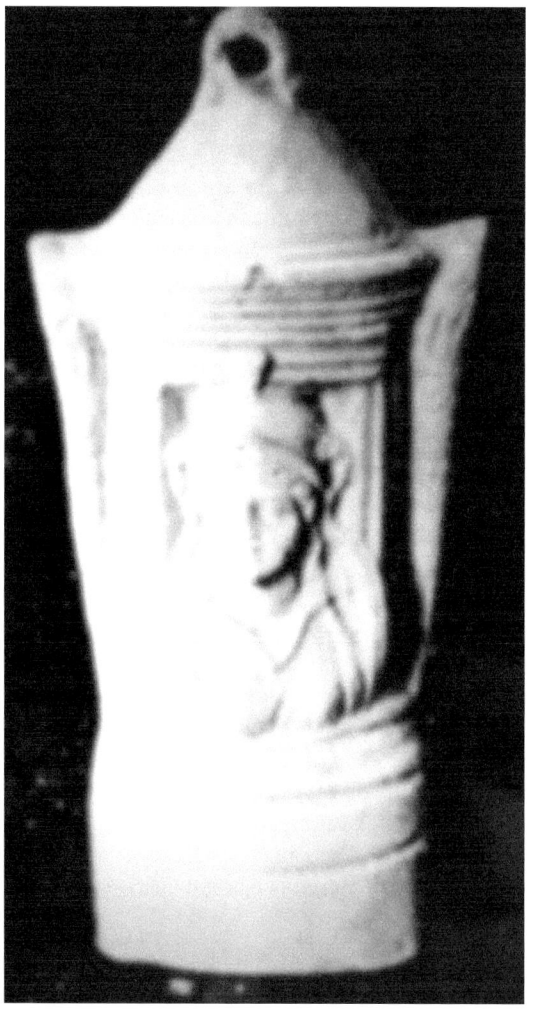

FIGURE 30. LANTERN OF HELMETED ATHENA INSIDE A GREEK TEMPLE IN THE MUSEUM OF ALEXANDRIA.

---

[82] Perlzweig 1963; Camp 1980, 4, fig.3, 10; Bernal 2006, 551-2.
[83] Neils 1992, 15.
[84] Bernand 1969, 110.2 (the Roman period). On the myth, *Pl. Ti.* 4.180; Dio. Sic. 1.12.8.
[85] Quaegebeur et al 1985, 223.
[86] Liszka 2012, 2501.
[87] Dunand 1976, pl. 6.2.
[88] Dunand 1976, pl. 10.1.
[89] Quaegebeur 1983, 318-19; Dunand 1976, 73-74.

Thoeris, reflects the integration of Greek and Egyptian religious traditions, something that similarly exists in the syncretistic cults of Hermes-Thoth and Hermanubis.[90]

IV.5. The Symbolism of the Illumination of Lamps

At the end of his passage on the *Lychnocaia*, Herodotus states that 'there is a religious reason assigned for the special honour paid to this night, as well as for the illumination which accompanies it'.[91] I have already suggested that the presence of 'the grave of Osiris' at Sais and the performance of the sufferings of the god as a mystery by night on an adjacent lake was one of the reasons, if not the main reason for the illumination of lamps on 13 Epeiph.[92] The embalmment of the body of Osiris, the search for and the discovery of his corpse, and the birthday of the Eye of Horus identified with the lamp occurred along Epeiph. On 13 Epeiph, lamps were kindled in Sais, Esna, and throughout the country not only for Athena-Neith, but also for Osiris. The *Lychnocaia* on 13 Epeiph commemorated the time when Isis managed to regenerate the mutilated body of Osiris by the power of light, and this is why lamps were illuminated at full-moon night. It was by the power of light, which symbolised the life-giving power of the Moon, that Isis rekindled life in her dead husband Osiris.[93] The 'sacred tale' attached to the Saite festival was that the lights were to assist Isis in her search for the body of Osiris and returning him back to life. The light of lamp, or symbolically the Eye of Horus, used in the Lychnocaia could destroy the powers of Seth. Thus in Chapter 137B of the Book of the Dead, which is entitled kindling a lamp, the birth-goddess Ipet drives off Seth using a flaming lamp: 'The white Eye of Horus comes. The brilliant Eye of Horus comes. It comes in peace, it sends forth rays of light unto Re in the horizon, and it destroys the powers of Seth according to the decree (?). It leads them on, and it takes possession [of him], and its flame is kindled against him [Seth]'.[94] As Isis succeeded in reviving the body of Osiris, the participants probably wanted to guarantee the same destiny by annually lighting lamps on 13 Epeiph.

The *Lychnocaia*, according to the Saite religious calendar, occurred when 'the [Nile] river gives indication of rising'. According to Plutarch, 'the wiser of the priests call not only the Nile Osiris and the sea Typhon [Seth], but they simply give the name of Osiris to the whole source and faculty creative of moisture, believing this to be the cause of generation and the substance of life-producing seed; and the name of Typhon they give to all that is dry, fiery, and arid, in general, and antagonistic to moisture'. He also adds 'not only the Nile, but every form of moisture they call simply the effusion of Osiris; and in their holy rites the water jar in honour of the god heads the procession'.[95] Thus, the Nile water was the discharge of Osiris' body. Chapter 137A of the Book of the Dead corroborates this notion: 'The [Nile] water is yours and the flood is yours, that is to say, the emanations which come forth from the God, the excretions which come forth from Osiris'.[96] The *Lychnocaia* occurred at the beginning of the flood season, which normally starts in mid-July. This interplay between Egyptian religious ideas is interesting. In the search for Osiris' body, lamps were kindled on 13 Epeiph, when the Nile-Osiris began to rise. The light of lamps equally mirrored the light of heavenly stars, symbolising the creation of a pathway to the starry fields of heavens, the domain of Osiris.[97] Since the crypt chambers at the temples of Edfu and Dendera were particularly connected with the cult and mysteries of Osiris,[98] the rite of lamp-lighting perhaps similarly took place in a subterranean chapel in the temple of Neith at Sais, where lamps were carried in procession around the coffin of Osiris. At night of the *Lychnocaia*, Neith-Athena similarly drew aside her veil, guiding the wandering souls to their true home with her living light.[99] The lamps of Neith-Athena illuminated the route to those who undertake their journey into the underworld, and this is why land donations were allocated for maintaining lamps for Neith at Sais.[100]

On 30 Epeiph the festival of the birthday of the Eye of Horus was performed. Plutarch reports that 'in the sacred hymns of Osiris they call upon him who is hidden in the arms of the sun; and on the thirtieth of the month Epeiph they celebrate the birthday of the Eye of Horus, at the time when the Moon and the Sun are in a perfectly straight line, since they regard not only the Moon but also the Sun as the eye and light of Horus'.[101]

The above mentioned Chapter 112 of the Book of the Dead supports Plutarch's passage, where Suti [Seth] had transformed himself into a black pig and aimed the blow of fire [the thunderbolt], which struck the eye of Horus.[102] One can notice the interconnection of Egyptian religious ideas. During the famous battle over the inheritance of Osiris, Seth stole and damaged the left eye of Horus associated with the moon. With the help of other deities, Thoth later restored it. The festival of the birthday of the Eye of Horus on 30 Epeiph undoubtedly symbolised this part of the Osirian myth. The left eye of Horus was associated with the moon, the right eye with the sun. Again, Selene (the Moon) is Isis and Osiris is the Sun.[103]

---

[90] Fowden 1986; Benaissa 2010.
[91] Hdt. 2.62.1-2; Bernal 2006, 551.
[92] Hdt. 2.171.
[93] Harding 1971, 130.
[94] Budge 1898, 228-9; Taylor 2010, 252.
[95] Plut. *De Is. et Os.* 33, 36. See also Assmann 2005, 355-63; Abbas 2010, 4-13.
[96] Budge 1898, 223-8.
[97] El-Sayed 1982.
[98] Fairman 1954, 170-1.
[99] Durdin-Robertson 1982.
[100] Leahy 1981: 37-46.
[101] Plut. *De Is. et Os.* 52.
[102] Faulkner 1972, 85.
[103] Dio. Sic. 1.11.1: Now the men of Egypt ... conceived that two gods were both eternal and first, namely the sun and the moon, whom they called respectively Osiris and Isis. Plut. *De Is. et Os.* 52: There are

Other festivals related to the death and rebirth of Osiris were conducted in different months of the year. Plutarch states that the mourning for Osiris occupied four days, 17-20 Athyr, but refers the production of the sacred boat to the third day, that is 19 Athyr (Julian: 15 November). On that date, the keepers of the robes and the priests 'go down to the sea at night-time and bring forth the sacred chest containing a small golden coffer, into which they pour some portable water which they have taken up, and a great shout arises from the company for joy that Osiris is found'.[104] The Athyr festival symbolised the discovery of the body of Osiris after Seth had thrown it into the river. The interment and resurrection of Osiris occurred in Khoiak. Since the Ptolemaic period, the Khoiak festival of Osiris was lengthened and began on 12 Khoiak and lasted until the end of the month.[105] An illumination of lamps accompanied the erection of the *djed*-pillar on 30 Khoiak.[106] These interconnected ceremonies symbolised important events in the lifecycle of Osiris: the sorrow over his death, the search for and the discovery of his corpse, the interment of his body, and the magic of Isis returning him to life. A passion-play was annually enacted to commemorate these tragedies of Osiris, where actors would impersonate Isis, her son Horus, and various other gods who searched across the world for the dismembered parts of Osiris. Then, the reassembly, burial, and rebirth of Osiris as a newly immortal god were performed.

IV.6. The Illumination of Lamps: An Ethnic Perspective

The *Lychnocaia* for Athena-Neith survived into the Graeco-Roman period. However, the ethnic or legal status of the participants was not given any prominence in the written evidence of the festival. I use ethnicity here to designate the expression of the self-conscious adherence to group identity.[107] The Egyptianness of the festivity in the Pharaonic period is unquestionable, yet there is no evidence that the ceremony was celebrated only by those who were legally defined as Egyptian in the Graeco-Roman period. In Roman Egypt, the inhabitants were marked by their legal status, which determined their social, political, and economic privileges until Caracalla's extension of Roman citizenship to all free citizens in AD 212.[108] The Romans, Alexandrians, and other citizens of the Greek *poleis*, Naukratis, Alexandria, Ptolemais and, from AD 130 onwards, Antinoopolis, came at the top of the Roman legal structure. These groups were exempt everywhere from the poll-tax (*laographia*), levied on males between the ages of fourteen and sixty-two.[109] Roman and Alexandrian citizenship of the parents was indispensible for their offspring to qualify for the same status.[110]

The rest of the population was referred to as the Egyptians (*Aiguptioi*). That is, the Roman authority applied the label 'Egyptian' to everyone living in Egypt, who was neither a Roman nor a citizen of the Greek poleis or Jew (*Ioudaios*), a designation that applied to metropolites and villagers alike.[111] There were also various status divisions within this group. Even though many of them will have been of Greek ethnic origin, citizens of the metropoleis of the chora paid the *laographia* at a reduced rate,[112] while the ordinary people who inhabited the villages (komai) paid the full rate of the poll-tax.[113] The metropolite group included members of the gymnasium, who are known in papyri as 'those from the gymnasium' and had to prove in their examination (*epikrisis*) that their ancestors were members of the gymnasium.[114] In the Fayum, the equivalent group to the gymnasial class was 'the 6475 Hellenes of the Arsinoite nome',[115] who were presumably the descendants of Greek and Hellenised mercenaries settled in the Fayum by the early Ptolemies.[116]

Apart from the legal definition of identity, there are no other reliable markers by means of which individuals can be recognised as Roman, Greek, or Egyptian. Similarly, the relationships between members of ethnic or legal groups are vague. That is, the cultural and social boundaries between these groups, if any, cannot be easily outlined. Although there is a huge number of documentary papyri which show day-to-day interaction between the persons involved, nomenclature is again an unreliable ethnic signifier. Given the ethnic and cultural plurality of the Egyptian society in the Graeco-Roman period, it is not impossible that members of different legal or ethnic groups, who were interested in the Festival of Lamps at least as a social occasion, could partake of it, if they wanted. Romans, Alexandrians, and citizens of Greek poleis like Antinoopolis offered private donations to traditional Egyptian cults and temples, which were treated as part of their own religious culture.[117] Greek and Roman citizens were buried according to the 'Egyptian fashion'.[118] In an epitaph of Lycian, an Alexandrian citizen, he is represented saying that 'I

---

some who without reservation assert that Osiris is the Sun; Bonnet 1952, 691.
[104] Plut. *De Is. et Os.* 39.
[105] Fairman 1954, 182-92; Chassinat 1966, 69-73.
[106] Gaballa and Kitchen 1969, 71.
[107] Morgan 1991, 131. The group must be larger than that of the immediate economic and social community. Priests, for instance, cannot be seen as an *ethnos*, but they can be members of an ethnic group or of different *ethnoi*.
[108] Bell 1942.
[109] On Alexandrian citizenship: El-Abbadi 1962; Delia 1991. On Antinoite citizenship: Johnson 1914; Hoogendijk and van Minnen 1987; Malouta 2009.
[110] Gilliam 1978.
[111] *CPJ* II.156c.ii.25-7.
[112] Lewis 1983, 26-64; Hanson 1992.
[113] Cf. *CPJ* II.156c.ii.25-7.
[114] Nelson 1979, 22-4; *P.Oxy*.XVIII.2186.
[115] Bowman and Rathbone 1992.
[116] Bell 1940, 136.
[117] *P.Mert.* II.63.
[118] On the mummy of Titus Flavius Demetrius, whose citizenship is inferred from his *tria nomina*, see Riggs 2005, 146. On papyrological reference to the *aiguptos taphos*, see Montserrat 1997.

dwell near the throne of Osiris of Abydos and have not to tread the halls of the dead'.[119] In AD 58 the temple of Souchos in Arsinoe could demand pious contributions from Romans, Alexandrians, and other inhabitants of the nome.[120] Investigations of the archaeology of poleis and metropoleis have also confirmed that urban centres were multicultural milieus, where Graeco-Roman and Egyptian cultural traditions were closely integrated.[121] Many Egyptian religious rituals were preserved into the Roman period through their incorporation into the dominant Hellenic milieu.[122] The traditional sacrifices of the 'most sacred Nile' and of the months of Tybi and Pachon respectively occurred in such distinctively classical structures as the hippodrome and theatre at Oxyrhynchus.[123] Similarly, the birthday of the god Kronos alias Souchos was held in the Temple of Jupiter Capitolinus at Ptolemais Euergetes.[124] This is probably related to a late third-century AD text from Oxyrhynchus, containing an invitation from the *gymnasiarch*, *prytanis*, *exegetes*, *archeries*, and *kosmetes* to an actor and Homericist to a celebration of the birthday of Kronos alias Souchos.[125]

Given that some traditional festivals were held in classical-style public buildings, public and religious occasions were thought of as the property of the inhabitants of the local community, regardless of their ethnic affiliation or legal status. This is also confirmed by documentary evidence of the *Lychnocaia* for Athena-Neith, which is portrayed as one of many in the religious calendars of Sais and Esna. The Saite calendar lists a number of Graeco-Egyptian festivals without any emphasis on the ethnic or legal status of the participants: the festival of Osiris on 26 Khoiak, an assembly of Athena [Neith] at Sais on 16 Mecheir; the festival of Promethcus-Iphthimis [Nefertem?] on 22 Mecheir; the festival of Hera [Mut?] on 11 Pharmouthi; the festival of Bubastis on 16 Pauni; an assembly and illumination of lamps for Athena [Neith] on [13?] Epeiph; the festival of Anubis on 23 Epeiph; and the birthday of Isis on the fourth intercalary day. Like the Esna festival calendar, the Saite religious calendar identifies the *Lychnocaia* by the patron goddess and the locale.

Another problem relating to the *Lychnocaia* for Athena-Neith is the identification of the place/space, where the participants illuminated lamps outside or within their houses. Herodotus uses the phrase *peri ta domata*, meaning 'round about the houses'. However, most houses in Egypt were attached to each other, such as those excavated in the Fayoum sites, particularly Karanis (fig. 20), and the Dakhla Oasis, especially Kellis, sharing in many cases the same wall with neighbours.[126] This suggests that lamps were simply kindled in front of the house or a night procession of lamps went around the city.[127] The terracotta figurines found in Egypt showing Athena-Neith holding a torch were probably used in this night procession, though this cannot be easily proven.[128]

There is no mention as to the space/place where lamps were illuminated within houses. Yet domestic shrines were the most appropriate arenas for this cult activity. Papyri indicate that children were taught to honour the gods and maintain their household shrines: 'Please light a lamp for the shrines and spread the cushions', wrote Apollonia and Eupous in a domestic context to their younger sisters, Rhasion and Demarion.[129] The domestic shrine of House C119 at Karanis is flanked on either side by a plain square opening for holding the brackets by which the oil lamps of the shrine could be clasped (figure 32).[130]

At first glance, the architecture of the shrine shows specifically classical features, resulting from the Graeco-Roman presence at Karanis,[131] a village with a high number of veterans, 'the vast majority of whom owed their [Roman] citizenship to military service'.[132] Archaeology indicates that Karanis was a multicultural village, where Graeco-Roman and Egyptian cultural and religious traditions were equally evident. Worshipping gods in domestic space had a long history in Graeco-Roman and ancient Egyptian cultures. The presence of what *we* now refer to as "Graeco-Roman" and "Egyptian" deities at Karanis is confirmed in papyri, on wall paintings, and from terracotta figurines.[133] A mural representation which survives in Karanis on the eastern side of a niche in the southern wall of House B50 has been interpreted as representing Isis holding Harpocrates (Horus the Child) to her breast and suckling him (figure 33).[134] The Thracian god Heron is riding a horse beside the goddess. The blending of Graeco-Egyptian cults and religious themes in one single mural painting shows the mixed cultural traditions of the house occupants.[135]

The depiction of Isis recalls the bust of Isis depicted on the ceiling of House B/3/1 at Kellis, where she is shown with

---

[119] Kaibel 1878, 414.
[120] *P.Mert.* II.63.7-10.
[121] Abdelwahed 2015, Chapter One.
[122] Alston 1997b, 89.
[123] *P.Oxy.* XXXI.2553.21.
[124] *BGU* II.362 = *Sel. Pap.* II.348.
[125] *P.Oxy.* VII.1025.
[126] Karanis: Boak 1926, Boak and Peterson 1931; Husselman 1979; Gazda 1983. Kellis: Knudstad and Frey 1999; Boozer 2005.
[127] Cf. Ach. Tat. 5.2.1-2: the night torch-bearing of Serapis in Alexandria. See also, Abdelwahed 2016.
[128] Lloyd 2007.
[129] *P.Athen.* 60.5-8 (323-30 BC).
[130] Husselman 1979, 30, fig. 54.
[131] Husselman 1979, 48.
[132] Alston 1995: 180. For papyrological references to these veterans, see Boak 1955; Husselman 1971.
[133] Gazda et al 1978; Allen 1985; Gazda 1983.
[134] Gazda 1983, 39, fig. 68.
[135] The facial features of the goddess (the round face, the wide open eyes, and the thick eyebrows) are similar in style to those of many of the mummy portraits uncovered from the Fayum (Bierbrier 1997, pls. 2.1, 8.2).

Chapter IV The Illumination of Lamps (Lychnocaia) for Athena-Neith on 13 Epeiph (Julian: 24 June)

Figure 32. The domestic shrine with holes for holding lamps in House C119 at Karanis, Kelsey Museum Archives 812.

Figure 33. The Thracian Heron and Isis suckling Harpocrates in House B50 at Karanis, Kelsey Museum Archive 5.2159.

her characteristic headdress, consisting of two bovine horns and solar disc and two plumes in between. Next to Isis, the god Serapis-Helios is depicted with a thick beard and a modius upon his head, suggesting that the god played a role in the domestic sphere.[136] Along with Soknopaios and Isis, Serapis-Helios was worshipped in the North Temple at Karanis, where a large 'Greek' horned altar bearing the head of the god was found in the outer court.[137] Based on their consideration of the archaeology and mural paintings of House B/3/1 at Kellis, Colin Hope and Helen Whitehouse concluded that the occupants had a shared cultural heritage with Graeco-Egyptian features.[138] By contrast, the representational media in the House of Serenos in Trimithis visualised Graeco-Roman heritage through mythology.[139] Nothing can be said about the legal or ethnic status of the occupants, however. The fusion of material and visual remains in houses and the variety of ritual activities mirror the complexity of the Graeco-Romano-Egyptian society, and suggest that many inhabitants experienced a culture in which Graeco-Roman and Egyptian traditional features were intermingled.

IV.7. Conclusion

On 13 Epeiph, an evening festival was held in honour of Neith-Athena at Sais, Esna, and throughout Egypt, where lamps were illuminated in great quantity inside her temples. Other participants kindled countless lamps around and within their houses. The festival of lamps displays a remarkable continuity with the past by maintaining traditional Egyptian religious beliefs. The illumination of lamps (*irt tk3* or *stj tk3*) began and continued as one of the rites associated with Osiris, and was confirmed in Middle Kingdom and later burial inscriptions. Probably at the Saite Period, the *Lychnocaia* was also connected with the creator goddess Neith, the patron goddess of Sais, because the city was one of the sacred graves of Osiris. In the Graeco-Roman period, however, the picture became more complicated with the identification of Neith and Athena, who had similar responsibilities in Egyptian and Greek religions. During that time, there was no barrier for any worshipper of Neith, Athena, or Athena-Neith to take part in the *Lychnocaia*, regardless of ethnic affiliation or legal status. Reference to the close relationship between the *Lychnocaia* on 13 Epeiph and the Osirian myth cannot be taken out of the equation. The illumination of lamps symbolised an important part of the Osirian myth: the search for Osiris' body and driving away the destructive forces of Seth using the light of lamp, the Eye of Horus, at night. Like the pilgrimage to Abydos and Busiris, the journey to Sais was essential for the passage of the deceased, who had to attend a tribunal at Sais before his or her admission to the next life. The pilgrimage to Bubastis, as Ian Rutherford argued, may have been a 'truly pan-Egyptian phenomenon because of the syncretism of various Egyptian goddesses'[140] and this seems to be the case of the *Lychnocaia* on Epeiph.

---

[136] Hope and Whitehouse 2006.
[137] Gazda 1983, 41, fig. 71.
[138] Hope and Whitehouse 2006.
[139] Mills 1980, 1993, 1998; Walter 2005; Whitehouse 2005; Boozer 2005.
[140] Rutherford 2005, 132.

Chapter V
The House as Social Space

The interior of houses functioned as a social, religious, and funerary space, where different forms of ritual activities were enacted. Based on Greek papyri uncovered from Graeco-Roman Egypt, this chapter considers the use of the house as the locus of social ceremonies associated with dining, birthdays, the mallokouria, the epikrisis, and marriage.

V.1. Dining in the House

As in the Pharaonic period, there was an intimate relationship between the house and its occupants in the Graeco-Roman period.[1] The house was not only identified by its major architectural and physical features,[2] but also by the name of its owner, a male person in most cases.[3] Houses of named individuals were also mentioned in directions given to letter carriers, where they served as important physical markers on the public space of the street.[4] Domestic properties in Egypt sometimes had a tower-gateway (*pylon*) at their frontage, acting as a physical marker of the house.[5] Different forms of social and commercial activities were performed in the public space. Business contracts, for example, were conducted in the street, where the house had no importance for such business acts.[6] By contrast, the domestic space served as the arena for many social activities. The triclinium, symposion, and andron are papyrologically confirmed within the domestic pylon, suggesting that the physical arrangement of pylon-houses was not only meant to assert social status, but also limited access to the interior of the house.[7] However, triclinia were also probably arranged to take maximum advantage of views. Although there is no archaeological evidence for a dining room in houses at Karanis, which might indicate how they were decorated and used, there is no reason for doubt that dining rooms referred to in papyri were used during festivals and social gatherings.[8] Symposia, the Greek equivalent of triclinia, are also mentioned in Greek papyri uncovered from Egypt.[9] For example, 'two rooms which are symposia' are mentioned in a rental agreement from Oxyrhynchus.[10] The occurrence of a symposion in an upper storey of a domestic pylon indicates that symposia could be approached and used 'without breaching the privacy of the rest of the house'.[11] The decoration and furnishing of triclinia and symposia might have asserted the social status of the occupants. A third-century AD letter from Oxyrhynchus asks for the retrieval of a cushion from a symposion.[12] A second letter, of the same period, asks for a basket to be brought from the symposion.[13] Undoubtedly, triclinia and symposia were fitted with good furnishings.[14]

It is unclear whether men and women dined together in Graeco-Roman Egypt. Dinner invitations were normally held by men;[15] however, some invitations were also issued by women.[16] The existence of a male dining area (andron), which is infrequently mentioned in late papyri, is insufficient in itself to suggest that the internal arrangement of houses reflected any gender differentiation.[17] The presence of an andron in the second floor of a pylon does not indicate that women dined separately.[18] In Greek houses like those at Olynthos, dinner parties were presumably held in the andron and were probably limited to males.[19] The andron was sometimes so separated that it could be entered without approaching the main house (oikos).[20] In Roman society, women participated in private dinner parties, and this practice is taken for granted as a major distinctive feature of Roman social life.[21] Dining rooms were a major feature of Roman houses, and were important space for the display of wealth and luxury.[22]

Surviving dinner invitations are issued by individuals who invited unnamed guests to celebrations, usually the next or the same day.[23] The invitations to dine attested in *SB* X.10496 and *P.Oxy*. LII.3694, however, are notionally sent by the god Serapis and Amun respectively.[24] A dinner party was held on the occasion of the birthday of a son in a private house[25] and the first birthday of a daughter in the Oxyrhynchite Serapeum.[26] Another dinner invitation

---

[1] Alston 2001.
[2] *P.Oxy*. XXIV.2406.
[3] *P.Oslo*. III.111.
[4] Llewelyn 1994.
[5] *P.Oxy*. XXIII.2406.
[6] Alston 1997, 38.
[7] *SB* VI.8988, 57-58; *P.Lond*. III.978.13; *P.Mich*. V.295.4; Abbas and Abdelwahed 2015.
[8] Husson 1983, 279-81.
[9] Husson 1983, 267-71. Symposion also designates an architectural and physical term in Luc. *Dial D.* 4.1.
[10] *P.Oxy*. VIII.1129.10 = *Sel. Pap*. I.46 (AD 449).
[11] *SB* VI.8988, 57-8; Alston 2001, 84.
[12] *P.Oxy*. VIII.1159.25-6.
[13] *P.Oxy*. XXXVI.2784.24-5.
[14] Husson 1983, 267-71, 279-81.
[15] *P.Oxy*. XIV.1755.
[16] *P.Oxy*. XII.1579; *P.Coll. Youtie* I.52 (the second or third century).
[17] On attestations of the andron in Greek papyri: Husson 1983, 37-40.
[18] *P.Flor*. III.285.12.
[19] Robinson and Graham 1938, 75-80.
[20] Nevett 1994, 1995. For the architecture of Greek houses in general: Nevett 2005.
[21] Vitr. *De arch*. 6.4.
[22] Clarke 1991; Salter 1991.
[23] Milne 1925; Youtie 1948; Koenen 1967; Skeat 1975; Alston 2001, 81-3.
[24] Serapis: *SB* X.10496 = *P.Köln* I.57 (the third century). Amun: *P.Oxy*. LII.3694 (218/25).
[25] *P.Oxy*. IX.1214 (the fifth century).
[26] *P.Oxy*. XXXVI.2791 (the second century).

issued by the exegetes was held 'in the temple of Demeter'.[27] A feast organised 'in the Thoereion' of the same city was related to a coming-of-age ceremony.[28] A dinner party was located in the unidentified birth house (loxion)[29] and in the Sebasteion in connection with marriage.[30] The Hadrianeion was a venue for a dinner invitation issued by the agoranomos.[31] A banquet is also confirmed 'in the gymnasium' in relation to the crowning of a son (as a magistrate?).[32] Like temples and other public structures, houses provided dining facilities for a variety of important social occasions.

Many invitations to dine at Oxyrhynchus are connected with the kline of Serapis 'in the Serapieion'[33] or 'in the oikos of the Serapieion'.[34] Some of the regular monthly banquets of guilds appear to have been held in temple dining halls.[35] Four square dining halls of unfired bricks have been identified along the dromos of the Temple of Soknebtunis at Tebtunis. Based on the presence of a stone altar in front of each building on the dromos and architectural similarities to dining halls in other sanctuaries of the Fayum, these structures have been identified as deipneteria.[36] A mud brick deipneterion with a stone portal is confirmed within the religious precinct of Petesouchos and Pnepheros at Karanis but separate from the temple proper.[37] Seats and tables must have been essential physical features of dining halls. The dining room in the temple at Karanis apparently had thirteen tables[38] and a dining club at Tebtunis could meet in a hall that accommodated 22 persons, of whom 18 were members and 4 were guests.[39]

Banquets were sometimes organized by religious as well as trade clubs.[40] The kline of Anubis at Oxyrhynchus was probably a funerary feast 'in the oikos of the Serapeum' in the presence of a statue of the god.[41] Grafton Milne claimed that the kline of Serapis was an exclusively secular affair.[42] However, Herbert Youtie reasonably argued that it referred to social and religious banquets, around which the hosts and guests celebrated a variety of social occasions and perhaps honoured the god with a sacrifice of some kind.[43] Although dinner invitations organised by clubs were nominally held for sacrifices, drinking remained the most distinctive feature of the gathering.[44] Thus, 'sodalities and clubs constantly hold feats under pretext of sacrifice in which drunkenness vented itself in political intrigue', writes Philo.[45] In addition to temples, the kline of Sarapis occurred in private houses like those of Sarapion, a former magistrate, and Claudius Sarapion,[46] suggesting that it was not necessarily held in the Serapieion or in a temple at all.[47] Yet the difference between the kline of Serapis in temples and those organised in houses remains unclear.

V.2. Birthdays

Birthdays are also attested in Greek papyri uncovered from Graeco-Roman Egypt on different accounts and letters. They are always referred to as genethlia or genesia.[48] Genethlia strictly applies to birthdays, whereas genesia is primarily a celebration in honour of the dead, but it also occurs in Greek papyri, especially in imperial times, to mean the 'feast of the birth'.[49] The two terms are confirmed from the third century BC to the seventh century AD. However, genethlia is the most common term for birthday in the Byzantine Period.[50]

The first anniversary of birth was of particular importance for families in Graeco-Roman Egypt.[51] One dinner party was held on the occasion of the first birthday of a young girl at Oxyrhynchus.[52] Perpillou-Thomas has explained the importance of the first anniversary of birth by the strong infant mortality during the first year after birth.[53] The first anniversary was marked by the presentation of a pair of golden earrings as a gift for the nurse in recognition for her care for the infant.[54] It was a time of happiness for not only parents and family members, but also for relatives and friends, who were invited to this social occasion.[55]

The ancient Egyptians celebrated the birthday of gods like Apis, but it is unlikely that they celebrated that of humans before the Ptolemaic period.[56] Although the Pharaoh's birthday had been celebrated by the priests, the custom of anniversaries of the common people in ancient Egypt was perhaps associated with the arrival of

---

[27] *P.Oxy.* XII.1485.
[28] *P.Oxy.* I.110; *P.Oxy.* XII.1484; *P.Oxy.* XXXI.2592; *P.Oxy.* XXXVI.2791; *P.Oxy.* LII.3693; *PSI* XV.1543; *SB* XVIII.13875.
[29] *P.Köln* I.57.3; *P.Oxy.* VI.927; *P.Oxy.* XII.1484 (the second or third century).
[30] *P.Oxy.* XXXIII.2678 (the third century).
[31] *SB* XVI.12596 (the second century).
[32] *P.Oxy.* XVII.2147 (the early third century).
[33] *P.Oxy.* I.181 (the third century); *P.Coll.Youtie* I.51 (the second or third century).
[34] *P.Oxy.* XIV.1755 (the second or third century); *P.Coll.Youtie* I.52; *SB* XX.14503 (the third century).
[35] *P.Mich.* V.243.1; *P.Mich.* V.244.14-5; *P.Mich.* V.245.34-5; Boak 1937, 216; Alston 2001, 208-9, 212.
[36] Anti 1931, 389; Rondot 2004.
[37] *SB* VIII.10167.
[38] *IGRR* I.1120.
[39] *P.Tebt.* I.118.3-4.
[40] *P.Tebt.* I.118.
[41] *SB* XX.14503 (the third century); Montserrat 1992.
[42] Milne 1925.
[43] Youtie 1948, 14.
[44] *P.Tebt.* I.118 (the second century BC).
[45] Philo, *In Flacc.* 4.
[46] *P.Oslo.* III.157 (the second century); *P.Oxy.* III.523 (the second century).
[47] Milne 1925, 6.
[48] Perpillou-Thomas 1993, 3-13.
[49] *P.Princ.* III.165.12-13.
[50] Perpillou-Thomas 1993, 3-13.
[51] *PSI* XII.1242.2, 9; *P.Oxy.* XXXVI.2791.2.
[52] *P.Oxy.* XXXVI.2791.
[53] Perpillou-Thomas 1993, 4.
[54] *CPGr* I.30.
[55] *BGU* I.333.5; *BGU* II.632.18. *P.Ryl.* IV.627.284; *P.Oxy.* IX.1214.4.
[56] Boddens-Hosang 1985.

Greeks.[57] Inhabitants in Graeco-Roman Egypt celebrated the birthdays of Graeco-Roman as well as Egyptian deities. The birthday of Souchos *alias* Kronos, for example, was held in the temple of Jupiter Capitolinus at Ptolemais Euergetis in AD 219 and was called for by the gymnasial and bouleutic elites.[58] The birthday of the god Soknopaios on 7 Athyr (Julian: 4 November) was apparently accompanied with a spectacular festival, which was referred to in Greek papyri as the Soucheia.[59] The birthdays of Osiris, Horus, Seth, Isis, and Nephthys were successively celebrated on the five epagomenal days of the year, following Mesore, the fourth month of harvest and the last of the year. The birthday of Isis on the fourth intercalary day (Julian: 12th August) was characterised with a lamp-lighting ceremony (Lychnapsia) in Egypt;[60] this festival is also confirmed in the calendar of Philocalus in imperial Rome.[61]

The birthday of the Emperor and members of the imperial family are also confirmed in papyrological documents. The birthday of Severus Antoninus was connected with the temple of Jupiter Capitolinus at Ptolemais Euergetis.[62] At Oxyrhynchus, the birthday of the deified Verus was marked with sacrifices by the gymnasiarch in the Sebasteion and Lageion.[63] The anniversaries of magistrates like Boethos, the epistrategus, and Callimachus, the strategus of the Thebaid, also appear in papyri.[64]

Papyri indicate that the celebration of anniversaries occurred mainly in metropoleis. In AD 325, the archive of Theophanes, for example, mentions the anniversary of a daughter at Hermopolis Magna.[65] The surviving attestations of birthdays from villages are always associated with wealthy landowners and ex-magistrates, suggesting that the celebration of anniversaries was probably used as a marker of social status within the local community.[66] As in Rome, funerary meals could be celebrated in Graeco-Roman Egypt on both the birthday and the day of death of the deceased.[67] Most papyrological references to birthdays, however, concern common individuals who are alive. Surviving dinner invitations are issued by individuals who mostly invited unnamed guests to celebrations, usually the next or the same day.[68]

Different venues are known for the anniversaries of sons and daughters. The location of the first anniversary of a daughter was the Serapeion at Oxyrhynchus.[69] Another invitation to the kline of Serapis in the same temple was issued on the occasion of the birthday of a son.[70] Many dinner invitations at Oxyrhynchus were held 'in the oikos of the Serapeum', presumably a dining hall within the enclosure.[71] It seems that temples possessed dining halls (deipneteria), which could be rented for such social occasions, as the archaeological evidence for dining halls along the dromos of the temple of Soknebtunis at Tebtunis and within the precinct of the North Temple of Petesouchos and Pnepheros at Karanis suggest.[72]

It appears that the most common site for the celebration of birthdays was the house of the parents. Invitations to dine in houses in relation with birthdays are confirmed in Greek papyri. A dinner party on the occasion of the birthday of a son was held 'in the private house' of the sender.[73] The dietary habits of such banquets in houses and elsewhere are well documented in papyri. Dining and drinking were the most prominent features of birthday gatherings. In AD 251, the archive of Heroninos mentions the sacrifice of pork in relation to the birthday of a daughter.[74] An account of a swineherd similarly records the supply of pigs for two birthdays.[75] In AD 265, one papyrus orders to give two chickens and twenty eggs for Panares for his birthday.[76] Two other papyri request the delivery of wine for the anniversaries of one Hyperechios[77] and the daughter of the owner of a superintendent.[78]

The consumption of wine rather than beer in banquets associated with birthdays is insufficient in itself to suppose the Hellenisation or Romanisation of the kline. Pigs were also among the most common domesticated animals since the Pharaonic period.[79] In Graeco-Roman Egypt, pig breeding continued to be a relatively important economic activity.[80] Pigs were reared alongside other domesticated animals in the courtyards of houses in both towns and villages.[81] This activity led to the emergence of a 'pig tax' levied from those breeding or trading on pigs[82] and even from those sacrificing pigs.[83] Pigs played a role in the diet of the inhabitants[84] and were consumed

---

[57] Perpillou-Thomas 1993, 5.
[58] *BGU* II.362.vi.22-4 = *Sel.Pap.* II.404.
[59] *SPP* XXII.183.iii.68-9; Perpillou-Thomas 1993, 140.
[60] *P.Hib.* I.27.76 (Mecheir), *P.Hib.* I.27.166-9 (Epeiph).
[61] Salem 1937, 166.
[62] *BGU* II.362 = *Sel.Pap.* II.348.
[63] *P.Oxy.* XXXI.2553.1-15, 21; Sijpesteijn 1969, 113.
[64] *GGIS* I.111.29; *GGIS* I.194.27
[65] *P.Ryl.* IV.627.284-5.
[66] Perpillou-Thomas 1993, 6-7.
[67] Rome: *CIL* VI.10248 (the second century); Hopkins 1983, 226-34; Carroll 2006, 180-6. Egypt: *P.Oxy.* III.494.22-5 (A.D. 165).
[68] Milne 1925; Youtie 1948; Koenen 1967; Skeat 1975; Alston 2001, 81-3.

[69] *P.Oxy.* XXXVI 2791.2.
[70] *SB* XVI.12596, 7-8.
[71] *P.Oxy.* XIV.1755; *P.Coll.Youtie* I.52; *SB* XX.14503.
[72] *SB* VIII.10167; Anti 1931, 389; Rondot 2004.
[73] *P.Oxy.* IX.1214.4.
[74] *SB* VI.9410.5-7.
[75] *P.Mert.* I.40.4-6.
[76] *P.Oxy.* XII.1568.2.
[77] *CPR* VI.62.2.
[78] *P.Jand.* VIII.153.3-5.
[79] On textual, pictorial and zooarchaeological evidence for pigs in ancient Egypt: Hdt. 2.14; Newberry 1928; Houlihan 1996, 25-8, 2001.
[80] *P.Ryl.* II.229.12, 19. Cf. *BGU* III.949.8 (AD 300, Herakleopolis).
[81] Bowman 1986, 102.
[82] *P.Oxy.* IV.733 (AD 171).
[83] *P.Giss.Bibl.* I.2 (the second century BC).
[84] Pedding 1991, 20-30.

at least by the lower classes.[85] Due to their connection with Seth, however, pigs had an ambiguous status in ancient Egyptian religion and culture.[86] Pork was never used in traditional temple offerings, though pigs were included in lists of temple properties.[87] On the night of 15 Pachon, the Egyptians used to sacrifice pigs before the front door of their houses for the god Osiris.[88]

V.3. The Mallokouria

Private letters and invitation letters to dine are sometimes issued on the occasion of the mallokouria (or coming-of-age),[89] which was a ceremony of the haircut of children in announcement of their adulthood, usually at the age of fourteen.[90] It has been suggested that mallokouria is a combination of the word *koura*, which seems to have stemmed from the verb *kerein*, or 'to cut', and the word *mallos*, which means 'a lock of hair'.[91]

The mallokouria was an important social rite for the inhabitants, and perhaps carried a religious significance as well. Thus, a papyrus of Nero's time reads 'My son Theon will shave off his lock of hair in honour of the city on 15 Tybi of this year in the great Serapieion in the presence of the priest, the hypomnematographos, and the exegetes'.[92] The social and religious dimension of the mallokouria is paramount by the presence of civic officials and priests. The mallokouria was an institutionalised initiation ritual for adolescent boys in Graeco-Roman Egypt, marking the transition from childhood to adulthood.[93] In second or third century AD Oxyrhynchus, one Apollonius invited an unnamed individual to the kline of Serapis in the temple of Thoeris on the occasion of the mallokouria of his son.[94] Contemporary is the letter of Serenos to Apollinarius, informing the hair-cutting of Isidoros, presumably the sender's son.[95]

The mallokouria as such seems to have had an Egyptian precedent. Group initiation rituals for boys, centring around circumcision and hair-cutting, are known since Pharaonic Egypt.[96] In 25 BC, Strabo visited Egypt and gave the first extant literary mention of male circumcision and female genital mutilation: One of the customs most zealously observed among the Egyptians is this, that they rear every child that is born and circumcise the males and excise the females.[97] Strabo considers the practice a distinctively Egyptian one. Even when he attributes it to the Jews as well, he considers them Egyptian in origin.[98] Other ancient physicians of the Roman and Byzantine periods like Galen, who lived in the second century AD, and Aetios, the Greek physician of the emperor Justinian I, had definitively placed the practice in Egypt.[99]

There is no papyrological evidence for common male circumcision in the Graeco-Roman period, though circumcision was still a prerequisite for priests at the end of the second century AD.[100] The word therapeuteria occurs in three papyri of the Roman period to refer to the excision of unmarried girls, which was usually followed by feast in the father's house.[101] Scholars presented different interpretations of female genital mutilation in ancient Egyptian society. Some viewed it not as a medical, curative procedure per se, but perhaps as a religious rite associated with temple life.[102] A papyrus of 163 BC mentions an Egyptian girl named Tathemis, who was authorized by the temple of Serapis at Memphis to collect alms. The letter concerns money earmarked for Tathemis's circumcision, for which she needed a dowry and a suitable dress, all indications of her entering into womanhood:

> Sometime after this, Nephoris defrauded me, being anxious that it was time for Tathemis to be circumcised, as is the custom among the Egyptians. She asked that I give her 1300 drachmas from what [Tathemis] had paid me ... to clothe her ... and to provide her a marriage dowry, and [she promised that] if she did not do each of these or if she did not circumcise Tathemis in the month of Mecheir, year 18, she would repay me 2400 drachmas on the spot.[103]

In fact, there is no ground for assuming that Tathemis's association with a temple was connected with her excision, since the letter indicates that the rite was an Egyptian custom preparatory to marriage.[104] One should also bear in mind that Tathemis was already involved in temple life before her excision. Marriage did not disqualify priests and others affiliated with the temples from continuing their service. The papyrus itself seems to support the interpretation that female excision may have been performed in preparation for marriage as a curative operation rather than as a prerequisite for priesthood.

Circumcision was closely associated with generative ability in ancient Egyptian textual evidence, as in the Book of the Dead, chapter 17, which glorifies and praises the creator god Re and all his creation: What is this? It

---

[85] Hecker 1982, 59-71.
[86] Helck 1984, 764.
[87] Newberry 1928, 211.
[88] Hdt. 2.47-48, Plut. *De Is. et Os.* 8; Ael. *NA* 10.16. For a full discussion of this festival: Abdelwahed 2015, 88-91.
[89] *P.Mil.Vogl.* II.60.11-16; *P.Oxy.* XII.1484.
[90] Legras 1993.
[91] Oslon 1927.
[92] *P.Oxy.* XLIX.3463.6-9.
[93] *SB* XIV.11944.
[94] *P.Oxy.* XII.1484.
[95] *BGU* I.38.22-4.
[96] Janssen and Janssen 1990, 90-99.
[97] Strabo 17.2.5.
[98] Strabo 17.2.5.
[99] Knight 2001, 326-8.
[100] *P.Tebt.* II.292-293.
[101] Montserrat 1990, 1991.
[102] Knight 2001, 329-30.
[103] *P.Lond.* I.24.ii.9-18.
[104] Wendland 1903.

is the blood that fell from the phallus of Re when he mutilated himself. It became the gods Hu (Authority) and Sia (Wisdom), who follow Re and who accompany Atum daily and every day'. Re's self- mutilation is understood by most commentators as a reference to circumcision. The visible sign of blood from circumcising becomes the physical sign of generative power.[105] It is notable that circumcision was practiced on boys at about the same age as girls. Philo indicates that the operation was done when children entered adulthood at the age of fourteen: The Egyptians by the custom of their country circumcise the marriageable youth and maiden in the fourteenth year of their age, when the male begins to get seed, and the female to have a menstrual flow.[106]

In the Pharaonic period, the cutting of the so-called sidelock-of-youth at the age of fourteen similarly marked the transition from childhood to puberty. In Graeco-Roman Egypt, several mummy portraits show that the Graeco-Egyptian bourgeoisie had adopted the wearing of the youth or Horus-lock, so they could also have adopted any customs attendant on its shearing at adulthood, especially since there was also a strong Greek tradition of making hair-offerings at puberty.[107] Hair was closely associated with Osiris and Isis in ancient Egyptian culture.[108] On hearing of the murder of Osiris, Isis cut a lock of hair and wore mourning clothes.[109] The two virgin girls selected to represent Isis and Nephthys and recite the lamentations for the departed Osiris in the Khoiak mysteries were obliged to remove the hair of their body.[110] Diodorus also recounts 'when all his preparations had been completed, Osiris made a vow to the gods that he would let his hair grow until his return to Egypt and then made his way through Ethiopia. This is the reason why this custom with regard to hair was observed among the Egyptians until recent times'.[111] The Egyptians also make vows to certain gods on behalf of their children who have been delivered from an illness, in which case they shave off their hair and weigh it against silver or gold, and then give the money to the attendants of sacred animals.[112] In Egypt as well as in the classical world, a lock of hair could be presented as a gift for the gods, whether given in the hope of obtaining divine protection or in thanks for divine services already rendered.[113] The excavations of the Graeco-Roman necropolis of Doush in the Kharga oasis have yielded hair or shaving hair among the offerings deposited in the tombs.[114] The mallokouria was perhaps an Egyptian adaptation of the ritual cutting of the youth-lock in the Pharaonic period.

V.4. The Epikrisis

The epikrisis was an examination of the fiscal status of males at the age of fourteen. It considered whether the child's ancestors (parents, grandparents and beyond) belonged to the metropolite group or the more prestigious gymnasial class. The recognition of this allowed the young man to pay only a reduced capitation tax. This examination was an opportunity to reaffirm social status of families within the local community.[115] Like the mallokouria, the epikrisis marked the transition of males from a child to adult status, but mainly for tax concessionary purposes. Yet it was also an access to official responsibilities and bureaucracy. Before AD 212, a peregrine child in Roman Egypt ceased to be a minor at the age of fourteen, and boys were then enrolled in the poll tax lists. For a Roman citizen, the age of legal majority was twenty-five. After the promulgation of the Constitutio Antoniniana, the Roman age of twenty-five became the norm in Egypt, and under that both men and women were legally under age. For peregrines in Egypt, patria potestas was considered just a form of guardianship. For boys it ended with their coming of age at fourteen.[116]

The examination took the form of a public status declaration before various city officials, and an oath was sworn that both parents of the boy 'entering the class of thirteen-year-olds' belonged to one of the privileged tax-groups. The boy's ancestors on both sides were enumerated, sometimes as far back as seven generations, to prove that the boy was unimpeachably worthy of the fiscal privilege. The declaration was followed by celebrations such as the ritual garlanding of the boy and banquets.[117] Two third-century AD papyri from Oxyrhynchus concern invitation to dine in relation with the epikrisis. In one papyrus, Heratheon invited an unnamed person to dine on the next day in his house on the occasion of the epikrisis, apparently of his son.[118] In the other papyrus, Horeios similarly invited an unnamed individual to dine tomorrow in his private house in relation with the epikrisis of his son.[119] Unfortunately, the proceedings and dietary activities of these social festivities are not mentioned in the documentary record. There is no room for doubt, however, that they did not differ from other social gatherings such as the mallokouria discussed above. The ceremony probably focused on eating and drinking in the host's house. The epikrisis emphasised the importance of the transition of children to adulthood, and the ritualised significance attached by the metropolites to their social and economic status.

---

[105] Knight 2001, 336.
[106] Philo, *QG* 3.4.
[107] Montserrat 1991, 46.
[108] Robins 1999.
[109] Plut. *De Is. et Os.* 39.
[110] Faulkner 1936, 122.
[111] Dio. Sic. 1.18.3.
[112] Dio. Sic. 1.83.2. Cf. Hdt. 2.65.
[113] Ammerman 1991, 203.
[114] Wagner et al 1985, 188.

[115] Perpillou-Thomas 1993, 27.
[116] Malouta 2012, 298.
[117] Montserrat 1991.
[118] *P.Oxy.* VI.926.
[119] *P.Oxy.* XXXVI.2792.

V.5. Marriage

Although marriage contracts from Graeco-Roman and Byzantine Egypt are well documented in papyri, the festivities related to this important event are hardly mentioned. The majority of the invitations to the wedding banquet come from Oxyrhynchus and date to the second and third centuries AD.[120] In Greek papyri, marriage is referred to as *gamos*, which means the 'wedding' or the 'wedding feast'.[121] In 153 BC, Sarapion sent a letter to his brothers Apollonius and Ptolemaios and invited Apollonius to his marriage with a Memphite girl.[122]

In Graeco-Roman Egypt, the regulations of commercial corporations provide a contribution to the wedding party of the member who arranges to marry.[123] The hunters' corporation at Aphrodites Kome (Antaiopolites), for example, stipulated the contribution of two bottles of wine in case of the marriage of a member, suggesting the existence of a drinking assembly at the wedding party of the colleague.[124] This drinking assembly could be held either in the host's house or in the dining halls associated with temples. Thus, the majority of invitations to dine on the occasion of wedding were associated with private houses.[125] However, a feast was also held in the Sebasteion in relation with marriage.[126]

Prior to the Macedonian conquest, Egyptian marriage was fulfilled through the acknowledgment of the cohabitation between the husband and his wife. In other words, marriage was not a codified rite, unlike Greece or Rome. Greek and later on Roman settlers imported their legal conceptions of marriage and their ceremonial customs. Unfortunately, Graeco-Roman ceremonial traditions of marriage scarcely appear in papyrological documents, making it impossible to infer their influence in the Egyptian society.[127] There is evidence for the popularity of the traditional practice of the marriage between brothers and sisters in Graeco-Roman-Egypt. In the second century AD, Dionysius invited an unnamed person to dine on the occasion of the wedding of his children at Oxyrhynchus.[128] The inhabitants' desire to keep the properties and inheritance within the family was one of the socio-economic reasons for such a practice. It can be said that the indigenous custom of incestuous marriage served the material interests of the metropolites.

Since marriage has always been an important social activity and rite of passage, where family members, relatives, and friends would meet together, the house was the most appropriate arena for wedding parties.[129] The celebration of wedding ceremonies in private houses suggests that the undesignated location at which a guest was invited to attend a wedding party, whether a marriage with a written contract (*graphos gamos*) or without (*agraphos gamos*), was the house of the host.[130]

Some practical details of weddings in wealthy families are known, especially in second and third century AD Oxyrhynchus, but they certainly apply to other places as well. The family of the young man or the girl invites their relatives and friends to the dinner wedding. The days selected for the ceremony ranged throughout the month.[131] Servants were responsible for delivering the invitation cards of the wedding banquet to the guest's home the day before marriage or even on the same day of marriage.[132] Since the main purpose of the invitation card was to commemorate the wedding party, it seems unlikely that guests exposed their invitation cards on entry the host's house. Yet they perhaps had to do so in case of dining in temples halls given the measurement limitation of temple dining rooms. The dining room in the temple at Karanis only had thirteen tables[133] and a dining club at Tebtunis met in a temple dining hall that accommodated 22 persons.[134]

Floral decoration was a prominent feature of wedding parties, whether in houses or temple dining halls. In the second century AD, Apollonius and Sarapias were unable to attend a wedding ceremony, but they were keen to send thousands of roses and daffodils for the party.[135] The exact significance of the lamps used for the wedding of one Apollonius in the late third century AD remains uncertain. They probably had a decorative purpose or used in some related, though unidentified, rituals.[136] The oil that Sarapion requested from his brothers Ptolemaios and Apollonius in relation with a wedding party was perhaps used to replenish such lamps.[137] There is little evidence for the gifts offered to the new couples. The congratulation label on a fifth or sixth century AD vase suggests that it was a wedding present by one Theodorus to a new couple.[138]

V.6. Conclusion

The rituals associated with such highly important social events as birthday, coming-of-age, epikrisis, and marriage occurred largely within the house. Hence,

---

[120] Perpillou-Thomas 1993, 15-19.
[121] *P.Giss.* 31.16.
[122] *UPZ* I.66.
[123] Boak 1937.
[124] *SB* III.6704.18-19 (In AD 538).
[125] *P.Oxy.* XII.1579.
[126] *P.Oxy.* XXXIII.2678.
[127] Perpillou-Thomas 1993, 17.
[128] *P.Oxy.* III.524.

[129] On marriage in ancient Egypt: Pestman 1961.
[130] For wedding invitations to unstated locations: *P.Oxy.* VI.927; *P.Oxy.* XII.1486; *P.Oxy.* XII.1487.
[131] Perpillou-Thomas 1993, 16-17.
[132] *P.Oxy.* III.524; *P.Oxy.* XII.1580.
[133] *IGRR* I.1120.
[134] *P.Tebt.* I.118.3-4.
[135] *P.Oxy.* XLVI.3313.
[136] *P.Oxy.* XVII.20-21.
[137] *UPZ* I.66.
[138] *O.Ashm.Shelt.* 196.

they offered the house occupants or hosts opportunities to articulate the wealth of their home and assert their social status and position to their guests. Although the precise location of such social activities within the house remains uncertain, the central light-courtyard or the domestic pylon could be easily used for such ceremonies, particularly given the presence of triclinia within the pylon and the spacious measurement and use of the courtyard as the kitchen of the house. Heavy tables in courtyards were used at family meals and on other social occasions. Like the domestic pylon, the court was also multifunctional.

Chapter VI
The House as Religious Space

VI.1. Domestic shrines

Houses were not only significant social places, but also important religious spaces. The religious role of the house is confirmed by the presence of terracotta figurines of Graeco-Roman and Egyptian deities and wall niches serving as domestic shrines.[1] The niches of the houses in Karanis provide the best, if not the only surviving examples. They have been divided into two types: cupboard niches and domestic shrines. Cupboard niches are usually found on the first floor of the house below the windows with their sloping sills (figure 34).[2] In most cases, they measure one meter in height, and are located about one meter above floor level. They often have shelves for keeping small portable objects and holding lamps, as carbon deposits on the niches' walls and sills indicate.

The domestic shrines were probably used to hold the small figurines of deities and once had paintings of religious themes.[3] Since the paintings are so badly obliterated, it is not possible in most cases to determine their subject-matter. Based on their occurrence in houses at Karanis, domestic shrines were closely connected to the rest of the house. They occurred in different rooms and at prominent positions within houses, and were built out of different material and took numerous forms.

Domestic shrines sometimes took the form of small niches hewn in the walls. For example, in the north wall to the left side of the doorway into room B in House C60 in Karanis, and on the same level as the lintel of the doorway, there is a rectangular shrine-niche, which has a frame of moulded mud plaster and is surmounted by a projecting cornice of plaster (figure 35). Domestic shrines of mud-brick also took the form of temple gateways. At floor level in the south wall of House C71 in Karanis, for example, there is a small niche, made of mud brick and plaster, in the form of a portal (figure 36). It rests on a rectangular base, measuring 41 cm in width, 39 cm in length and 20 cm in height. The shrine measures 36 cm in width and 43 cm in height; it consists of two pillars supporting a lintel, the top of which is moulded into a concave pattern in imitation of a cavetto cornice. At the front of each pillar is an attached column in relief.[4] Even such simple examples of domestic shrines demonstrate how important religion was for the domestic life of inhabitants in Graeco-Roman Egypt.

There were more elaborate niches used as domestic shrines in Karanis, such as that in House C119 (figure 32), where the architecture of the shrine shows specifically classical features, which resulted from the Graeco-Roman presence at Karanis. It is known that Karanis was a village with a high number of veterans, 'the vast

FIGURE 34. A CUPBOARD NICHE IN A HOUSE AT KARANIS

FIGURE 35. THE DOMESTIC SHRINE IN ROOM B OF HOUSE C60 AT KARANIS.

---

[1] Gazda et al 1978; Allen 1985.
[2] Gazda 1983, 25-6.
[3] Husselman 1979, 47-8.
[4] Husselman 1979, 47.

Chapter VI The House as Religious Space

Figure 36. The domestic shrine in house C71 at Karanis.

majority of whom owed their [Roman] citizenship to military service'.[5] Archaeology indicates that Karanis was a multicultural village, where Graeco-Roman and Egyptian traditions were evident. Such domestic shrines indicate that worshipping gods in houses was not limited to a particular group of inhabitant. The back of the niche in House C119 is curved and flanked by two engaged, fluted columns similar, for example, to those in the House of the Labyrinth at Pompeii.[6] The columns rest on high pedestals and support capitals with helices, beneath which are narrow bands moulded into a zigzag pattern. The helices look like those of Alexandrian Capital Type II, where these are set back to back and spring directly from the collar of acanthus leaves, but in this example are suspended from the arch and held upside down.[7]

The top of the curved niche takes the shape of a shell framed by an arch, which consists of four decorated bands surmounted by a projecting arched course of bricks. Both the niche and its surrounding frame are covered with a thin coat of white lime wash, and it measures about 1.5 m in width and 2.15 m in height.[8] Like the domestic shrine in room D of House C57 (Appendix 1), this shrine is flanked on either side by a plain square opening, which was meant to hold brackets by which lamps for the shrine could be clasped. Since domestic shrines are the most decorated spaces of houses, it is clear that there was a tendency to visualize and illuminate the religious space in the house. The decoration of domestic shrines also shows the significance of architectural ornament in some houses in Graeco-Roman Egypt.

VI.2. Wall Paintings and Figurines

Worshipping gods in domestic space had a long history in Graeco-Roman and ancient Egyptian cultures. The presence of Graeco-Roman and Egyptian deities at Karanis is confirmed in papyri, on wall paintings, and from figurines made of terracotta, stone, and other materials.[9] A mural representation which survives in Karanis on the eastern side of a niche in the southern wall of House B50 represents the goddess Isis holding Harpokrates, Horus the Child, to her breast and suckling him (figure 33). The Thracian god Heron is shown riding a horse beside the goddess. The blending of Graeco-Egyptian cults and religious themes in one single mural painting shows the different cultural traditions of the inhabitants of this house. It is noteworthy that the facial features of the goddess (the round face, the wide open eyes, and the thick eyebrows) are similar in style to those of many of the mummy portraits uncovered from the Fayum.[10] Egypt in the Graeco-Roman period was a notable example of a place in which different ethnic groups were intermingled. The fusion of Graeco-Egyptian representational media in houses in the post-Pharaonic period was a natural result of the cultural contact and intermarriage of Greek new comers with native Egyptian inhabitants. This hybrid figurative theme may appear puzzling to modern scholars, whose main concern was to classify material objects into classical (Graeco-Roman) versus Egyptian. Such a distinct classification was not important for the occupants of houses in Karanis and elsewhere in Egypt, who experienced a culture in which there was no barrier or clear-cut distinction between Graeco-Roman and Egyptian traditional features.

The depiction of Isis in Karanis recalls the bust of the same goddess on the ceiling of House B/3/1 at Kellis (Appendix 1.1.2), where Isis is shown with her characteristic headdress, consisting of two bovine horns and a solar disc and two plumes in between. Next to Isis at Kellis, the god Serapis-Helios is depicted with a thick beard and a modius upon his head, suggesting that the god played a role in the domestic sphere. Along with Soknopaios and Isis, Serapis-Helios was worshipped in the North Temple at Karanis, where a large horned altar bearing the head of the god was found in the outer court of the temple.[11] The popularity of Serapis is the Graeco-Roman period was in part due to his role as a redemptive deity.[12] The sanctuaries of the god Serapis across Egypt were the destinations for the inhabitants

---

[5] Alston 1995, 180. For an example of papyrological reference to those veterans: Husselman 1971, Text 571, 121-2. See also Boak 1955; Husselman 1971.
[6] McKenzie 2007, 90 (fig. 143). Although fluted columns are used in the Third Dynasty in the colonnade of King Djoser at Saqqara, they are rarely used in Egyptian architecture. On the remains of a fluted column uncovered from Tell el-Amarna: Borchardt 1897, 50, fig. 79.
[7] McKenzie 2007, 87 (fig. 132).
[8] Husselman 1979, 48.
[9] Gazda et al 1978; Allen 1985; Gazda 1983.
[10] Cf. Bierbrier 1997, pls. 2.1, 8.2.
[11] Gazda 1983, 41, fig. 71.
[12] Bell 1948, 93-5.

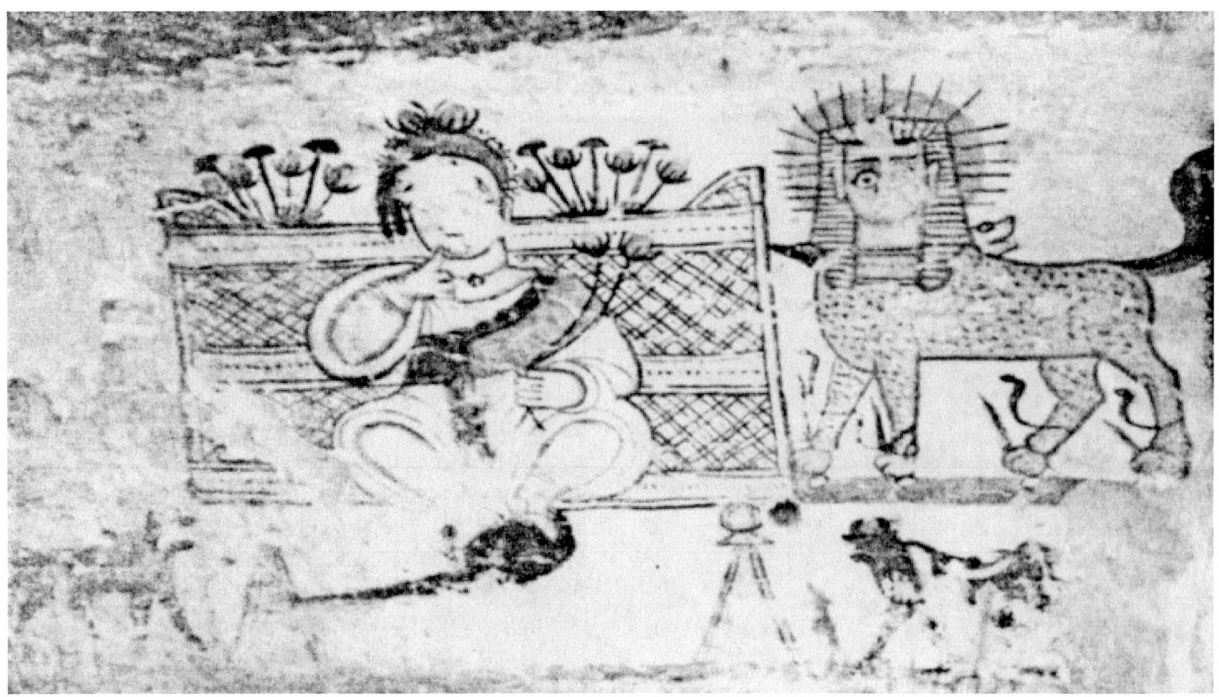

FIGURE 37. HARPOKRATES AND TITHOES ON THE SOUTH WALL OF ALCOVE CF4 OF HOUSE C65 AT KARANIS.

looking for healing. In 26-25 BC, Canopus contained the temple of Serapis, who was 'honoured with great reverence and produces such healings that even people of the greatest merit believe in him and come to sleep in it for their proper recovery or send others to sleep there in their stead. Some write down their recovery, others the proof of the effectiveness of the oracle of Serapis'.[13] The presence of Serapis in domestic contexts is not surprising. Based on their consideration of the archaeology and mural paintings of House B/3/1 at Kellis, Colin Hope and Helen Whitehouse concluded that the occupants had a shared cultural heritage with Graeco-Egyptian features.[14] By contrast, the representational media in the House of Serenos in Trimithis visualised Graeco-Roman cultural heritage through mythology (Appendix 1.2.1).[15] Nothing can be said about the legal or ethnic status of the occupants of such houses, however. The variety of material remains mirrors the complexity of the Romano-Egyptian society and suggests that the occupants of many houses experienced a culture in which Graeco-Roman and Egyptian traditional features were intermingled.

The presence of Isis in the domestic sphere seems a natural result of her widespread cult in the Graeco-Roman period, and of her maternal aspect that appears to have appealed to women in post-Pharaonic Egypt.[16]

Following her syncretism with the cobra goddess Thermouthis, whose particular duty was to protect the harvested grain, Isis-Thermouthis was particularly worshipped in houses. Sculptures of the goddess with serpentine tail were found, for instance, in House 5021F at Karanis. As the economy of Karanis was dependant on agriculture, Isis-Thermouthis had unsurprisingly gained popularity in the village. A bronze statue of the goddess Aphrodite was also found in House 418 at Karanis, confirming her presence in the domestic sphere.[17] The crocodile god Soknopaios is depicted on the right side of the domestic shrine in House II 204 at Dimê, where the deity holds a palm branch in his upraised left hand and faces the centre of the shrine. Next to the god are an altar and a tall palm branch (Appendix 1.2.2). The presence of Soknopaios in houses at Dimê is natural, but his depiction here suggests that the occupants wanted to have his figure while they performed their prayers or perhaps made sacrifices around the domestic shrine.

An interesting religious theme is painted on the south wall of alcove CF4 of House C65 in Karanis (figure 37). As it stands, the wall painting is typically Egyptian and attests for traditional religious subjects in domestic architecture, as mural paintings with purely classical themes elsewhere do. The painting measures 1.14 m wide and 68 cm high. In the middle of the scene the god Harpokrates is shown sitting upon a throne-like chair. Harpokrates is depicted with his distinctive attributes:

---

[13] Strabo 17.1.17.
[14] Hope and Whitehouse 2006.
[15] Mills 1980, 18-25, 1993, 192-8, 1998, 84-91; Walter 2005; Whitehouse 2005; Boozer 2005.
[16] On the cult of Isis in the Roman Empire: Witt 1972; Donalson 2003. On the cult of Isis among women in the Graeco-Roman world: Heyob 1975.

[17] Isis-Thermouthis: Gazda 1983, 40, fig. 69. Aphrodite: Gazda 1983, 41, fig. 72.

a lock of hair hanging down on the right side of his head, a finger to the mouth and a bulla suspended on a cord around his neck. Harpokrates wears red sandals, anklets and bracelets. He holds two long stemmed lotus flowers in his left hand. On each side of his head above the chair are shorter stemmed lotus flowers. To the left of Harpokrates a striding sphinx is depicted with a lion's body, a long curved tail, and a human head with a radiant *nemes* headdress. It possibly represents the sphinx god Tithoes. In each paw, the sphinx holds a black dagger, while a black cobra is entwined about each leg. A black head of a jackal projects from the right side of the sphinx's head. On each side of the legs of the chair stands a black Apis bull with a sun disc between the horns of each bull. Before each bull stands an altar, however, little remains of the altar on the left side.[18]

It is difficult to determine the exact significance of such a religious theme in a place that was primarily used for storage. No fewer than eight figurines of the god were uncovered from the sacred precinct of the South Temple at Karanis, a clear testimony to his cult in the village.[19] A faience figurine of Harpokrates (the son of Isis) was similarly recovered from a street (Layer A, Area 200) in Karanis.[20] The close association of Harpokrates with abundance suggests one possible reason. Owing to his connection with fertility, the inhabitants perhaps thought that Harpokrates would amplify the supplies stored in alcoves, and this may be why the god is shown with the lotus flower, the symbol of fertility. The visual and physical presence of Harpokrates in houses is also connected with his role as a patron deity of childhood. It is known that infant mortality was a profound concern in Roman Egypt: an infant had a one in three chance of dying before the first birthday, although after this first year the chances of survival to adulthood increased.[21] This explains the inhabitants' care for the celebration of the first anniversary of birth.[22] Considering these realities of child mortality, it is probably no coincidence that there was a robust community honouring the child-god Harpokrates at Karanis. Ample testimony to this cult is offered by the numerous terracotta figurines representing the deity found in both residential and temple contexts at the town and by two domestic wall paintings, one of Harpokrates with the god Tithoes (figure 37) and one depicting him nursing at the breast of Isis, his mother (figure 33).[23]

Classical themes are also evident in domestic architecture, though they are less represented than traditional Egyptian programmatic content in domestic contexts. Graeco-Roman subjects are hybridised with Egyptian themes, like the above example of Isis and Heron in Karanis. However, they also occurred on their own, like the mythological programme used in the house of Serenos at Trimithis in the Dakhla oasis, which has managed to capture the attention of specialists. Archaeological investigations of the site have revealed a temple of the Egyptian god Thoth, a necropolis filled with barrel vaulted tombs and a Roman-dated pyramid, a church, and the fourth-century AD house of Serenos.[24] The house or villa of Serenos, who was likely a town councillor of Trimithis, has particularly received the attention of a multitude of scholars, because of the decoration of its walls with a selection of scenes drawn from Graeco-Roman mythology.

The house of Serenos (House B1, R1, Area 2.1) was first discovered in 1979 in the course of test excavations at Amheida by the Dakhla Oasis Project, but the walls were reburied and had to wait for proper excavations. It was in 2004 when a team sponsored by Columbia University under direction of Roger Bagnall that the wall paintings in the house were properly studied by a number of scholars. Dorothea Schulz, Susanna McFadden, and Anna Boozer have provided full description of the subject matter of the scenes in the house. However, the meaning of many parts of the iconography remains unclear.[25] Overall, the house is unparalleled in Egypt and beyond in the compositional format of its visual media. Most of the iconographical programme of the central 'painted room' in the house is drawn from Homer's *Odyssey*, however. On the north wall, in the half-lunette west of the room's entrance, there is a representation of Perseus rescuing Andromeda from a sea monster. The lunette on the north wall east of the main entrance contains a scene from the story of Odysseus' return to Ithaca, when his old nurse, Eurykleia, recognises him.[26] In the lower register of the east wall of the room Polis and other identifiable Olympian gods are shown headed towards Aphrodite and Ares, a composition that has been identified as the adultery of Aphrodite and Ares (figure 38).[27] A papyrus from nearby Kellis recording that Trimithis achieved the status of Polis in AD 304 suggested that Serenos had referenced Polis and other related gods and heroes in the wall painting of his house to promote civic pride and identity centred on the ideals of wealth and Hellenism.[28]

Of Special concern to our topic in the iconographical programme of the house of Serenos is the representation of the banquet scene on the west wall of the central painted room. This scene shows the owner of the house and his family enjoying a festive meal, accompanied by a musician playing the double *aulos* (figure 39).[29]

---

[18] Husselman 1979, 61-2.
[19] Gazda 1983, 38, fig. 65.
[20] Johnson 2004, 56.
[21] Bagnall and Frier 1994, 77, 100.
[22] See chapter five.
[23] Allen 1985, 137, fig. 13; Boak and Peterson 1931, 34.
[24] Davoli and Kaper 2006; Aravecchia et al 2015.
[25] Schulz 2010, 2011, 2015; McFadden 2014; Boozer 2015.
[26] McFadden 2014, 363.
[27] Schulz 2015, 24.
[28] McFadden 2014, 364.
[29] Bagnal et al. 2006, 27, fig. 6.

Figure 38. Polis and Olympian deities watch the adultery of Aphrodite and Ares.

Figure 39. Serenos and his family at a meal, accompanied by a flautist.

On the proper right side of the composition, the seated musician plays a double flute. To his left is a small standing figure, either another child entertainer or a servant. The two figures look towards four figures, three men and a woman, holding goblets and probably reclining on a banqueting couch (*stibadium*).[30] Although the scene shows a woman dining with three men, it remains unclear whether women were admitted to dining parties with male strangers in Roman Egypt. Above all, the figures have been identified as Serenos and members of his family. In any case, the painting visualises some features of dining parties held in relation with different social ceremonies and ritual activities identified in the papyrological record.[31]

In addition to wall paintings of religious themes, figurines uncovered from domestic contexts clearly show that religion was essential to house-dwellers in

---

[30] McFadden 2014, 365.

[31] See chapter 5.

Graeco-Roman Egypt, where houses were not merely living quarters. Boozer has drawn attention to the capacity of the figurines found in a Romano-Egyptian house at Trimithis (Amheida) in the Dakhla oasis, House B2, to express issues of identity, sexuality, status, and human representation. Figurines are generally defined as anthropomorphic, zoomorphic, or geometric figures, which are typically made of terracotta or stone. Although these objects have the potential to convey information about the men, women, and children who once lived in houses, they can only give elusive answers for their exact use-context and meaning.[32]

Terracotta figurines were used for a variety of reasons in the ancient world. The most notable use of terracottas was their offer as gifts to the gods, whether given in the hope of obtaining divine protection or given in thanks for divine services already rendered. As far as the archaeological record s concerned, votive gifts made of terracotta have generally proved to be excellent survivors due to the durable nature of fired clay. This is not generally the case for ex-votos made of such perishable materials as wax or wood or for those made of valuable metals, which were often melted down to be recycled. Owing to their lack of utility for purposes of recycling, terracottas are instead preserved in large numbers.[33] There is no clear evidence to either support or reject the use of terracotta or stone figurines of Graeco-Roman or Egyptian deities found in houses in Graeco-Roman Egypt in ritual activities performed within or around the domestic space. However, it is tempting to suggest that terracotta lamps taking the shape of Osiris as a mummiform figure or having the representations of Athena-Neith might have been used in the illumination of lamps for Athena-Neith in commemoration of the search for the body of Osiris on 13 Epeiph, though this cannot be proven.

It is completely untenable that such religious physical representations of divinities as figurines were in any way used as decorative objects in the house or toys of children. Toys are well documented in many houses in Karanis, Kellis, Trimithis, and elsewhere in Egypt. They usually take the form of quadruped toys (horse, donkey, camel), which were typically made of stone, terracotta, wood, or, rarely, textile and papyrus dolls.[34] About nineteen figurines made of textile and papyrus, dating from the first through fourth centuries AD, have been found in Karanis (figure 40). The majority of these contexts were houses, but one figurine was also found in a street. Based on their stylistic characteristics, textile and papyrus figurines have been interpreted as miniatures of the human form, which were used as toys by children.[35] The same function is attributed to a group of six textile dolls uncovered from various sites in Egypt, all dating from the first through fourth centuries AD, the same timespan as the Karanis dolls.[36]

FIGURE 40. SWADDLED DOLL-FIGURINE, 8 × 3 CM, KELSEY MUSEUM, 26413.

As important archaeological objects, figurines are important attestations that augment our knowledge of the daily-life activities of the inhabitants of Graeco-Roman Egypt. Numerous artefacts were recovered from Room E of House C54 at Karanis. These include a badly denuded terracotta figurine of Isis and Harpokrates, ivory dice, several kinds of faunal remains, a fragment of a muzzle, a wooden tethering stake, flint grinders, a whetstone, a fragment of a weaver's comb, and a wooden doll. That there are several items related to the keeping of animals and the grinding of grain is not surprising since this room opened out into a courtyard area where such activities took place. It is, however, intriguing that a textile doll (Kelsey Museum No. 7512) is found in general association with the figurine of Isis and Harpokrates, the ivory dice, and a

wooden doll. The dice and the textile and wooden dolls are both suggestive of games and leisure activities. Yet these possible associations are tantalizing in terms of the kinds of domestic activities with which the terracotta figurine may be associated. The terracotta figurine is interesting since there is a wall niche in the adjacent room, which has been posited to be both of a utilitarian nature and indicative of domestic ritual.[37] Based on the striking similarity of the Karanis dolls with the Egyptian *tit* and *sa* amulets, Karen Johnson has recently interpreted the textile and papyrus figurines as amulets. The *sa*-sign embodied protective forces, and the large loop at the top of the symbol almost seems to correspond to the head of the Karanis dolls. The *tit*, or 'girdle of Isis', in amulet form also shares structural characteristics with the dolls. Hence, the Karanis figurines were perhaps used as amulets that were manufactured for the protection of unborn and newborn children.[38]

Judging from the great number of his figurine-amulets that were found in houses, the dwarf-god Bes, the patron of women in childbirth, had a strong presence in the domestic sphere. A papyrus of AD 144 from Oxyrhynchus

---

[32] Boozer 2015, chapter 10.
[33] Ammerman 1991, 203. For general discussions of votive offerings in the Classical world: Rouse 1902; van Straten 1981.
[34] Husselman 1979, 7-32; Malouta 2012, 299, fig. 18.2.
[35] Johnson 2004, 54, fig. 7.
[36] Janssen 1996.
[37] Johnson 2004, 57.
[38] Johnson 2004.

records a complaint about the theft of a golden statue of Bes, which probably stood in a domestic shrine.[39] The god Osiris is also attested in houses at Karanis and elsewhere in Graeco-Roman Egypt. A terracotta figurine found in House C11 at Karanis has been interpreted as Osiris in the form of a bust-length mummy (figure 25).[40] Given that religious symbols were common in houses, it is not surprising that Osiris, the principal god of death and of the underworld, was esteemed in the domestic sphere. Osiris was the principal deity from whom the living as well as the dead sought protection.[41]

The presence of domestic cults of Graeco-Roman and Egyptian deities in the Roman period suggests that religion was 'not limited by the sacred precincts of a temple or the liturgy of a priest'.[42] The visual and physical presence of deities in houses was an integral part of the domestic religious life of the inhabitants. Mural representations, statuettes, and figurines of several deities probably served to extend the protective powers of these deities to the house occupants. Papyri indicate that children were taught to honour the gods and maintain their household shrines:[43] 'Please light a lamp for the shrines and spread the cushions', wrote Apollonia and Eupous in a domestic context to their younger sisters, Rhasion and Demarion.[44] In the light of oil lamps, cushions were spread, prayers were performed by family members, and offerings were perhaps made to the protector deities of the family. The small sculptures of deities, made in stone, bronze, or clay, uncovered from houses were probably deposited in domestic shrines. These family ceremonies were 'rites of intensification', which provide recurrent times of family gatherings around the domestic shrines. Domestic shrines probably helped inhabitants to adhere to their religious values and cultural traditions. A father or mother might have found it a good opportunity to teach his or her children their own religious ideas and practices. It is known that children learn the basic, but important information about their culture in the house. Above all, culture is a 'learned behaviour' comprising a set of shared practices, beliefs, customs, and habits. Religious ideas and cultural practices are constructed by individuals and passed on over generations through enculturation or socialization.[45]

The Kelsey Museum's collection houses more than 250 figurine-amulets from Karanis alone, several of which are representations of such gods as Serapis, Osiris, Isis, Horus, and Harpokrates. A group of terracotta objects of Roman date have been found in the Athenian Agora. The types include grotesques, which are images of men and women with distorted and exaggerated features thought to represent actors and dwarfs, animals, and, more important, lamps, figurine-amulets, and busts of Greek and Egyptian deities.[46] Egyptian deities included Isis, Serapis, Osiris, Harpokrates, Anubis, and other minor Egyptian deities, whose cult seems to have been introduced to Athens in the fourth century BC by traders coming into Piraeus. Once installed, the Egyptian gods enjoyed great popularity in and around the city. Though their shrines lay beyond the limits of the Agora, small objects such as these demonstrate Athenian interest in Egyptian cult.[47] It is no coincidence that the most frequent figurines of Egyptian deities uncovered from houses in Karanis and elsewhere belonged to Isis, Serapis, Osiris, Horus, and Harpokrates. This seems to suggest that Egyptian deities played similar roles abroad and that the Athenian figurines of Egyptian divinities might have been crafted in Alexandria and later they were transported to Athens or that they were simply imitated in local Athenian workshops.[48] Other amulets uncovered from houses in Karanis and elsewhere in Egypt also take the form of dangerous animals, such as crocodiles and lions, as if to harness their ferocity on behalf of the protection of an individual. While amulets were often made of particular kinds of stone or metal, they were also manufactured from organic materials as well.[49] In 1979, Françoise Dunand has considered aspects of popular religion in Roman Egypt, with the focus on the widespread devotion to the various manifestations of Isis and Harpokrates. He argues that invoking symbols of fertility was especially important to rural populations, such as that of Karanis, both for agricultural production and for human reproduction.[50]

Egyptian deities were popular subjects in local terracotta production since the foundation of Naukratis and represent a continuation of Late Period practice, though in a more 'naturalistic' Hellenistic style that mixed Greek and Egyptian cultural symbols, as was common elsewhere in Ptolemaic Egypt. They remain popular throughout the Ptolemaic and Roman periods, though their production declines with time, as does the manufacture of figurines at Naukratis in general. Of the Egyptian deities, Harpokrates is by far the most frequent, though his mother Isis-Hathor or Isis-Aphrodite (figure 41), the Sothic dogs associated with her cult and his protector, Bes, were also popular, with hundreds of examples found in Naukratis.[51] As in the Late Period, the majority of figurines come from domestic contexts, which is unsurprising as these were deities associated

---

[39] P.Oxy. X.1272.10-11.
[40] Gazda 1983, 40.
[41] On the role of Osiris in the funerary sphere, see Venit 2002; Smith 2009.
[42] Bowman 1986, 183.
[43] Gazda 1983, 31.
[44] P.Athen. 60.5-8 (323-30 BC).
[45] Sewell 1999, 40-1.

[46] For a Ptolemaic grotesque in the Petrie Museum at University College London (UC 49909), see Booth 2005. Dwarf figurines, the prototypes of grotesques, are known in Egypt since the Predynastic Period: Ucko 1965, 217, pl. ii.
[47] Camp 1980, 20.
[48] Burr 1933, 192.
[49] Aune 1997.
[50] Dunand 1979.
[51] Thomas 2015b, 2, fig. 1.

FIGURE 41. TERRACOTTA FIGURE OF ISIS-HATHOR OR ISIS-APHRODITE, C. 300-100 BC, © BRITISH MUSEUM, 1888, 0601.110.

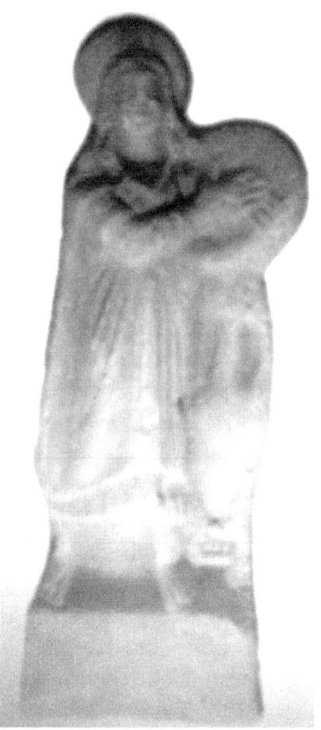

FIGURE 42. TERRACOTTA FIGURE OF FEMALE TAMBOUR PLAYER, C. AD 1-200.

with protection, fertility and childbirth. They represent a continuity of Egyptian domestic religion from the Late Period, concerned with family health and protection. Terracottas of the god Serapis and the Apis bull are generally rare in Ptolemaic Egypt. Representations of Serapis, the Sothic dog, and busts of Apis were proportionally increased in the Roman period, when Serapis began to appear more frequently on figures, medallions, lamps, and other moulded terracottas. In sharp contrast to the Late period, terracotta figurines from Greece and Cyprus are rare in Ptolemaic Naukratis, and the last imported Hellenistic figures probably arrived in the early third century BC. In contrast, the large quantities of locally produced 'Graeco-Egyptian' terracotta figures (Greek style figurine of Egyptian deities) found in domestic contexts in Ptolemaic Naukratis suggest that Egyptian domestic religion was practised by the local population on a large scale.[52]

At Naukratis, models of Egyptian votive objects, animals, figure vases, and representations of nude and pregnant women were popular local products. They have not been found in large quantities, but remained popular until the Roman period. Paul Perdrizet interpreted the particular pose of these squatting women figures in the light of a passage from Plutarch, according to which Egyptian religion obliged women to celebrate the rite crouching on the ground, just as the Athenian women did for the Thesmophoria.[53] The depictions of such figurines may represent a continued use of this symbolism in the Egyptian practice of magico-medical rites from the Late Period. They have been intended as apotropaic amulets, particularly given that the majority of them come from houses and graves and some had loops for suspension for this reason. Marcella Pisani has interpreted such figurines as votive offerings to the goddess Isis, either presented to the deity by pregnant women or spouses praying for their fertility, or intended to represent Isis herself. The squatting female terracottas discovered in graves were linked to religious tendencies which developed in Ptolemaic times, bringing about the fusion of Demeter with Isis and Dionysus with Osiris.[54]

The most common representations of human figures in Naukratis are depictions of lay celebrants, festival-goers, and priests. This rather evocative group of festival celebrants is full of fun and energy, such as the terracotta figure of female tambour player, c. AD 1-200, pertaining to a festive procession (figure 42).[55] They often wear festival wreaths, play instruments or carry offerings or statues to their deity. Sometimes a relationship with a specific deity can be identified, for example in the 'water carriers', who are possibly devotees of Demeter. Other figures have been interpreted as priests and lay followers of Ptah or Harpokrates because of their distinctive shaven head and side-lock. However, the precise association remains uncertain in most cases. The iconography represents festival-goers, and is often not specific enough to discern which festival of which deity is referred to, if it was ever intended to be so specific. They may simply concern the festivals of various deities undertaken at different times of the year.

During festivals and processions, a range of performers was hired, including musicians and actors, for Graeco-Roman and traditional Egyptian festivities. In the late second century AD, 6000 drachmas were spent on sacrifices and shows held in the theatre, where a *mimus*, a musician, a dancer, and a Homericist conducted their performances in connection with the traditional festivals of Tybi and Pachon at Oxyrhynchus.[56] Graeco-Roman performances were probably also held at traditional festivals in theatres at Memphis, Krokodilopolis, Apollonopolis Heptakomia, and Panopolis.[57] The development of the theatre reflected a high degree of urbanisation in the second and third centuries AD, where

---

[52] Thomas 2015b, 2-3, 6.
[53] Plut. *De Is. et Os.* 69; Perdrizet 1921, 122.
[54] Pisani 2006, 101, 290, 366-67, no. 162. See also, Török 1995, 132-3.
[55] Thomas 2015b, 8, fig. 20.
[56] *P.Oxy.* XVII.2127.
[57] Sear 2006, 300-1.

ambitious inhabitants assimilated themselves with Greek institutions.[58]

Other Graeco-Roman and Egyptian festivals and sacrifices were also conducted in the hippodrome, which gave its name to an amphodon as early as AD 22.[59] Taken over from a traditional ceremony is the festival of 'the most sacred Nile' on 30 Pauni (Julian: 24 July), for which the strategos was supplied with items like a calf, sweet wine, garlands, pine-cones, and green palm-branches.[60] A second-century AD papyrus records payments for a *mimus*, a musician, a dancer, and a Homericist in a procession related to this festival, which was probably held in the hippodrome.[61] During the second and early third century AD, the political and administrative power in cities was transferred from the Egyptian priests to the gymnasial and later bouleutic elites, who organised and summoned Greek entertainers to games and a variety of religious and public festivals, centring on the gymnasium, theatre, and hippodrome.[62] The festivities and their architectural backdrops helped the participants to construct a sense of belonging to their city.[63] Metropoleis competed against each other in athletic contests, which were elevated to 'sacred' status.[64] In AD 199/200 Aurelius Horion, a wealthy Oxyrhynchite, petitioned the emperor to be allowed to establish a fund of 10000 Attic drachmas to provide prizes for the ephebic games to rival those offered at Antinoopolis, showing the familiar civic rivalry among Greek cities. Horion supported his request by stating that Oxyrhynchus still celebrated the emperor's victory over the Jews in the rebellion of AD 115/17.[65] The metropolis already developed new festivals to reinforce its local identity in competition with other cities.[66]

Like Graeco-Roman festivals and sacrifices, Egyptian festivities were held in classical structures such as the theatre and hippodrome, not to mention civic temples. Cult centres in the city were meant to serve worshippers of the deities and members of the local community, without regard for their legal status. Egyptian legal traditions, for example, were available for everyone who wanted to take advantage of them. Greeks had the chance to go to an Egyptian notary and had legal or business documents drawn up in demotic.[67] Yet it should come as no surprise that the priests and priestesses of these temples bear Egyptian names[68] and the rituals and cult practices within these temples remained traditional, where image-bearers, ibis-feeders, ibis-embalmers,[69] lamplighters of the temples of Serapis and Thoeris,[70] and hieroglyphic-carvers continued to perform their long-standing duties.[71] Both classical and traditional monuments were equally used as landmarks and gave their names to districts and streets.[72]

It has been suggested that traditional cults and temples were preserved through their incorporation into the dominant Hellenic milieu.[73] The metropolitan magistrates were involved in the organisation of festivities in the city, including the festivals of Serapis; Nilus, Tybi, and Pachon.[74] Religious festivals and processions represented the ideal religious moments in the life of the inhabitants. David Frankfurter argues that 'the festival's significance lies principally in its effective linking of temple and cities, where the sacred images exited the temples and were carried on priests' shoulders to embellish and demarcate space or render oracles'.[75] The inhabitants of Graeco-Roman Egypt constructed their local sense of time around the festival calendar, which included a huge number of classical and traditional festivities. One Petosiris writes to Serenia: make every effort, lady, to come out on the 20th for the birthday of the god.[76]

Similarly, the temples and sanctuaries dedicated to Greek deities such as Demeter, Dionysus, Hera, Nemesis, Kore, the Dioskouroi (Castor and Pollux), Apollo, Zeus, and Tyche must have been important to the inhabitants of the city as a whole.[77] A papyrus already attests a festival in honour of 'the stars of Hera', i.e. Venus, which was granted three days of public holiday.[78] Equally, temples built for the imperial cult must have been important to almost all inhabitants. It was only in AD 406 that the Caesareion was converted into a church, reflecting the growing supremacy of Christianity in the early fifth century.[79] Roman cults in Oxyrhynchus included a temple of Mars[80] and a Kapitolium.[81] Another cult of Jupiter Capitolinus is attested in AD 215 at Ptolemais Euergetis, where a

---

[58] Bowman and Rathbone 1992; Bowman 1995, 2000; Alston 1997c.
[59] *P.Oxy.* II.288.17, 26, 30; *P.Oxy.*II.311.2; *P.Oxy.*X.1258.2; Humphrey 1986, 516-9.
[60] *P.Oxy.* IX.1211.
[61] *P.Oxy.* III.519. The papyrus mentions that the ἱπποκόμοις participated in the festival, though his role cannot be ascertained.
[62] Alston 1997b, 141-59.
[63] Alston 1997b.
[64] Rigsby 1977.
[65] *P.Oxy.* IV.705.
[66] Alston 1997c, 88.
[67] On the Demotic Legal Code of Hermopolis West: *P.Oxy.*II.237; *P.Oxy.*XLVI.3285; Mattha 1975.
[68] Lewis 1983, 87.
[69] *P.Fouad* I.16.2-4.
[70] *P.Oxy.* XII.1453.4-5, 8.
[71] *P.Oxy.* VII.1029.15-16.
[72] Rink 1924, 25-42, with papyrological references.
[73] Bowman and Rathbone 1992; Alston 1997c.
[74] Serapis: *P.Oxy.* XLIII.3094 = *SB* IV.7336. Nilus: *P.Oxy.* XI.1211 = *P.Oxy.* III.519 = Vandoni 1964, 46. Tybi and Pachon: *P.Oxy.* XVII.2127 = Vandoni 1964, 46.
[75] Frankfurter 1996, 304. Cf. the festival of the *Navigium Isidis* in Rome (Apul. *Met*.11).
[76] *P.Oxy.* I.112.
[77] Turner 1952, 130 = Krüger 1990, 103-5.
[78] *P.Oxy.* IV.731.6 = Vandoni 1964, 141 = Whitehorne 1995, 3087.
[79] *P.Mert.*I.41.12.
[80] *P.Oxy.* VI.984.149-150.
[81] *P.Oxy.* I.43, verso, iv.3; *P.Oxy.* XVII.2109.8-9; *P.Oxy.* XVII.2128.4; *P.Oxy.* LIV.3758.78, 156.

festival of Kronos/Sobek was celebrated and called for by the gymnasial and bouleutic elites, reflecting the incorporation of traditional festivals into Roman sanctuaries.[82]

The Greek and Roman terracotta figurines from Naukratis comprise a large and varied group of artefacts, including figures, vases, models, and coffin fittings dating from the fourth century BC to the seventh century AD, reflecting the continued significance of the settlement into the Roman and Byzantine periods. There is archaeological evidence for at least two terracotta workshops operating in the north-east part of Naukratis. The majority of what *we* now call classical figurines included Greek deities and mythological characters (satyrs and maenads), male and female cult followers and priests, votive models of animals and objects, figure vessels and ampullae, and coffin fittings.[83] Clearly, this reflects the dominance of religion in daily-life activities of the inhabitants.

During the late fourth and early third century BC, Greek deities, mythological scenes, and characters were not particularly popular and rarely produced locally in Naukratis. Figurines of deities are usually imported representations of Greek goddesses: Demeter, Aphrodite, Artemis, and Athena. Male Greek deities are rare, with Dionysus, Eros, and Priapos being the most popular represented during that time. It seems that Egyptian subjects, even if made in a Greek style, were most suited in Ptolemaic times to settings in the home. Figurative art was popular during the Ptolemaic period as a form of decoration used to embellish the household and terracotta household objects. Representations of Isis enthroned with Harpokrates, or nude standing Isis-Hathor, Harpokrates, 'Sothic' dogs and riders continued to be popular from the mid-first to the early third centuries AD.[84]

The large and varied groups of terracotta figurines of Graeco-Roman Egypt come from sanctuaries, cemeteries, industrial production areas, and domestic contexts. The contexts in which figurines were found is significant for understanding how they were used by the inhabitants. The divine figurines uncovered from Graeco-Roman shrines or Egyptian temples were used as votive offerings and/or ritual foundation deposits, while those found in cemeteries were utilised in burial rituals and/or coffin-fittings deposited within graves. The majority of religious and divine figurines were associated with houses across Egypt. These were undoubtedly used in popular or domestic religion, including magico-medical rites and festivals held in or around the domestic property. By the Roman period, for example, household lamps and vessels were used as containers for eulogia (blessings of oil, water or dirt), although they can be only identified in the archaeological record through the word 'εὐλογία' written on the objects, as is the case with one example from Naukratis, now kept in the British Museum (figure 43).[85] The figurines represent the requirements and concerns of the inhabitants of Graeco-Roman Egypt. A significant proportion of domestic terracottas comprises representations of popular deities, particularly Harpokrates, and his protector Bes, his mother Isis-Hathor and her dog, Sothis. Also popular are the figurines of pregnant women, actors, and priests and worshippers dressed for religious festivals or rituals. In sharp contrast to 'classical' style sanctuaries, which contained a large number of figurines of Greek and, to a lesser extent, Roman divinities, Graeco-Roman subjects are rare in domestic contexts, other than those that concern the 'Greek' theatre and women wearing Greek dress. It may well be the case that these were incorporated into daily Egyptian life without carrying the same meaning as in other parts of the Hellenistic and later Roman world. Instead, representations of actors and satyrs, reinterpreted for an Egyptian audience, may have been thought of as referencing performers in the Egyptian religious festivals attested in documentary sources.[86]

The general impression given by the terracotta assemblage uncovered from houses is that figurine iconography across Egypt reflects predominantly the

FIGURE 43. POTTERY VESSEL MARKED 'EULOGIA', C. AD 100-300, BRITISH MUSEUM, OA.9431.

---

[82] *BGU* II.362.vi.22-4 = *Sel.Pap.* II.404.
[83] Thomas 2015b.
[84] Thomas 2015b, 7-12.
[85] Thomas 2015b, 11, fig. 31.
[86] Montserrat 1996, 170.

local worship of Egyptian deities. Representations of Greek deities declined from the beginning of the Ptolemaic to the Roman periods. Local demand remained strong for representations of lay worshippers and priests of Egyptian deities. However, there was a change in how terracotta figures were produced and used in Egyptian religion over time. In the Roman period, the subjects represented in figurines remained largely the same, at least as far as the range of Egyptian deities were concerned, although their diversity and quantity declined significantly. Figurines of pregnant women became relatively popular and representations of cultists and priests declined in Byzantine Egypt.[87]

VI.3. Conclusion

Archaeology and papyri confirm that the interior parts of houses in Graeco-Roman Egypt were used as religious space. This is represented in the presence of a variety of domestic shrines in different parts of the house. Wall paintings with religious themes of Graeco-Roman and Egyptian divinities also appear in domestic space and even in attached domestic structures such as alcoves in the Nile Valley and beyond. Terracotta figurines of Isis, Isis-Thermouthis, Osiris, Serapis, Hera, and Harpocrates, and amulets of Bes affirm the religious side of the domestic sphere.

---

[87] Thomas 2015b, 15.

Chapter VII
The House as Funerary Space

In addition to serving as a social and religious place, the internal space of houses had an important funerary role. This is represented in the rituals performed within the house following the death of animals associated with traditional deities and of family members whose mummies would be kept in houses at least for a short period before burial.[1]

VII.1. Mourning rituals for Dead Animals: the Case of Dogs

Aelian's comprehensive work on animals encouraged scholars to address animals in the ancient world.[2] Based on textual, pictorial, and zooarchaeological evidence, Patrick Houlihan systematically collected the different species of ancient Egyptian fauna, providing information about their character, environment, and domestication.[3] Dieter Kessler turned attention to animal cult and hypogea at Tuna el-Gebel, the necropolis of Hermopolis Magna.[4] Perhaps the most beloved animal to ancient as well as modern inhabitants is the dog.[5] Scholars considered the history of dogs in ancient Egypt and the Mediterranean.[6] Salima Ikram, a passionate of animals, presented valuable studies on animals, with special focus on animal mummification and dogs in the dynastic period.[7] This article deals with dogs in Graeco-Roman Egypt based on literary, archaeological, and papyrological documents. It argues that the dog enjoyed reverence from the Pharaonic to the Roman period mainly through its role in the myth of Isis and Osiris. Dogs' mummies in Egypt symbolised and perpetuated the role of Anubis and the dog in the Osirian legend. Additionally, they served as guardians and companions of the givers/dead in their journey to the underworld. The paper begins with animal cult and the dog's function in the Osirian myth, followed by consideration of dogs in Pharaonic and Graeco-Roman times to highlight continuity in dogs' symbolism. It finally addresses the death and burial rituals, which the owners of dogs performed after the demise of their pets, closely matching those offered to Osiris by Isis and Anubis.

VII.1.1. Animal Cult in Ancient Egypt

Animals played a dominant role in ancient Egyptian religion and culture.[8] Nearly 176 of the 777 hieroglyphs in Alan Gardiner's Signlist revolve around animals.[9] Ancient Egypt was full of animals.[10] Not all animals were revered throughout the country, however. While some animals were equally honoured in different nomes of Egypt, others enjoyed supreme rank in some areas and held only a subordinate place elsewhere. However, the bull, the dog, the cat, the hawk, the ibis, the fish lepidotus, and the fish oxyrhynchos were venerated countrywide.[11] For classical writers, the transmigration of the soul from human bodies into living creatures, including animals, was a theological reason for animal cult in ancient Egypt. According to Herodotus, 'the Egyptians were the first to teach that the human soul is immortal and, at the death of the body, it enters into some other living thing then coming to birth; and after passing through all creatures of land, sea, and air, it enters once more into a human body at birth'.[12] Diodorus similarly states that 'Pythagoras learned from Egyptians his teachings about the gods, his geometrical propositions and theory of numbers, as well as the transmigration of the soul into every living thing'.[13]

Diodorus gives three other explanations for animal veneration in ancient Egypt: the first says that the original gods, being few in number, took the shape of animals to escape from the savagery and violence of humankind, and afterwards, when became masters of the whole world, consecrated these animals to themselves out of gratitude. According to the second, the images of animals were fixed on spears as ensigns to distinguish the corps of the army and prevent confusion, victory followed, and the animals became objects of worship. The third reason is that animals were venerated due to the benefits they make to humans.[14]

The ancient Egyptians venerated many animals. At Kynopolis, the dog-headed Anubis was particularly honoured and a form of worship and sacred feeding was organised for all dogs.[15] For Greek and Roman visitors, the use of animals as representatives of deities was an excessive superstition and expression of the Egyptian 'otherness'. Plutarch reports that when the Kynopolites had eaten the fish oxyrhynchos, the Oxyrhynchites took revenge by consuming dogs sacred at Kynopolis. A fight between the two nomes broke out before Roman soldiers intervened and brought the inhabitants apart.[16] Juvenal

---

[1] On animals: Diod. Sic. 1.84.2. On mummies: Diod. Sic. 1.92.6; Cic. *Tusc.* 1.45.108; Sext. Emp. *Pyr.* 3.226; *P.Princ.* III.166.4-7.
[2] Ael. *NA* I-XVII.
[3] Houlihan 1996.
[4] Kessler 1989.
[5] Lazenby 1949, 245-7.
[6] Brewer et al 2001; Routledge 2004; Gransard-Desmond 2004.
[7] Ikram 2005, 2007a, 2008, 2013.
[8] Arnold 1995; Houlihan 1996.
[9] Gardiner 1957; Te Velde 1980, 67.
[10] Hdt. 2.65.
[11] Strabo 17.1.40.
[12] Hdt. 2.123.
[13] Diod. Sic. 1.98.2.
[14] Dio. Sic. 1.86-7.
[15] Strabo 17.1.40.
[16] Plut. *De Is. et Os.* 72.

narrates a more brutal fight between the Tentyrites and Ombites, resulting in an act of cannibalism.[17] However, there is no evidence for Egyptian cannibalism at any date.[18]

Greek and Roman writers, philosophers, and politicians employed the religious practice of animal cult to emphasise their cultural superiority over the Egyptian 'barbarians'.[19] Thus, Juvenal writes 'Who knows not what monsters demented Egypt worships? One district adores the crocodile; another venerates the ibis that gorges itself with serpents... In one part cats are worshipped, in another a river fish, in another whole township venerates a dog'.[20] Juvenal denounces the Egyptian custom of regarding animals as incarnations of deities with biting sarcasm.[21] One encounters the same attitude in Philo's *Dekalogue*: What can be more ridiculous than this cult? The first foreigners who arrived in Egypt were quite worn out with laughing at and ridiculing these superstitions.[22] In line with this criticism is Octavian's speech to his soldiers before the Battle of Actium, 'should we not be acting most disgracefully, if, after surpassing all men everywhere in valour, we should then meekly bear the insults of this throng, who, oh heavens!, are Alexandrians and Egyptians, who worship reptiles and beasts as gods'.[23] The reason for Greek and Roman denouncement of the Egyptian practice of animal veneration was the ignorance or misunderstanding of the complex relationship between ancient Egyptian deities and their associated animals. Like the statues in the shrines and temples, it was believed that the gods would reside in the animals. The animal-headed masked priests, for example, were representations of ancient Egyptian deities in rituals and ceremonial processions.[24]

Mummified animals excavated throughout Egypt are classified into four categories: household pets interred with their owners; food offerings; sacred animals; and votive animals.[25] In the Teti Cemetery at Saqqara, dogs buried in the Graeco-Roman period with humans have been interpreted as amuletic animal mummies, adding a fifth category.[26] Yet, as will be shown later, there was no contradiction and/or difference between the use of dogs as votive or amuletic animals. Dogs are confirmed as household pets buried with their owners;[27] sacred animals of Anubis and other related deities; and as votive/guardian mummies.[28] Yet dogs are not attested as food offerings, because they were never used in Egyptian diet. In most cases, pets lived out their natural lives and when dead, were carefully mummified and interred with their owners. Often these pet mummies were placed in theriomorphic coffins of their own or sometimes even with their owner.[29]

Most dog mummies in ancient Egypt fall in the category of sacred and votive animals. Sacred animals were incarnations of Egyptian deities: the Egyptians worshiped the power that is over all, which each of the gods exhibited, by means of the animals, which shared the same nomes with them.[30] They are faunal representatives of given deities and are attested from the earliest times of Egyptian history.[31] Scared animals were honoured with temples, religious precincts, sacrifices, solemn assemblies, and public processions.[32] They were kept in the sacred precinct of their associated gods' temples, 'which are surrounded with groves and consecrated pastures',[33] normally covered with grass or other plants suitable for feeding the sacred livestock. Men of distinction gave the sacred animals the most expensive care. The food was placed before them, cakes of fine flour, seethed in milk or smeared with honey, the flesh of ducks, boiled or roasted, and that of birds and fish uncooked for the carnivorous animals. They were bathed in warm water, anointed with costly perfumes, and were furnished with expensive jewellery and clothes.[34] Pilgrims and worshippers partly covered this cost: the Egyptians make vows to certain gods on behalf of their children who have been delivered from an illness, in which case they shave off their hair and weigh it against silver or gold, and then give the money to the attendants of sacred animals.[35]

A sacred animal was identified by certain defined markings; it was worshipped as an incarnation of god during its lifetime and, after death, was mummified and buried as a divinity.[36] Only one divine creature was selected as the god's physical manifestation.[37] The sacred animal of a god living in the temple was an oracle-giver and dream-interpreter. Examples of Demotic oracular petitions addressed to Thoth were uncovered from the baboon/ibis catacombs at Tuna el-Gebel.[38] The Apis bull at Memphis was honoured as an image of the psyche of Osiris,[39] which was supposed to migrate from one Apis to another in succession.[40] Death was penalty for

---

[17] Juv. *Satire* 15.
[18] Alston 1996, 101.
[19] Alston 1996; Feder 2003.
[20] Juv. *Satire* 15.1-3, 5-8.
[21] Smelik and Hemelrijk 1984.
[22] Philo, *Deka.* 16.80.
[23] Cass. Dio 50.24.
[24] Wolinski 1987.
[25] Ikram 2005.
[26] Hartley et al 2011.
[27] Ikram 2007a.
[28] Kessler 1986; Ikram 2005.
[29] Petrie 1902, 39-40, pl. lxxx.
[30] Euseb. *Prae. evang.* 3.4.
[31] Dodson 2009.
[32] Philo, *Deka.* 16.76-9.
[33] Clem. Al. *Paedag* 3.2.
[34] Dio. Sic. 1.84.5-6.
[35] Dio. Sic. 1.83.2. Cf. Hdt. 2.65.
[36] Ikram 2007a, 418.
[37] Strabo 17.38.
[38] Kessler 1986; Kessler 2003, 41, 52; Kessler and Nur el-Din 2005, 136-7; Ikram 2005, 4-14.
[39] Dio. Sic. 1.85.1-4; Strabo 17.1.31; Plut. *De Is. et Os.* 39; Kessler 2003, 40-1.
[40] Hdt. 3.28.

intentionally killing a sacred animal, but if someone killed it by mischance, he would pay whatever penalty the priests appoint.[41] In the late first century BC, when a Roman accidentally killed a cat, the inhabitants rushed to his house and 'neither the officials sent by the king (Ptolemy Auletes) to beg the man off nor the fear of Rome which all people felt were enough to save the man from punishment'.[42] This fanatical fury recalls a parallel at Athens, where the people condemned a man to death for killing a sparrow sacred to Asklepios.[43]

After death, sacred animals were ceremonially buried in special cemeteries near the temple of their associated deity.[44] The death of Apis was a season of general mourning; and his interment was accompanied with most costly ceremonies. When the Apis died of old age, the curator of the sacred animal not only spent on his funeral the large sum appropriated to this purpose, but also borrowed fifty talents from king Ptolemy I Soter.[45] The Apis was mummified and buried in a special cemetery at Memphis and another creature with special markings was selected.[46] The mummification of the dead Apis took place at the 'Embalming House of the Apis Bull' of the temple of Apis at Memphis.[47] The new selected animal was kept in seclusion, except for women, for forty days, during which the people did not cease their mourning over the dead bull.[48] Similarly, when the sacred crocodile died in the Arsinoite nome, one creature was selected to replace the dead animal.[49] This selection was apparently accompanied with a spectacular festival called in Greek papyri the Soucheia.[50]

Other creatures were killed and mummified as votive items offered by pilgrims to deities. Votive animal mummies are only attested from the Late Period onwards.[51] They were the most prolific of all animal mummification. The votive animal has no special defined markings; it was embalmed and dedicated to its corresponding deity, who was thought to fulfil the prayers attached to it.[52] A prayer inscribed on a jar containing an ibis mummy asks Thoth to be benevolent toward the woman who embalmed his sacred bird.[53] Millions of ibises were offered to Thoth at Tuna el-Gebel to bring pilgrims closer to god.[54] Since the Ptolemaic period, the ibis-cult was associated with the Serapeum at Oxyrhynchos, where the ibioboskos and ibiotaphos respectively kept and embalmed ibises,[55] as was the Serapeum at Tuna el-Gebel.[56] There was a quarter named after the Ibiotaphieion at Oxyrhynchos.[57] At Saqqara, Buto, Abydos, and Kom Ombo, complexes were dedicated to mummified falcons, representing the manifestation of Horus.[58] At Abydos, Asyut, the Kharga oasis, and Saqqara, mummified dogs were buried in special cemeteries as votive animals of Anubis.[59]

VII.1.2. The Dog in the Myth of Isis and Osiris

The ancient Egyptian word for dog is 'iw', which refers to the animal's barking, while 'Tsm' designates the hunting 'hound'.[60] Ancient Egyptian names of dogs in Pharaonic tomb reliefs and stelae included the Brave One, Reliable, Healthy, Grabber, Pleasant One, Good Herdsman, Cook-pot, and even the Useless.[61] Many of the epithets represent endearment, but others merely convey dogs' abilities. Dogs also acquired theophoric names such as "Amun is Valiant".[62] There is little evidence for dogs' names after the 26th Dynasty. A Ptolemaic situla in the Cleveland Museum of Art calls the dog beneath the chair of his master "the Beautiful" (figure 44).[63] There are two epitaphs for a hunting dog named Tauron in the Zenon archive.[64] The reason for the rareness of dogs' names in the Graeco-Roman period cannot be determined. The owners perhaps felt it unnecessary to record their pets' names on monuments or, most likely, dogs' names are accidently lost in the literary and archaeological record.

The mythological background for animal cult in ancient Egypt is rooted in the myth of Isis and Osiris. While Osiris left his Egyptian kingdom to subdue the world by means of peace, Isis governed in his absence. On his return, Seth and his seventy-two fellow conspirators imprisoned him by craft in a chest, which was flung into the Nile.[65] On hearing of the murder of Osiris, Isis cut off a lock of her hair and wore mourning clothes. Together, Isis and Nephthys mourned for the lost Osiris for four days (17-20 Athyr) before the chest containing his body was found by Isis near the mouths of the Nile.[66] Here it was buried for a while; but Seth, while hunting by night, discovered it and cut the body into fourteen or twenty-six pieces, which he scattered to the winds.[67]

---

[41] Hdt. 2.65.
[42] Dio. Sic. 1.83.9.
[43] Ael. *VH* 5.17.
[44] Dodson 2009.
[45] Dio. Sic. 1.84.8.
[46] Hdt. 3.28.
[47] Jones 1990.
[48] Dio. Sic. 1.85.1-3.
[49] Strabo 17.38.
[50] Perpillou-Thomas 1993, 140.
[51] Dodson 2009.
[52] Ikram 2005, 10-11.
[53] Lacovara and Trope-Teasley 2001.
[54] Kessler 2003, 42; Kessler and Nur el-Din 2005, 120-63.
[55] *P.Fouad* I.16.2-4.
[56] Kessler 2003, 45.
[57] *P.Princ.* II.46.
[58] Lauer 1976; Morgan and McGovern-Huffman 2008.
[59] Ikram 2007a, 418; Hartley et al 2011.
[60] Gardiner 1957, Signlist No. 14, 459.
[61] On names of animals in the Roman Empire: Toynbee 1948.
[62] Phillips 1948, 9; Janssen 1958; Fischer 1961; Simpson 1977. Dogs were not only given personal names by the Coast Salish peoples in Washington State and British Columbia, but they were also buried ceremonially like humans and were sometimes interred with their owners (Elmendorf 1992, 99; Barsh et al 2006, 1-2).
[63] Fischer 1978, 174, fig. 1.
[64] Purola 1994; Pepper 2010.
[65] Plut. *De Is. et Os.* 13.
[66] P*lut. De Is.* et Os. 39.
[67] Plut. *De Is. et Os.* 87; Dio. Sic. 1.21.2.

FIGURE 44. A DOG BENEATH ITS MASTER'S CHAIR ON A PTOLEMAIC SITULA IN THE CLEVELAND MUSEUM OF ART.

Then Isis took boat and searched for the pieces, until she had recovered them all save one, the privates.[68] Isis and Nephthys carefully put the pieces together. Anubis then embalmed the whole body and made the first mummy in the ancient world.[69] The rejoining of the limbs of Osiris became the prototype for the overcoming of death and furnished the mythical precedent for mummification.[70] Isis placed coffins of Osiris beneath the earth in several places, but only one of them, and that unknown to all, contained the body of Osiris. She did this because she wished to hide the body from Seth, fearing that he might find it and cast it out of its tomb.[71] Having buried Osiris in different nomes, Isis commanded the inhabitants and priests of Egypt to pay honour to Osiris and consecrate some animal from their district to Osiris; to pay to the animal the same honour as to the god during its life and bestow the same kind of funeral they had given to Osiris after its death.[72]

Dogs function in the Osirian myth in two passages. In the late first century BC, Diodorus states:

Again, the dog is useful both for the hunt and for man's protection, and this is why they represented the god whom they call Anubis with a dog's head, showing in this way that he was the bodyguard of Osiris and Isis. There are some, however, who explain that dogs guided Isis during her search for Osiris and protected her from wild beasts and wayfarers. They also helped her in her search, because of the affection they bore for her, by baying; and this is the reason why at the festival of Isis the procession is led by dogs, those who introduced the rite showing forth in this way the kindly service rendered by this animal of old.[73]

In the early second century AD, Plutarch similarly narrates:

They relate also that Isis, learning that Osiris in his love had consorted with her sister Nephthys through ignorance, in the belief that she was Isis, and seeing the proof of this in the garland of melilote, which he had left with Nephthys, sought to find the child for the mother, immediately after its birth, had exposed it because of her fear of Typhon (Seth). When the child had been found, after great toil and trouble, with the help of dogs, which led Isis to it, it was brought up and became her guardian and attendant, receiving the name of Anubis, and it is said to protect the gods just as dogs protect men.[74]

The Osirian legend clearly gives the sacerdotal reason for dogs' veneration. Here dogs are associated with the most known chthonic deities: Osiris, Isis, and Anubis. Due to its chthonic nature, the dog was assumed to belong to the upper and the underworld. Dogs helped Isis in her search for Osiris' body and later acted as their bodyguard. They also assisted the goddess in her search for the infant Anubis, who later became the guardian of Isis and the embalmer of Osiris. Anubis was associated with mummification since he was responsible for the wrapping of Osiris, king of the underworld. He was the way-finder who guided the dead from the land of the living to the realm of the dead.[75] In Greece, dogs were similarly associated with the chthonic goddesses Artemis and Hekate, who were active at the edge of the upper and the underworld.[76] Dogs' chthonic associations also appear in Kerberos, the watchdog of Hades,[77] who stopped living persons from entering the underworld and prevented the souls of the dead from exiting.[78] The dog was consequently related to the magic sphere of dreams and omens.[79]

---

[68] Dio. Sic. 1.22.6.
[69] Sayce 1903, 142.
[70] Assmann et al 1989, 138.
[71] Strabo 17.1.23.
[72] Dio. Sic. 1.21.6.

[73] Dio. Sic. 1.87.2-4.
[74] Plut. *De Is. et Os.* 14.
[75] Griffiths and Barb 1959, 367.
[76] Karouzou 1972, 66-7.
[77] Hom. *Il.* 7.368, *Od.* 11.623.
[78] Scholz 1937, 16-18.
[79] Sergis 2010, 64-5.

The dog was linked to Anubis, who guided the deceased to the Hall of the Two Truths, where the soul was judged by Osiris. Sculptures of theriomorphic Anubis emphasised the importance of the god of the necropolis.[80] Dogs were the most common scavengers in ancient Egyptian towns and villages.[81] In a passage in the Book of the Dead the deceased appeals to Re, the sun god, for protection from 'this god who carries off souls, who gulps down decayed matter, who lives on carrion, who is attached to darkness and dwells in gloom, of whom the feeble are afraid'.[82] Despite the sentimental attachment to dogs in the description of Argos, Odysseus' faithful dog who recognised his master after 20 years and died happily,[83] the *Iliad* and *Odyssey* similarly portray dogs as devourers of dead bodies.[84] Persistent also are the references in Latin literature to dogs' mangling the corpses.[85] As canids inhabited the liminal space between the desert and the cultivation and, by extension, the transitional area between the land of the dead and that of the living, they could disturb the body during embalming and disinter burials.[86] This gruesome ability of dogs enabled their veneration to avoid the exhumation of cemeteries and the annihilation of corpses. Dogs were therefore associated with Anubis, who presided over the liminal zone between this life and the hereafter and guided the soul from this life to the next.[87]

Since wolves, jackals, and dogs are closely related, all species of canids living at the margins of the desert were associated with Anubis.[88] The canids of the Nile Valley developed from two genetic lines: *canis familiaris Leineri,* known for greyhounds and sight hounds, and *canis familiaris intermedius,* known for smaller house dogs.[89] The classification of Egyptian canids causes problems even for zoologists. Apparently the ancient Egyptians did not distinguish particular canid species in their representation of Anubis, the god of the necropolis; Duamutef, one of the four sons of Horus; or Wepwawet, the god of Asyut.[90] A jackal or dog head could serve to depict any of these deities. Thus, a canine-headed god in the Tomb of Soldiers at Asyut has been loosely interpreted as Wepwawet or Anubis.[91] Millions of canids were offered as votive mummies in different cemeteries throughout Egypt. Canid cult was particularly popular in Abydos and Asyut, the cult centres of Anubis and Wepwawet.[92]

VII.1.3. Other Capabilities of Dogs

In addition to sacerdotal association with Anubis, dogs were consecrated on account of their benefit in hunting and warfare, as friendly companions, and of their outstanding abilities. The dog was recognised as a cunning, persistent partner in hunting.[93] It is shown on Pharaonic monuments as a hunting companion and a protector of the flocks. In the New Kingdom, hunting dogs were part of a tribute gift from Nubia.[94] In the tomb of a huntsman of the 18th Dynasty, Maiherpri, buried

FIGURE 45. A RELIEF OF THE 5TH DYNASTY SHOWS A DOG CATCHING A GAZELLE BY THE LEG, WHILE ANOTHER ATTACKS A HYENA FROM THE NECK, THE METROPOLITAN MUSEUM OF NEW YORK.

---

[80] Ischlondsky 1966, 21-4.
[81] Dixon 1989, 194.
[82] Allen 1974, 21; Dixon 1989, 197.
[83] H*om*. Od. 17.292-322.
[84] Scott 1921.
[85] Suet. *Dom.* 15.3; Burriss 1935, 37.
[86] Ikram 2007a, 419.
[87] Assmann 2001, 81-8. The North American Indians similarly attached effigies of dogs to the forehead of the dead to guide their souls to heaven (Mangold 1973).
[88] Vilà and Wayne 1999.
[89] Bunson 2002, 103; Gransard-Desmond 2004.
[90] Arnold 1995, 15, no. 10.
[91] El-Khadragy 2006, 152.
[92] Kahl 2007, 39-58, Kahl 2012, 4, 19.
[93] Ael. NA 6.53.
[94] Phillips 1948, 8.

at Thebes, two dog-collars were part of the funerary equipment.[95] Scenes of hunting dogs are not confined to Pharaonic tombs and stelae, because they occur on a ring-stand from the Ptolemaic temple of Min at Coptos.[96] The connection between dogs and Min, the Egyptian god of fertility, cannot be determined. In ancient Greece, however, huntsmen dedicated dog-collars to the god Pan, the lord of mountains and patron of hunters, who was identified with Min in Graeco-Roman Egypt.[97]

The dog has a reasoning power in hunting.[98] A relief of the 5th Dynasty in the Metropolitan Museum of New York shows a dog catching a gazelle by the leg, while another attacks a hyena from the neck (figure 45).[99] Hunting was a religious act in which forces of chaos and enemies were assigned to animals, which must be hunted down and even destroyed that the world order may stand. The disordered representation of animals in ancient Egyptian art has been interpreted as a metaphor of the impending evil forces, potential menace for the humanity. The archetypal dualism of the Egyptian religion finds its reuniting element in the concept of Maat, which signified law and order. Since the king is the primary agent of order preservation, the ruler is shows hunting animals and birds, the chaotic elements of nature.[100] Dogs assisted Pharaohs in hunting lions, as shown in a sketch of the 20th Dynasty from Thebes in the Metropolitan Museum of New York, where a Pharaoh spears a lion with the help of his well-trained leaping dog (figure 46).[101] As the lion embodied the forces of chaos and thus belonged to a world beyond the ordered realm of the Egyptian king, the dog, in this context, personified the forces of law and order. Tomb paintings of Ramesses II depict him with hunting dogs, presumably in the Field of Reeds, and dogs were often buried with their masters to provide this kind of companionship in the afterlife. Hunting representations are the replica of sacrificial rituals, which were performed to establish symbolic control of man over nature and its phenomena.[102] Dogs helped in hunting other animals and guaranteed the preservation of order. In this context, dogs were not chaotic creatures, but guarantors of order.

There is literary evidence for the use of dogs for military purposes in the ancient world.[103] When Cambyses invaded Egypt in 525 BC, the defenders of Pelusium used darts, stones, and fire against him. Cambyses, thereupon, placed in his front line dogs, sheep, cats, and other animals held sacred by the Egyptians, who instantly ceased using their

FIGURE 46. A SKETCH OF THE 20TH DYNASTY SHOWS A PHARAOH SPEARING A LION WITH THE HELP OF HIS DOG, THE METROPOLITAN MUSEUM OF NEW YORK.

weapons. Thus, Cambyses took Pelusium and opened the way into Egypt.[104] Pharaonic temple reliefs depict dogs participating in military actions against the enemies of Egypt. In the temple of Beit el-Wali Ramesses II attacks his Libyan enemy with a sword, while the royal dog named "Anath Is a Defender" bites the kneeling enemy.[105] The dog's apotropaic name invokes the aid of the goddess Anath. The dog supported the king in battle and emphasised victory over enemies and other chaotic forces. Apart from positive aspects of dogs, the animal has also acquired negative ones in ancient Egyptian society. Their fawning, cringing nature was sometimes attributed to Egypt's enemies. On two pillars from Merenptah's palace at Memphis in the University Museum of Philadelphia, the submission of the enemies to the king's rule are expressed in the statement "we are indeed your dogs".[106] The Ptolemies perhaps used dogs for military purposes for 2400 dogs appear in the Great Procession of Ptolemy Philadelphos.[107]

Dogs enjoyed other outstanding capabilities. For instance, they served as household pets and personal guards. Very well-known in the ancient world is the devotion of dogs to their masters.[108] The dog of Erigone [daughter of Icarius] died upon the body of its mistress; the dog of Silano [a Roman soldier] died upon the body of its master; and the dog of Darius [the third], the last king of Persia, remained faithfully at his master's corpse, unwilling to abandon, as though he was still alive.[109] Tauron lost his life in defence of his master

---

[95] Reisner 1938, 12.
[96] Kemp 1989, 128-9.
[97] Douglas 1928, 9-10, 16.
[98] Ael. NA 6.59.
[99] Arnold 1995, No. 2.
[100] Kemp 1989, 46; Baines 1995, 115.
[101] Arnold 1995, No. 12.
[102] Raffaele 2010, 255.
[103] Polyaenus, *Strat*. 7.2; Hdt. 7.187; Forster 1941. For the use of dogs in modern wars: Johnston 2012.

[104] Polyaenus, *Strat*. 7.9.
[105] Fischer 1978, 176, fig.3.
[106] Fischer 1978, 177.
[107] Ath. 5.31-2; Hubbell 1935, 75.
[108] Sext. Emp., *Pyr*. 1.68.
[109] Ael. *NA* 6.25.

Zenon against a wild boar.[110] Dogs were also so keen-scented that they never touched the roasted flesh of other dogs[111] and clearly distinguished between strangers and acquaintance people.[112] They also gave warning of the approach of dangers by barking,[113] and served as guardians in the temple of Asklepios at Athens.[114]

VII.1.4. Dogs in the Dynastic Period

Animals were of paramount importance in ancient Egyptian culture.[115] They feature prominently in Egyptian representations, texts, and burials.[116] In the Predynastic Period, the ancient Egyptians regarded wild and domesticated animals with great interest, judging from theriomorphic implements and iconography (zoomorphic palettes, animal figurines, animal graffiti, carvings, depictions, and single signs).[117] Bones of dogs dating to the fifth millennium BC were uncovered in different parts. The earliest surviving representation of dogs occurs on the Moscow cup from the Badarian culture (4500-4000 BC).[118] An ivory comb of *c.* 3200 BC in the Metropolitan Museum of New York shows registers of animals, including elephants, antelopes, and dogs.[119] On a predynastic slate palette from Hierakonpolis (Kom el-Ahmar), a king is shown in a hall littered with decapitated bodies of his foes, while four standards are carried before him. On the first two are the hawks of Horus, on the third the canid of Anubis, on the last a lock of hair, presumably of Isis.[120] Clearly, these symbols are derived from the legend of Isis and Osiris.

In the Early Dynastic Period, the Two Dog Palette, now in the Ashomlean Museum of Oxford, dating to Naqada II (3500-3000 BC), was deposited in the cache of votive items in the temple of Horus at Hierakonpolis.[121] As dogs helped Isis in her search for Osiris and served as her bodyguard, dogs' plaques were deposited in a temple of Horus for apotropaic reasons. The dog of Anubis was also recognised as guardian of equilibrium, which is balanced by the presence of the chaotic Seth at the bottom of the palette. At Abydos, rulers of the Early Dynastic Period were successively buried with their animals, including dogs.[122] During that time, animals apparently had some totemic and cultic significance, as animal processions on ceremonial knives and maces uncovered from temples and burials indicate.[123]

During the First Intermediate Period and Middle Kingdom, dogs became an increasingly popular motif in tomb reliefs and stelae. The popularity of dogs also appears in the game 'Hounds and Jackals', the canids of Anubis, which comprised a board with ten pins, five with flat-eared dog heads and five with pointed-eared jackal heads.[124] Stelae from Gebelein and Asyut, belonging to Nubian archers and spearmen, often depict dogs, presumably used in warfare.[125] In the Middle Kingdom tombs of Beni Hasan, dogs are often seen in hunting and battle settings. A small wooden coffin from tomb 17 at Beni Hasan bears the Htp-di-nsw formula for its owner, a dog called Ob.[126] The royal dog Abuwtiyuw received its own tomb at Giza as a reward for being in the bodyguard of Khufu.[127] The dog of Amenhotep II or Horemheb, which was buried in tomb 50 in the Valley of the Kings, was royal.[128] In contrast, Ob was not a royal dog as Beni Hasan was the necropolis of the monarchs of the sixteenth nome of Upper Egypt. The Htp-di-nsw prayer to Osiris and Anubis is only preserved for humans, but here it is devoted for a dog. Ob was probably a sacred animal of Anubis in one of his temples in the region. The adjacent seventeenth nome was called Inpwt, the 'Anubis Nome', with Kynopolis 'the City of the Dog' as the capital.[129]

Iconographically, dogs are normally faithful companions to humans. Thus, Inyotef II (*c.* 2069 BC) of the 11th Dynasty appears in a funerary stela with his five dogs[130] and a man is shown in the tomb of Ipy at Thebes (*c.* 1250 BC) irrigating a garden while his dog appears behind him.[131] At Abydos Cemetery G in tomb G61 of Hapimen dated to 30th dynasty, a mummified dog was buried at the feet of his master.[132] Dogs, however, are sometimes shown as harmful animals in literature, probably because of their association with chthonic divinities. In the Tale of the Doomed Prince, a king and queen were granted a son after many prayers to gods, while the goddesses of destiny decreed that he would die by crocodile, snake, or dog.[133] This ambivalent nature of dogs also occurs in the Tale of the Two Brothers of the 19th Dynasty. When Bata, a predynastic god, convinced Anup, believed to represent Anubis, that he did not seduce his wife, Anup goes home to kill his wife and throw her body to the dogs.[134]

From the Late Period, Saqqara was the arena for mass burials of mummified animals in catacombs.[135] Next

---

[110] Purola 1994; Pepper 2010.
[111] Ael. *NA* 4.40.
[112] Hom. *Od* 16.1.
[113] Burriss 1935, 36.
[114] Ael. NA 7.13.
[115] Phillips 1948.
[116] Houlihan 1996.
[117] Raffaele 2010, 244.
[118] Bunson 2002, 418.
[119] Arnold 1995, 8, no. 1.
[120] Quibell 1898, pls. xii-xiii; Sayce 1903, 96.
[121] Kemp 1989, 80, 94, fig. 31; Bunson 2002, 418.
[122] Dreyer et al. 1996, 59.
[123] Ciałowicz 1992; Dreyer et al 1996, 59; Raffaele 2010.

[124] Tooley 1988, 210.
[125] Kemp 1989, 27-8, fig. 6.
[126] Tooley 1988, 207-11.
[127] Reisner 1938, 8.
[128] Mark 2004, 30-5; Ikram 2013, 301.
[129] Gauthier 1925, 84.
[130] Bunson 2002, 181.
[131] Davies 1927, pl. xxix; Kemp 1989, 13, fig. 3.
[132] Petrie 1902, 39-40, pl. lxxx.
[133] Frandsen 2008, 53.
[134] Bunson 2002, 394.
[135] Other catacombs in Saqqara included the Bubastieion, the Serapeion, the burials of the Mother and Brother of Apis, the Falcon

to the Teti pyramid on North Saqqara there is a huge complex called the Anubieion.[136] The Anubieion was a temple complex in honour of Anubis with millions of mummified dogs. A processional route once connected the Anubieion with the Serapeion, the cult complex of Osiris-Apis. Based on coins and lamps uncovered from the site, the Ptolemaic settlement within the Anubieion was occupied into the Roman period.[137] There is textual evidence for different social groups and professions in this community.[138] In Teti's Cemetery at Saqqara, some Roman-period deposits were not votive as they consisted of human burials with no grave goods, but with dogs placed near the entry as amuletic guardians.[139]

Gebel Asyut el-Gharbi was also used as an animal necropolis, where mummies of sacred and votive animals were buried.[140] The so-called Tomb of the Dog housed thousands of mummified animal remains dating from the Late Period to the Roman Period. The most identified animal species was the dog, flowed by the cat, the fox, and the jackal, reflecting the supremacy of the canids of Wepwawet and Anubis, the main deities of the district.[141] The canine burials attest to the popularity of Anubis or more likely a conflation of Khentamentiu, Wepwawet, and Anubis. All these divinities are associated with death, cemeteries, and voyages between this world and the next. Khentamentiu, the 'Foremost Among the Westerners'; Wepwawet, the 'Opener of the Ways'; and Anubis, the 'Lord of the Sacred Lands', were all represented as canine creatures.[142]

Although most cemeteries at Abydos contain a variety of mummified animals, some graveyards are devoted only to dogs.[143] A dog hypogeum has been found at Abydos in the Middle Cemetery next to the Sacred Well. The cemetery has been dated by pottery lamps found with the dogs to the period between the first century BC and the fourth century AD.[144] As the mythological grave of Osiris' head, Abydos was the seat of the Osirian cult and the gate to the netherworld. Given the absence of cult temples for different gods at Abydos, the connection between Osiris and Abydos encouraged pilgrims to build cemeteries with votive animals associated with gods of the netherworld. As incarnations of Anubis, canids may protect and lead the mummy to the next life, while raptors, shrews, serpents, scarabs, and ibises may assist in re/creation through their association with Re, Sokar, and Thoth.[145]

VII.1.5. Dogs in the Graeco-Roman Period

This section highlights some remarks on the position of dogs in Egyptian society in the Graeco-Roman period, with special focus on the rituals performed upon the death of the animals in houses and beyond.

VII.1.5.1. Anubis/Hermes (Hermanubis)

The Egyptian jackal or dog-headed god Anubis guided souls on their way to the kingdom of Osiris, the judge of the dead. As an icon of Egypt, Anubis occurs in rabbinic texts that refer to the dogs guarding the Egyptian tomb of Joseph in a necropolis.[146] Socrates' famous oath, 'by the dog, the god of the Egyptians', is a clear reference to Anubis, who appears as a chief assistant of Osiris in the judgment of the dead as he weighs the heart of the dead against the feather of Maat.[147] In the Graeco-Roman period, Anubis was assimilated with the Greek Hermes, the messenger of Zeus, creating the syncretistic god Hermanubis, the psychopompos of the dead.[148] In mythology, Anubis and Hermes conducted souls to the underworld. Also at times Anubis is associated with Kerberos, the three-headed watchdog of Hades.[149] As the souls were believed to follow the paths of the planets on their way to paradise, Anubis/Hermes possessed words of power, which enabled him to pass through all the gates and overcome on their behalf the resistance of any opposing spirit. Anubis-Hermes is referred to in a Greek papyrus of the third century AD as 'the one who holds the key to the netherworld', a reference to his funerary role as Psychopompos,[150] and he is often shown holding a key (*ankh*) in his hand on coffins and shrouds.[151]

VII.1.5.2. The "Dog-headed One" in Greek Papyri

Anubis is represented in a theriomorphic shape[152] or as canine-headed anthropomorphic figure.[153] In the latter, Anubis is depicted with hands raised and performs purification and transfiguration rites over a mummy, as a Ptolemaic statuette in the Metropolitan Museum of New York shows (figure 47).[154] During the mummification process and other related ceremonial processions, a priest wearing a canine mask plays the role of Anubis, such as the terracotta Anubis mask in the collection of the Roemer-Pelizaeus, Hildesheim, Germany (figure 48).[155] Tomb paintings and Greek papyri affirm that the embalmer of Anubis participated in funeral processions

---

and Baboon galleries, and the Ibis galleries (Thompson 1988; Ikram 2007a, 429).
[136] Jeffreys and Smith 1988.
[137] Smith and Jeffreys 1981, 22. The last datable coin belongs to Heraclius.
[138] Cannata 2007.
[139] Hartley et al 2011.
[140] Kahl et al 2009.
[141] Kahl 2012, 17-8.
[142] Ikram 2007a, 419.
[143] Ikram 2007a, 418-21, fig. 1.
[144] Peet 1914, 98-101; Ikram 2007a, 420.
[145] Whittemore 1914; Ikram 2007a, 429.

[146] Ulmer 2010, 199-201.
[147] Blackwood et al 1962.
[148] Benaissa 2010; Doxey 2001, 98.
[149] Hoerber 1963.
[150] *SB* IV.7452.3.
[151] Griffiths 1970, 61 n. 1, 517; Morenz 1975; Priese 1991, 216-17, no. 132.
[152] Kahl 2007, 153-4.
[153] Arnold, D. 1995, 15, no. 8, figure in page 14.
[154] Arnold 1995, No. 8.
[155] Wolinski 1987, 28. The dog head of St. Christopher in Byzantine iconography is connected with Anubis (Millard 1987).

Chapter VII The House as Funerary Space

FIGURE 47. A PTOLEMAIC CANINE-HEADED ANTHROPOMORPHIC STATUETTE OF ANUBIS IN THE METROPOLITAN MUSEUM OF NEW YORK.

FIGURE 48. A CANINE TERRACOTTA MASK OF ANUBIS.

to necropoleis. In the Ptolemaic tomb of Petosiris in Tuna el-Gebel, the embalmer of Anubis holds the mummy of Petosiris outside the tomb while the *sem*-priest performs the ritual of the Opening of the Mouth.[156] In *Stud.Pal.* XXII.56, the eight drachmas 'for the dog' probably refers to the embalmer of Anubis, wearing the mask of the god.[157] In *P.Ashm* I.17, the embalmer designated 'the man of Anubis' perhaps took part in the funeral procession to the cemetery.[158]

Priests and priestesses wearing animal masks that appeared artistically to be their head played an important role in ancient Egyptian rituals and ceremonial processions through villages or towns. They sometimes wore a symbol on top of their head to distinguish which divinity they represented. Perhaps the most commonly depicted masked priest was that of Anubis, who is usually depicted attending the mummy and plays the role of Anubis in death rituals and other related ceremonial and funerary processions.[159]

The man of Anubis always appears in public processions associated with the festivals of Isis and Serapis in Egypt and Rome. The 'dog-headed one' (κυνώπης) is a key player in the procession of Serapis at Oxyrhynchos. A late third-century AD papyrus gives an account of payments to a trumpeter, comedian, dancer, herald, the doorkeeper of the Serapeion, and the 'dog-headed one' in return for their duties in the festival of Serapis on 26 Khoiak,[160] which was associated with the Osirian mysteries of Khoiak.[161] The festival probably included a public procession through the city since the papyrus mentions gifts to the 'dog-headed one', who, since the New Kingdom, referred to 'the official who took the part of Anubis in the festival'.[162] This masked official

---

[156] Taylor 2010, 8.
[157] *Stud.Pal.* XXII.56.22.
[158] *P.Ashm.* I.17.1.
[159] Wolinski 1987.
[160] *SB* IV.7336.42.
[161] Abdelwahed 2016.
[162] Wormald 1929, 242.

FIGURE 49. DOGS BURIED WITH CHILDREN AT QASR ALLAM IN THE BAHARIYA OASIS.

of Anubis also appears in the procession of Isis in Rome.[163] The role of the dog and Anubis in the legend of Isis and Osiris was the basis for the participation of the priest/official wearing the mask of Anubis in religious processions.[164]

The dog-masked priest also played a role in the cult of Hermanubis, a cult that combined the worship of Anubis with that of Hermes (or Mercury). Juvenal scoffed at the priests of Hermanubis and found it both laughable and shocking to see a priest in a dog's mask. The Christian writer Cyprian similarly asked, 'How can a man who has been a member of the Roman Senate sink so low as to go around with a rattle in his hand and a dog's mask over his head?'. In both cases, the 'dog's mask' represented the priest personifying Anubis, the canine-headed god of mummification, in religious ceremonial processions.[165]

VII.1.5.3. Anubis and the Lunar Disc of Osiris in Birth-houses (mammises) of Egyptian Temples

In the legend of Isis and Osiris, dogs helped Isis in her search for the infant Anubis. Therefore, dogs were associated with childbirth in ancient Egypt and served as guardians of infants and children. In ancient Greece, dogs were similarly sacrificed in honour of Eileithyia, the goddess who watched over birth.[166] The Gauls equally associated dogs with goddesses of childbirth, such as Sirona, Epona, and Nehallenia.[167] In Deir el-Banat in the Fayum, the Graeco-Roman cemetery contains the burial of a child accompanied by several mummified dogs.[168] In Qasr Allam in the Bahariya oasis, dogs were similarly buried with the bodies of children (Figure 49).[169] At the Bahariya oasis, infants and children were also interred with mummies of dogs. In all cases, dogs probably served as guardians and companions of the deceased in the journey to the underworld.

In the Graeco-Roman period, Anubis was associated with *mammises* through the lunar disc of Osiris. As the embalmer of Osiris, Anubis played a central role in the rebirth of the god, which presumably took place at full-moon night.[170] This episode of the Osirian myth provided the rationale for the representation of Anubis with the lunar disc of Osiris in birth-houses of Egyptian temples, where the divine birth of the child god/king is represented. Representations of Anubis beneath the feet of mummies similarly show the god elevates the newly

---

[163] Apul. *Met*. XI.11.
[164] Dio. Sic. 1.87.2-4.
[165] Wolinski 1987, 28.

[166] Plut., *Quaest. Rom*. 52; Mazzorin and Minniti 2006, 63.
[167] Hondius-Crone 1955; Gourevitch 1968.
[168] Belova 2016.
[169] Ikram 2013, 305, fig. 6. See also Pantalacci and Denoix 2009.
[170] Dogs are restless in full-moon time, when they are given to howling (Burris 1935, 38).

reborn lunar Osiris into heavens and also the deceased by his own identification with Osiris. Since the lunar disc is equated with Osiris, the god's dismemberment and resurrection symbolised the moon's cycle: the wane/crescent and the wax/full.[171]

VII.1.5.4. Mourning Rituals for Dead Dogs in Houses

Homer emphasised in many instances the strong relationship between the dog, the house, and the master in the *Odyssey*.[172] Perhaps the most famous instance is the scene of Odysseus approaching his house at Ithaca and only recognised by his faithful dog, Argos, which soon died from joy at the return of his master.[173] This fundamental connection between the canine, the oikos, and the owner is clearly inherent in mourning rituals observed in Graeco-Roman Egypt by the house occupants after the demise of their faithful companion and beloved pet.[174]

It was customary for the Egyptians to keep animals in their houses, a practice that held to be unique by ancient classical authors: The Egyptians are the only people who keep their animals with them in the house.[175] The house was not only a residential place for humans, but also a home for animals. Anthropological studies suggest that domestic animals are usually given unlimited access to different interior parts of the house.[176] Yet it is unlikely that they were allowed into domestic shrines. According to Diodorus, 'the Egyptians venerate certain animals exceedingly, not only during their lifetime, but also even after their death, such as cats, ichneumons and dogs, and, again, hawks and the birds which they call ibis'.[177] Animal cult was a widespread practice in Egyptian religion of the Graeco-Roman period. Thus, sacred animals associated with traditional deities were not used in sacrifice.[178]

Certain animals were honoured during their lifetimes and likewise after death. When one of these animals dies, the Egyptians mourn for it deeply as do those who have lost a beloved child, and bury it in a manner not in keeping with their ability but going far beyond the value of their estates.[179] They also wrap it in fine linen and then, wailing and beating their breasts, carry it off to be embalmed.[180] Dwellers in a house where a cat had died a natural death shave their eyebrows and no more; where a dog has so died, the head and the whole body are shaven. Cats which have died are taken to Bubastis, where they are embalmed and buried in sacred receptacles; dogs are buried also in sacred burial places in the towns where they belong.[181]

Upon the death of certain animals, the Egyptians used to perform particular rituals of lamentation in their houses: Whenever a dog is found dead in any house, every resident of it shaves his entire body and goes into mourning. What is more astonishing than this, if any wine or grain or any other thing necessary to life happens to be stored in the building where one of these animals has expired, they would never think of using it thereafter for any purpose.[182] During this period of mourning, which presumably ended with the burial of the dead animal, it was expected that relatives and neighbours would come to the house to console its residents.[183] Great grief was displayed over the death of a family dog and the family would shave their body as a sign of sorrow. Dogs were highly valued in Egypt as part of the family and, when a dog died, the family, if they could afford to, would have the dog mummified with as much care as they would pay for a human member of the family.

VII.1.6. Mummification and Burial in Sacred Hypogea

The standard period for the mummification process of all animals was seventy days, like humans. When one of these animals dies, they wrap it in fine linen and then, wailing and beating their breasts, carry it off to be embalmed. After it has been treated with cedar oil and such spices as have the quality of imparting a pleasant odour and of preserving the body for a long time, they lay it away in a consecrated tomb.[184] At home, the animal was first wrapped with linen cloth, before it was sent off to the embalming place. Generally, dogs are not well embalmed for they were merely desiccated with natron or salt, before being wrapped in white linen. In ancient Egypt, mummified dogs guided human spirits into the next world. Thus, Abuwtiyuw, the royal dog of Khufu, was given a coffin from the royal treasury, fine linen in great quantity, incense, and ointment that he might be honoured before the great god Anubis.[185] In Graeco-Roman Egypt, canid species were continuously mummified as guides for the deceased.[186]

Animal mummification was widely practised, and it was customary to use the second procedure described by Herodotus. Like votive animals, household dogs were probably mummified in the embalming houses ($w^ʿbt$).[187]

---

[171] Ritner 1985, 145.
[172] Beck 1991.
[173] Scott 1948, 228.
[174] Diod. Sic. 1.84.2, 1.92.6; Cic. *Tusc.* 1.45.108; Sext. Emp. *Pyr.* 3.226; *P.Princ.* III.166.4-7.
[175] Hdt. 2.36.
[176] Bourdieu 1973.
[177] Diod. Sic. 1.83.1.
[178] Bell 1948, 82-97.
[179] Dio. Sic. 1.84.7.
[180] Dio. Sic. 1.83.5.

[181] Hdt. 2.66-7.
[182] Diod. Sic. 1.84.2.
[183] It is quite extraordinarily that in contemporary Egypt, especially in villages, whenever a cow dies people sometimes go to the owner of the cow to console him/ her. Of course, this modern custom has nothing to do with Islam or Christianity, but seems to have passed over generations through social tradition.
[184] Dio. Sic. 1.83.5.
[185] Reisner 1938, 8.
[186] Gautier 2007, 279.
[187] Nur el Din 1992; Kessler and Nur el Din 2005; Kessler 2003, 52;

Animal mummification closely matched the embalming method used for humans,[188] presumably imitating the mythological burial rituals offered to Osiris by Isis and Anubis. Both humans and animals were embalmed to preserve the body so that it could host the eternal soul in the hereafter. The most common and plausible method of mummification for animals began with evisceration through the belly, followed by desiccation using natron. This part of the preparation of the body took 40 days.[189] The massage of the body with resins and oils took a further 30 days. The final stage was wrapping the mummy in linen bandages, ranging from two up to ten layers of bandages.[190] After the 70 days of mummification were completed, the animal mummy was ready for burial in its tomb.[191] It was buried in the catacombs called 'Houses of Rest'.[192]

The ancient Egyptians mummified a variety of animals and birds for religious and ceremonial reasons.[193] The fish oxyrhynchos was believed to have eaten the phallus of the god Osiris, when Seth flung his body into the river. Out of devotion to Osiris, some nomes forbade the consumption of this sacred fish.[194] Animals were also mummified as epiphanies of particular deities. At Tune el-Gebel, selected baboons (sacred animals of Thoth) were given individual names and kept in a special pen at the temple of Osiris-Baboon. After death, they were mummified and buried in the catacombs, having been properly deified through the performance of the ritual of the Opening of the Mouth over them.[195] This ceremony was originally enacted over human mummies at the entrance of tombs in the day of burial to symbolically bring the dead back to life so that it could reunite with the soul, the *ba*.[196]

Literature and archaeology confirm that sacred, votive, and household animals were buried in private tombs.[197] Dead cats were taken away into sacred buildings, where they were embalmed and buried in Bubastis. Shrewmice and hawks were taken away to Buto, while the ibises were buried at Tuna el-Gebel[198] and Oxyrhynchos.[199] Dogs were also buried in several sacred burials.[200] Gebel Asyut el-Gharbi was a necropolis for mummified dogs.[201] Remains of dog mummies with wrappings have also been found in two cemeteries associated with the temple of El-Deir in the Kharga oasis, probably offered by the inhabitants or the travellers to the god Anubis.[202] The first/second century AD temple of Ain Dabashiya was also associated with the cult of the canine-headed god Anubis, where the remains of several hundred dogs, ranging from few-week-old puppies to adults, were found near the temple.[203] Oxyrhynchos also contained mummified remains of dogs.[204] Nearly 8 million mummies of puppies and old dogs were ceremonially buried in the Anubieion of Saqqara for Anubis,[205] the god responsible for taking the deceased from this world to the next.[206]

The ancient Egyptians associated animals and birds with their own deities.[207] They paid for embalming and keeping the dead animals and birds in hypogea. Demotic documents indicate that certain Egyptian priests journeyed the province to collect dead bodies of animals and birds and brought them for mummification and burial in hypogea at Tuna el-Gebel.[208] Animal cult, mummification, and burial were confirmed in the Pharaonic period[209] and were maintained in the Graeco-Roman period.[210] Funerary practices of combining dog and human burials or burying dogs in pits separate from their masters are documented in several cemeteries. These animals were probably intended to act as companions and/or guardians in the journey to the underworld or as beloved household pets.

Household dogs should be distinguished from votive dogs, which were embalmed and presented to gods as offerings and intermediary between men and gods and transmitters of human prayers, desires, and interests.[211] Generally, it has been suggested that the niched dogs in hypogea were sacred, while the remainder were votives.[212] Again, not all non-niched dogs were votive, because they must have included votive as well as family dogs, though it is difficult, if not impossible, to differentiate them in the archaeological record. Food and drink were offered to votive animals to keep them for the slaughter.[213] Mummies of animals were purchased by devout pilgrims and offered to the relevant deity as votive items and then buried in catacombs, en masse, at certain religious festivals. Votive animals were deposited for good omen along with human mummies, like family dogs. Millions of votive mummified dogs were sold to pilgrims by the gods' priests.[214] The popularity of votive

---

Ikram 2007a, 418.
[188] Vos 1993.
[189] Ikram et al 2013, 54.
[190] Ikram 2007b, 12.
[191] Ikram 2007b, 12.
[192] Ray 1976, 140.
[193] Kessler 2003.
[194] Bunson 2002, 292.
[195] Kemp 1989, 377.
[196] Lichtheim 1976; Smith 1987.
[197] Diod. Sic. 1.83.5-6; Vos 1993.
[198] Hdt. 2.66.
[199] *P.Oxy*. IX.1188.4.
[200] Hdt. 2.66-7.
[201] Kahl et al 2009.

[202] Dunand and Lichtenberg 2005.
[203] Ikram 2008, 39.
[204] Bunson 2002, 292.
[205] Ikram et al 2013, 51.
[206] DuQuesne et al 2007.
[207] Görg 2004, 433-43.
[208] Nur el Din 1992, 253-4.
[209] Diod. Sic. 1.69.2.
[210] Germer 2004, 469.
[211] Te Velde 1980, 80-1.
[212] Ikram et al 2013, 50.
[213] P*hilo. In* Flacc. 178.
[214] Nur el Din 1992; Kessler and Nur el Din 2005; Kessler 2003, 52;

animal burials was rooted in the upsurge of personal piety in the Late Period, and continued into Roman times until Egyptian temples were closed under the Edict of Theodosius in AD 391.[215]

The high number of votive neonates (75 percent) in the dog catacomb at Saqqara suggests that this was an almost industrial production, with entire litters being killed, perhaps by drowning or exposure immediately after birth, before being given a cursory mummification. Puppy farms and the mummification of animals were important for the economy of temples.[216] However, votive mummies, such as a bird mummy at Cape Town Museum, sometimes contained only plant material, mud, linen, and small stones.[217] Egyptians seem to have identified all dogs with the god Anubis, and at times domestic dogs were also interred in the Anubieion catacombs at Saqqara. The figure of Anubis is prominent in the funerary sphere of Graeco-Roman Egypt. On a second-century AD shroud painting in the Ägyptisches Museum of Berlin, the dog-headed Anubis attends to the deceased, a man in Roman dress representing the mummified Osiris.[218] Anubis is often depicted in the form of a dog or jackal watching over the dead. The falcon and dog on funerary stelea from Terenouthis (Kom Abu Bellou) definitely represented Horus and Anubis (figure 50).[219] At the Alexandrian tomb of Kom el-Shouqafa, Anubis is shown in Roman military garb as guardian of the necropolis, while in the Tigrane tomb the deceased is flanked by two dogs or jackals of Anubis.[220] The connection between dogs and Anubis finds the basis for mourning rituals for dead family dogs in houses and apparently for their mummification and burial in special cemeteries. While temple priests cared for sacred and votive dogs while alive or dead, family members similarly took charge of domestic dogs.

The mummified animals were thought to be holy and therefore accompanied their owners in the beyond as amuletic guardians.[221] The dogs buried with humans has also been interpreted as sacrifices to appease and invoke Hekate and Anubis as gods of the underworld, travel, and liminal areas, thus ensuring the safety of the deceased in his travels to the hereafter.[222] There was no contradiction between the use of dogs as votive animals or as amuletic guardians.[223] The problem of modern scholars is typically semantic and typological. The dog was a companion of Isis in her search for Anubis,

FIGURE 50. THE FALCON/HORUS AND THE DOG/ANUBIS ON A FUNERARY STELEA FROM TERENOUTHIS (KOM ABU BELLOU).

Ikram 2007a, 418.
[215] Ikram 2007a, 419.
[216] Ikram et al 2013, 62.
[217] Cornelius et al 2012, 144.
[218] Cannuyer 2001, 12.

[219] Hartley et al 2011, 28, fig. 7.
[220] Venit 2002, 143-44, figs. 123-4, 152-3, fig. 133.
[221] Hartley et al 2011.
[222] Ikram 2013.
[223] Hartley et al 2011; Ikram 2013, 304.

who later served as a guardian and companion of Isis in her search for Osiris. As the embalmer and guide of Osiris, the dog-headed Anubis analogously guided the common deceased in the hereafter. This episode of the myth tackles dogs' presence in cemeteries with or without human remains. In the Graeco-Roman period, an amulet in the form of Anubis was attached to corpses for apotropaic reasons.[224] The Egyptians similarly assigned this capacity to a physical dog, which, like the amulet, served as a theriomorphic manifestation of Anubis, the god of the necropolis.[225]

VII.2. Mourning Rituals for Dead Humans

Françoise Perpillou-Thomas has systematically collected papyrological references to festivals and rituals in Graeco-Roman Egypt. Among the rituals associated with the processing of the corpse from death to burial are the peristolē and kēdeia, often translated as burial and funeral.[226] Based solely on Greek papyri, Dominic Montserrat reconstructed prosperous funerals in the Fayum during the Roman period.[227] Surprisingly, little attention has been given to Egyptian material and classical literature on burial and funeral practices in Egypt.[228] Moreover, the relationship of the house with the different steps of the journey of the corpse from the house to the tomb (ekphora, peristolē, kēdeia, and apostolē) has not been highlighted. Integrating papyrological, literary, and archaeological evidence, this study hopes to reconstruct the rituals of the passage of the corpse from the moment of death to the interment in the necropolis, highlighting the role of the house in each stage.

VII.2.1. The Osirian Myth and Burial Rituals

Writing in the first century BC, Diodorus Siculus states:

> For the inhabitants of Egypt consider the period of this life to be of no account whatever, but place the greatest value on the time after death when they will be remembered for their virtue. While they give the name of "lodgings" to the houses, thus intimating that we dwell in them but a brief time, they call the tombs of the dead "eternal homes", since the dead spend endless eternity in Hades. Consequently, they give less thought to the furnishings of their houses, but on the manner of their burials, they do not forgo an excess of zeal.[229]

Diodorus's visit to Alexandria between 60-56 BC gives credibility to his testimony as an eyewitness. Egyptian tombs and temples were built of stone because they were intended to last for eternity, whereas houses were constructed of perishable materials such as mud-brick and wood because they were regarded as replaceable.[230] Because of the durability of the materials used in their construction, archaeology has revealed much more about tombs and temples than about houses.[231] There was no contradiction between the function of the house and that of the tomb. By contrast, the relationship between the house and the tomb is complementary. While the former provided a temporary residence for the living body, the latter offered it an everlasting abode. The Egyptians believed that when they died their body would exist in an afterlife similar to their life on earth. Since the dead required many articles for use in the eschatological life, they consequently equipped their tombs with a variety of burial goods.

Since the Pharaonic period, the legend of Osiris has left its impact on almost every aspect of Egyptian rituals of the burial and funeral.[232] While Osiris left his Egyptian kingdom to subdue the world by the arts of peace, Isis governed in his absence. On his return, Seth and his seventy-two fellow conspirators imprisoned him by craft in a chest, which was flung into the Nile.[233] There are two versions regarding the timing of the death of Osiris. One version suggests that the death of Osiris occurred in harvest time, when 'an offering of the first fruits was brought, whilst the men beat their breasts, lamenting and invoking Isis'.[234] On the other hand, Plutarch states that the ancient Egyptians commemorate the mourning for Osiris by Isis when the Nile started to rise in summer, when the inundation was caused by the tears of Isis. Very well-known is his description of the procession to the Nile in the night of 19th Athyr; the priests scopped water from the Nile in a precious pitcher and those present proclaimed loudly: 'Osiris has been found'.[235]

On hearing of the murder of Osiris, Isis cut off a lock of her hair and wore mourning clothes. Together, Isis and Nephthys mourned for the lost Osiris for four days (17-20 Athyr) before the chest containing his body was found by Isis near the mouths of the Nile.[236] Here it was buried for a while; but Seth, while hunting by night, discovered it and cut the body inside into fourteen or twenty-six pieces, which he scattered to the winds.[237] Then Isis took boat and searched for the pieces, until she had recovered them all save one, the privates.[238] Isis and

---

[224] Andrews 1994, chapter 5.
[225] Hartley et al 2011.
[226] Perpillou-Thomas 1993, 19-22.
[227] Montserrat 1997.
[228] Dawson has collected references to mummification in classical literature (Dawson 1928).
[229] Dio. Sic. 1.51.2. Cf. Prince Hordjedef, the son of Khufu, advised: 'Beautify your house in the necropolis since death is bitter and exalted for us, the house of death should be for life (Wente 1982, 18).

[230] Husselman 1979.
[231] David 2007, 51.
[232] Assmann 1977.
[233] *Plut. De Is. et Os*. 13.
[234] Dio. Sic. 1.45.
[235] Plut. *De Is. et Os.* 39.
[236] Plut. *De Is. et Os.* 39.
[237] *Plut. De Is.* et Os. 87; Dio. Sic. 1.21.2.
[238] Dio. Sic. 1.22.6.

Nephthys carefully put the pieces together. Anubis then embalmed the whole body and made the first mummy in the ancient world.[239] The rejoining of the limbs of Osiris became the prototype for the overcoming of death and furnished the mythical precedent for mummification.[240] Isis placed coffins of Osiris beneath the earth in several places, but only one of them, and that unknown to all, contained the body of Osiris. She did this because she wished to hide the body from Seth, fearing that he might find it and cast it out of its tomb.[241]

Following the death of Osiris, an eighty-two year dispute over the inheritance of Osiris broke out between Horus, the son of Osiris, and his uncle Seth, the archenemy of Osiris and the icon of chaos. Finally, the tribunal of the god at Heliopolis ordered the throne to Horus. This tribunal set the setting for the so-called negative confession, when the dead man turned to forty-two assessors and pleaded that he was innocent of forty-two sins. Not only ancient Egyptian funerary literature always connects the dead with Osiris,[242] but also Osirian eschatological imagery dominates tombs and coffins in Graeco-Roman Egypt.[243] The Osirian myth indicated that the physical and spiritual aspects of the dead, *ka* and *ba*, would be reunited with the body in the hereafter.[244] This is why the Egyptians were concerned to preserve the dead bodies. A Demotic funerary composition of the first/second century AD has the opening phrase as 'May the *ba* live' formulae, stressing the centrality of the soul to the post-mortem existence of the corpse and its transition into the following of Osiris.[245] As in the Pharaonic period, funerary texts of Graeco-Roman Egypt empower the postmortem individual through liturgical recitation by lector priests or mourners.[246]

The official cult never explains how the *Ba* and the mummy were united. In the so-called Hermetic books, which endeavoured to translate the theology of Egypt into Greek thought, the *ka* is equated with the intelligence (νοῦς), of which the *ba* or soul (ψυχή) was the envelope. The soul is imprisoned in the earthly tabernacle of the body, the intelligence is deprived of the robe of fire in which it should be clothed and its brightness is dimmed. The death of the body releases it from its prison-house; it once more soars to heaven and becomes a spirit (δαιμων), while the soul is carried to the hall of judgment to be awarded punishment or happiness according to the deeds it did on earth.[247] For modern Egyptians, death similarly has two inseparable meanings related to the two components of a person, the body and the soul/spirit. The first meaning is related to the condition of a person's body when his/her soul/spirit departs from it. The second meaning refers to death as the transition of the soul/spirit of a person from this life to another life or from one *dar* (house) to another.[248]

VII.2.2. Burial as Necessity and Obligation

The ancient Egyptians spent a considerable amount of time and money preparing for their death. The custom of Pharaonic kings granting the deserving persons assistance in founding and providing funerary equipment for their graves ceased by the Graeco-Roman period.[249] It is now the family's responsibility to commission the tomb and cover burial and funeral costs. Greek papyri and elaborate mummies in the necropoleis show the will of the dead and their families to allocate excessive expenditures on the funeral and burial.

Roman-period wills from the Fayum and Oxyrhynchus make clear the concerns of living testators about their funerals. In the second century AD, the joint will of a married couple at Oxyrhynchus states that whichever of the partners survives has the power to sell all or any of the slaves they owned mutually to 'defray the expense of the funeral and carrying-out of the body'.[250] Tamystha similarly stipulated that her daughter Taoresenouhpis would inherit her property on condition that she shall provide a fitting kēdeia and peristolē for her mother at Tebtunis.[251] In the second century AD, a woman in the Arsinoite bequeathed a room without rent in her house to her unmarried daughter on condition that she shall take care for the funeral and embalming of her mother's body.[252] A woman called Soueris, who made her will at Tebtunis in AD 125, stipulated that her heirs Onnophris and Tephersais should be responsible for her interment and laying-out 'as seem appropriate to them'.[253] In the third century AD, one Besas stipulates that his son should to arrange for the burial of his body (kēdeia) in Kysis, the Great Oasis.[254] Here, family members had full responsibility for the arrangement for the funeral and burial of their late relatives.

The inability of presumptive heirs to prepare the burial for the dead person may lead to the exclusion from inheritance. Thus, lines 10-11 recto of P.Bulaq X, which dates back to the late 19th or early 20th dynasties, states 'let the possessions (*sc.* of the deceased) be given to him who buries, says the law of Pharaoh'.[255] This text records a dispute over inheritance. When Tgemy died, she left

---

[239] Sayce 1903, 142.
[240] Assmann 1989, 138.
[241] Strabo 17.1.23.
[242] Smith 2009a.
[243] Edgar 1905.
[244] Lohmann 1998.
[245] Scalf 2014.
[246] Smith 2009a; Scalf 2014.
[247] Sayce 1903, 59-60.
[248] El-Aswad 1987, 211.
[249] Erman 1907, 124.
[250] *P.Oxy.* III.493.5.
[251] *SB* VIII.9642.12.
[252] *BGU* III.896.7: τὴν κηδείαν μου καὶ περιστολὴν τοῦ σώμ[ατος] μου.
[253] *SB* VIII.9642.3.13.
[254] *SB* I.4651.10.
[255] Janseen and Pestman 1968, 140.

some children and an inheritance. Since Huy, one of her sons, took care of her burial without the assistance of his brothers and sisters, the whole inheritance passed to him in accordance with the law of Pharaoh. At this point, the other children of Tgemy came forward and claimed a part of their mother's inheritance as being her heirs, claiming that Huy did not bury her alone.

The extraordinary care that heirs gave to burial and funeral arrangements of their testators suggests that this law probably survived into the Graeco-Roman period. In late second century AD Oxyrhynchus, Helen wrote rebuking her brother Petechons: 'You did not act properly by failing to come on account of your brother; you have allowed his funeral to be neglected. I think you should know that a woman from somewhere else has been made his heir'.[256] In all probability, the deceased left no children to care for the burial and inherit his possessions. The only case in which a strange woman would inherit his possessions is when she solely takes care of his burial and funeral. The papyrus does not mention whether Helen participated in the burial. The tone of anger and blame inherent in the letter suggests that she was unable to take care for the burial of her dead brother; possibly, she could not afford it. By not burying the dead, the heirs forfeit their rights to a share of the inheritance, while the one who undertakes the burial gets everything. Early in the New Kingdom, one Meniupu dies as a fugitive and without heirs; a woman buries him at the instance of her husband who says, 'bury him and act as an heir towards him'.[257]

VII.2.3. The Egyptian Mode of Burial

Individuals often leave precise instructions in their wills about how they wished to be buried.[258] At Oxyrhynchus, Sintheus, daughter of Diogenes, specified that 'I wish for my son and heir to make an equal outlay on my funeral and the treatment of my body in the Egyptian fashion (αἰγυπτιᾷ ταφῇ)'.[259] In a second century AD will from Tebtunis, an unknown man similarly writes 'Let my wife organise my funeral and the treatment of my body in the Egyptian fashion'.[260] A famous exception to this custom is the will of the son of Epimachos, who refused the Egyptian mode of burial for cremation, indicating the diversity of mortuary options at this time.[261] In an Egyptian context, the word ταφή encompasses a spectrum of meanings ranging from the burial,[262] the burial-place,[263] the burial-fee,[264] the mummy,[265] or even the sarcophagus.[266] Yet the 'Egyptian mode of burial' definitely included, among other things, the peristolē and the kēdeia.[267]

In the Egyptian mode of burial, the dead had to pass a journey of stages to face the final judgment before they would access the afterlife. If successful, they were required to provide eternal sustenance for their spirit. These things could be achieved if proper preparations were made during the person's lifetime and after death as well. Such arrangements could be made by purchasing small funerary goods for placement in the tomb, including amulets and funeral equipment; commissioning a coffin; and by constructing a tomb. From the moment of death to burial, other necessary preparations should be guaranteed for the dead body, which has to pass through successive and/or simultaneous rites of passage: The ekphora; the peristolē; the kēdeia; and the apostolē. The aim of these rites was the preparation of the deceased for a successful postmortem transition from this life to the next.

VII.2.3.1. The Ekphora

Death and funeral rituals start immediately after the death of a person. When people died away from home, their bodies were brought back to their place of origin to be buried. Numerous letters mention mummies being transported for this reason. As there is a passionate liaison between the body and the house, whenever a person dies out of his/her house, the body was taken to the house to be prepared for necessary burial and funeral rites.[268] In Rome, it was crucial to have the corpse rested in the house before the performance of burial and funeral rituals. The father of a Roman citizen who killed his sister for blaming him for murdering his cousins, including her lover:

> Neither permit his daughter's body to be brought into the house nor allow her to be buried in the tomb of her ancestors or given any funeral or burial robe or other customary rites (οὔτε κηδείας καὶ περιστολῆς καὶ τῶν ἄλλων νομίμων μεταλαβεῖν). But as she lay there where she had been cast, in the place where she was slain, the passers-by, bringing stones and earth, buried her like any corpse which had none to give it proper burial.[269]

Immediately after a death, relatives and friends sent letters of condolence to the bereaved. In late third or early fourth century AD, Eudaemon, an officer in the Roman

---

[256] *P.Oxy.* VII.1067.
[257] Gardiner and Sethe 1928, 26-7.
[258] Montserrat 2004, 475.
[259] *PSI* XII.1263.6-8 (AD 166-167) = *SB* V.7816: Β[ου]λομαι ὑπὸ τῶν [υἱῶν μου]καὶ κληρονόμων ἐξ ἴσου εἰς κηδείαν καὶ περιστολὴν τοῦ σώμ[α]τίου μου ταφησο[μένου Αἰγυ]πτίᾳ ταφῇ.
[260] *CPR* VI.1.14.
[261] *SB* V.7871.
[262] *OGI* 90.32.
[263] *SB* 6028.2.
[264] *P.Enteux.* 32.6.
[265] *P.Oxy.* 736.13.
[266] *P.Giss.* 68.7.
[267] *PSI* XII.1263 = *SB* V.7816.
[268] Game 1995, 202.
[269] Dionysus of Halicarnassus, *Antiquitates Romanae* 3.21.8. Translation: Cary 1961, 85.

army, sent a letter of condolence to Hermodorus, the exegetes of Alexandria, for the death of his daughter.[270] Such letters never refer to the recently dead people whose bodies are not already in the hands of the embalmers by name.[271] Instead, they use euphemisms such as *eumoiros*, 'the fortunate one',[272] or later on *makarios*, 'the blessed one'.[273] During the first three days after death, the corpse was presumably washed and shrouded in cloth at home. The corpse might also have been treated with substances thought to retard decomposition, as was the case in rural Egypt in the 1930s[274] or in Chinese death rites. The latter is characterised with the placement of a blackly shining pearl in the deceased's mouth to retard decomposition so that the soul might find an intact body for revival.[275] At home, the body was first wrapped with linen cloth. At the embalmers' workshop, however, the cadaver was subject to what the papyri call the 'second wrapping' (deutera taphē).[276]

Immediately after a death, the ancient Egyptians went through a mourning period and observed dietary and grooming prohibitions. In the fifth century BC, Herodotus writes:

> Whenever a man of some standing departs from his house by death, all the womenfolk of the house daub their heads or even their faces with mud. Then they leave the corpse lying in the house while they and all their female relatives wander here and there in the city lamenting, with their garments girt around them and their breasts exposed. The men too lament in their place, with garment girt likewise. After this phase of mourning, they take the corpse to be mummified.[277]

In the first century BC, Diodorus Siculus similarly gives a detailed description of mourning rituals in ancient Egypt in two passages:

> For whenever anyone dies among them, all his relatives and friends, plastering their heads with mud, roam about the city lamenting, until the body receives burial. Nay more, during that time they indulge in neither baths, nor wine, nor in any other food worth mentioning, not do they put on bright clothing.[278]

The inhabitants of Egypt mourn for seventy-two days. They plaster their heads with mud and wrap strips of linen cloth below their breasts. Women as well as men went about in groups of two or three hundreds, and twice each day, recite the dirge in a rhythmic chant, they sang the praises of the deceased, recalling his virtues. Nor would they eat the flesh of any living thing or food prepared from wheat. They also abstained from wine and luxury of any sort. In addition, no one would ever have seen fit to make use of baths or unguents or soft bedding, nay more, would not even have dared to indulge in sexual pleasures, but every Egyptian grieved and mourned during those seventy-two days.[279]

For Diodorus, the Egyptian mourning period was seventy-two days. Yet this was not, as many scholars think, the ideal time that the deceased should spend from death to burial. Rather, Egyptian and classical evidence confirm that the mummification process took seventy days. A passage in the Eighteenth Dynasty tomb of Djehuti reads 'A good burial comes in peace, when the seventy days are completed in the mortuary workshop'.[280] Herodotus similarly writes, 'When a dead body is brought to the embalming place, the embalmers conceal the body for seventy days, embalmed in saltpetre, no longer time is allowed for the embalming'.[281]

There is agreement in classical literature over the embalming period. For Herodotus, the Egyptians had observed a number of mourning rituals before they took the corpse to the embalming place, where it was concealed and embalmed for seventy days. Since Diodorus reports that the Egyptians mourn for seventy-two days, it is a reasonable suggestion that family members performed certain mourning activities for at least two days before the cadaver was carried forth to the mummification place. There are different interpretations for this seventy or seventy-two day embalming period. Scholars often connect the seventy-day period with the movement of the Dog Star Sirius.[282] The rising of Sirius marked the Egyptian New Year in the beginning of the inundation season. The time when Sirius disappeared in the sky until the time it returned was 70 days. The Egyptians perhaps equated this astronomical phenomenon with the time needed from death in the physical world to rebirth into the afterlife. However, the seventy-two day period surprisingly coincided with the number of the fellow conspirators of Seth, who participated in the assassination of Osiris. Possibly, it was thought essential to mourn and keep the body away from the followers of Seth for seventy-two days.[283] In a society where rituals were always tempered with symbolic meanings, the latter interpretation cannot be totally disregarded.

In all cases, the existence of the paterfamilias provided a sense of protection for the household. As death meant the departure of the patron, it represented a threat to the integrity of the household. Ancient Egyptian

---

[270] Rea 1986. Cf. *P.Oxy.* I.115; *P.Princ.* II.102; *PSI* XII.1248.
[271] Montserrat 1997, 33.
[272] *P.Haun.* II.17.
[273] *CPR* VI.81.
[274] Gamal 1937, 159-67.
[275] Grießler 1991, 12.
[276] Montserrat 1997, 36.
[277] Hdt. 2.85.
[278] Dio. Sic. 1.91.1.
[279] Dio. Sic. 1.72.2-5.
[280] Wilson 1944, 201-3.
[281] Hdt. 2.86.
[282] Smith 2009b.
[283] Cf. Hdt. 2.86.

lamentations clearly reflect this notion. In a Theban tomb on reads the following lamentation, 'My home has been wrecked in an instance'.[284] In the opening passage of the Ptolemaic Songs of Isis and Nephthys, one reads 'O fair stripling, come to your house ... O fair sistrum-player come to you house'.[285] This can be paralleled with modern Egypt, where female relatives of the deceased utter piercing shrieks saying '*ya kharab baiti*', which means 'O destruction of my house'.[286] Destruction of the house does not literally mean the demolition of the physical structure, but it signifies that the deceased's wife and children have now lost the patron and protector of their house. Undoubtedly, the departure of the deceased was a gruesome occurrence that may bring about the disintegration of the household.

The shrouded corpse remained in the home for several days, while people took time off their jobs to observe the time of mourning. The sender of a letter in AD 118 writes 'Because of the death of his daughter, your steward has stopped work until his period of mourning is over'.[287] The first stage of mourning rituals took up the first three or four days after death. Thus, the dead bodies 'are not given over to the embalmers, but only after they have been dead for three or four days'.[288] The four-days mourning period must have been borrowed from the mourning period for Osiris.[289] In modern Egypt, the family of the deceased set up a pavilion for three days after death, where they receive relatives, neighbours, and friends who come to offer condolence. This practice has nothing to do with Islam. In modern Greece, a dish of *kolyva* (a dry, crumbly sweet made of grains of wheat, almonds, sugar, and cinnamon) is similarly taken to the tomb for three days after death. The exact significance of the three days is uncertain. Yet, it has been suggested that it takes the soul three days to get where it is going.[290] In the tomb of Tutankhamen, three ritual couches (hippopotamus, lion, and cow) served to keep the mummy of the king overnight in the course of a four days'/three nights' ritual to prepare him for the new life in the netherworld.[291]

Death ritual, in particular, was a means to prevent disorder after the death of a family member had struck the hierarchical order of the family. In the performance of the death rites, the family structure was maintained and the position of each living member defined.[292] Many studies have revealed that the extended family (families who have common blood ties but live in separate houses) was a characteristic feature of the Egyptian society in the Graeco-Roman period, particularly in villages.[293] Members of an extended family were expected to participate in social occasions of other members of their family, such as wedding celebrations and death ceremonies.

Mourning rituals seem to have been determined by gender to some extent. During this mourning period, female relatives of the deceased were expected to show the utmost feelings of lamentation. They performed a repertoire of conventional nonverbal practices of grief, such as beating breasts, tearing clothes, and throwing dirt on heads within and outside the house.[294] It was apparently acceptable for women to mourn excessively, but not for men to do so. Judging from their frequency on Pharaonic tomb walls and mortuary vignettes, the exposure of breasts has been recognised as a 'typical' gesture of female mourning in contrast with other 'spontaneous' gestures like pouring dust or dirt onto the face.[295]

As a sign of mourning, men would shave the entire body, but others are expected to let their hair and bread grow.[296] A shaven head and body guaranteed cleanliness and was associated with ritual purity.[297] Herodotus writes that 'the priests shave the whole body every other day, that no lice or aught else that is foul may infest them in the service of the gods'.[298] The two virgin girls who were selected to represent Isis and Nephthys and recited the lamentations for the departed Osiris in the Khoiak mysteries were obliged to remove the hair of their body.[299] Many bodies were buried shaven and hairless, as in the 18th Dynasty tombs nos. 1370, 1379, and 1388 at Deir el-Medina.[300] Equally, hair growing seems to have been associated with Osiris: 'When all his preparations had been completed, Osiris made a vow to the gods that he would let his hair grow until his return to Egypt and then made his way through Ethiopia. This is the reason why this custom with regard to hair was observed among the Egyptians until recent times', writes Diodorus.[301]

Apart from the preliminary wrapping of the body and the mourning rituals, the ekphora seems to have encompassed the viewing of the corpse by relatives and friends and the arrangements for supplying the embalming.[302] During this period, family members notified the death of their relative to the royal scribe or the village scribe.[303]

---

[284] Bleeker 1958, 2.
[285] Faulkner 1936, 123.
[286] El-Aswad 1987, 216.
[287] *P.Brem.* 40. Three days seem to have been standard on different occasions. In the 18th dynasty at Deir el-Medina, a workman named Kasa took three days off work to be at home during the birth of his child (Meskell 2000, 426).
[288] Hdt. 2.89.
[289] Plut. *De Is. et Os.* 39.
[290] Cadbury 1990, 418.
[291] Beinlich 2006.
[292] Grießler 1991, 11.

[293] Alston 1997; Hobson 1985.
[294] Hdt. 2.85.
[295] Millward 2013.
[296] Hdt. 2.36.
[297] Robins 1999.
[298] Hdt. 2.37.
[299] Faulkner 1936, 122.
[300] Meskell 1999, 193.
[301] Dio. Sic. 1.18.3.
[302] Montserrat 1997, 38.
[303] Youtie 1976. See also *P.Oxy.* XXXVIII.2837; *P.Oxy.* XLI 2957; *P.Oxy.* XLIII.3104; *P.Oxy.* XLIII.3141;

Before the transportation of the body to the embalmer's workshop, the corpse remained within the house to be visited by relatives and friends.[304] This seems to be the situation behind the first century AD letter of Thaubas to her father Pompeius: 'On receiving my letter, please be so good as to come home promptly, because your poor daughter Herennia has died. She had already come safely through a miscarriage on 9th Phaophi. For she gave birth to a still-born child in the eight month, but herself survived four days; and only after that did she die. Now she has received from us and her husband the proper funeral preparations (peristolē) and has been placed in Alabanthis, so if you come and you so wish, you can see her'.[305] The father had the chance to see his daughter while her body was still at home before the ekphora. If he is absent, he still could see her when the embalmers returned her mummy.

The primary mourning period ends up with what Greek papyri call the ekphora, which refers to the carrying forth of the corpse to the embalming workshop on the third/fourth day after death.[306] Before the body was delivered to the embalmers, the heirs and family would provide the necessary embalming commodities to the mummification workshop.[307] Together with the corpse, these were probably carried forth from the house to the embalming workshop in the ekphora-procession.[308] The two moments preceding the coming out of the corpse from the house for mummification (ekphora) or burial (apostolē) are extremely distressing, where close female relatives, specifically the mother, sisters, daughters, and wife of the deceased, smite their breasts with both hands, tear their clothes, and smear dust on their heads.[309] There is no textual or pictorial description of the funeral procession to the embalming workshop in Graeco-Roman Egypt. Yet the procession of deities carrying linen and ointments for the mummification of the dead in the first century AD tomb of Petosiris in the Dakhla oasis probably invokes the ekphora-procession to the embalmers' workshop rather than the apostolē-procession to the necropolis.[310] Starting from the house, the body was presumably carried on a bier on the shoulders of family members, relatives, and friends to the mummification workshop. The procession must have been accompanied with female weepers and carriers of the embalming commodities. In that sense, the ekphora 'could be an effective means of exhibiting the prestige of the deceased and their family'.[311] The ekphora encompassed all forms of mourning rituals from the moment of death to sending-off the corpse to the morticians' workshop.

VII.2.3.2. The Peristolē

The next stage of the burial process, the peristolē, began with the transportation of the corpse to the mummification workshop. The Greek term *peristqlh/* literally means the 'wrapping up' or 'laying out' of a corpse.[312] This indicates the wrapping of the mummy with linen bandages or the use of other wrappings in case the body was not embalmed.[313] In an Egyptian context, the Peristolē refers to the embalming, wrapping, and adorning the body before it was delivered to the family.[314] It also constitutes the funerary rituals and recitations accompanying the mummification process. It was an important step in the processing of the deceased and the preparation of the body for the funeral. Greek documents suggest that the peristolē began when the body was taken to the embalmers on the third/fourth day after death.[315] The Demotic stela of Amenher similarly mentions that his mummification started four days after death on 1 May 73 BC.[316] Here it would be worked on for seventy or seventy-two days and then returned to the family. No mummification workshop has archaeologically been identified in Egypt. However, literary evidence suggests that embalming workshops at Alexandria were located within the necropolis together with graves and gardens.[317]

As elsewhere, inhabitants in Graeco-Roman Egypt did not adhere to a strict mortuary code, for their funerary practices display a variety of interment techniques.[318] Direct inhumation, cremation, and mummification were possibilities of the disposal of the body.[319] Mummification, however, remained the typical and ideal treatment of the body from the Pharaonic and down to the Roman period.[320] Lucian speaks of burning as the Greek custom, as contrasted with the burial of the Persians, the eating of the dead by the Scythians, and the embalming of the Egyptians.[321] The family was closely involved in every stage of processing the corpse to the necropolis, including the provision of some of the commodities needed for mummification. A third century AD letter requests various items needed for embalming: 'Because of the matter about which I wrote to you previously concerning the mourning of all of us necessitated by the death of my overseer Hermesion, come out and bring me resin and bitumen for the work and the basket about which I spoke to you'.[322]

---

[304] Hdt. 2.85.
[305] *P.Fuad* 75. The letter is dated 18 Phaophi.
[306] Montserrat 2004, 475.
[307] *P.Mich.Inv.* 3724.6-12 = *SB* XVIII.13613.
[308] Montserrat 1997, 38.
[309] Cf. Dionysus of Halicarnassus, *Antiquitates Romanae* 3.21.4.
[310] Osing et al 1982.
[311] Montserrat 1997, 38.
[312] *BGU* III.896.7.
[313] Cf. Dionysus Halicarnassus, *Antiquitates Romanae* 3.21.8.
[314] Montserrat 2004, 475.
[315] Hdt. 2.89; Montserrat 1997.
[316] Sauneron 1952, XV note 4; Shore 1992, 229-32.
[317] Strabo 17.1.10.
[318] Nabatea: Perry 2002. Rome: Counts 1996. Although cremation was the dominant rite in early imperial Rome, Poppaea, Nero's wife, was embalmed in the Egyptian style (Tac. *Ann.* 16.6.).
[319] Cartwright, Spaabaek, and Svoboda 2011.
[320] The Roman world: Nock 1932. Pharaonic Egypt: Smith 1906. Roman Egypt: Aufderheide et al 1999.
[321] Luc. *Luct.* 21.
[322] *P.Mich.Inv.* 3724.6-12 = *SB* XVIII.13613.

Herodotus describes three classes of prearranged mummification based on cost. The cheapest method involved the injection of an unspecified liquid via the rectum, followed by treatment with natron (a mixture of sodium carbonate and bicarbonate with some natural impurities). The second method (the one also used for animals) was similar, and included injection of cedar oil via the rectum and treatment with natron. The most expensive method involved the most complicated procedures. First, the viscera and abdominal contents were removed through an incision made in the flank. The heart was left *in situ* because it was the location of a person's intellect and emotions; also, the kidneys were not removed, but no religious explanation is given for this. Next, the body was cleansed and washed, the cavities were packed with bandages, herbs and spices, and the incision was closed. Both the viscera and the body were packed with natron to dehydrate the tissues.[323]

The mummification process lasted for seventy days from the arrival of the body at the embalmers' workshop to its eventual return to the family for burial.[324] Yet this seventy-day period was divided into two steps; the first step lasted for forty days; the second took up thirty days. Diodorus describes the first stage of the peristolē or the drying process of mummification:

When they have gathered to treat the body after it has been slit open, one of them thrusts his hand through the opening in the corpse into the trunk and extracts everything but the kidneys and heart, and another one cleanses each of the viscera, washing them in palm wine and spices. And in general, they carefully dress the whole body for over thirty days, first with cedar oil and certain other preparations, and then with myrrh, cinnamon, and such spices as have the faculty not only of preserving it for a long time but also of giving it a fragrant odour.[325]

Diodorus's narrative of Egyptian funeral procedures has been confirmed in modern times by papyrological evidence.[326] This stage of the peristolē involved washing and anointing the corpse, evisceration, dehydrating the body by means of dry crystals of natron, and packing its abdominal cavity with linen, sawdust, and other materials.

While the body was in the hands of the morticians, the relatives and friends went into mourning for forty days. They could visit the embalming workshop while the bodies of loved ones were being mummified.[327] The forty-day mourning period seems to have been associated with the god Osiris. Following the death of the Apis bull at Memphis, the people did not cease their mourning for forty days.[328] One has to remember that the Apis was thought to be the soul of Osiris.[329] The corpse is believed to decompose after forty days. In modern Egypt, the family, relatives, and friends of the deceased would gather on the fortieth day after death to commemorate his/her departure. This gathering is called al-Arbaien, which means the fortieth. For forty days after death, families refrain from participating in wedding ceremonies and other entertaining events and women keep wearing black clothes.[330] Apparently, this forty-day mourning period was borrowed from ancient Egyptian funeral traditions, as it has nothing to do with Islam.[331] In modern Greece, candles are similarly illuminated for forty days in the house after the death of a family member. After forty days, there is a short and less attended memorial service than was the funeral.[332]

After forty days, when the dehydration process was complete, the body was ready for the second step of the peristolē, which included the final application of resins and oils and swathing the body in linen bandages. The oil, ointment, and linen mentioned in Greek papyri related to funeral costs were almost certainly used in the mummification process. Since the religious upheavals of the Amarna period, the overall treatment of the body was more intricate, where the corpse was invested with time-consuming embalming procedures. In line with this was the shift in the burial goods that focus on life and the lived experience of individuals to a more visible focus on death-oriented and mortuary paraphernalia.[333] This is why family burials in the Roman period reveal a variety of expensive funerary equipment such as coffins, masks, and mummy shrouds.[334]

The preservation of the body meant that the deceased would enjoy another life in the hereafter. Mummification guaranteed that the dead body would continue to receive offerings. Thus, a dead child's prayer to Osiris in the Ptolemaic period asks, 'Give me bread and beer and incense and water, which are offered on your table'.[335] The physical transformation of the corpse into a mummy mirrored the spiritual transformation of the dead human into an empowered being.[336] For contemporaries and later generations, the mummy represented the personality of the dead person. Thus, Ptolemy I Soter used the mummy of Alexander the Great both as a physical presence and as memory in order to appear special in the eyes of his soldiers and subjects.[337] Augustus similarly visited the

---

[323] Hdt. 2.85-90.
[324] Hdt. 2.86; Wilson 1944, 201-3; David 2007, 96.
[325] Dio. Sic. 1.91.6.
[326] Merkelbach 1993.
[327] De Cenival 1972, 189.
[328] Dio. Sic. 1.85.1-3.
[329] Dio. Sic. 1.85.1-4; Strabo 17.1.31.
[330] El-Aswad 1987, 207.
[331] El-Aswad 1987, 224; Abu-Loughd 1993.
[332] Cadbury 1990, 418.
[333] Meskell 1999.
[334] Riggs 2005, 182-217.
[335] Erman 1915, 107.
[336] Hornung 1983.
[337] Erskine 2002. On the embalmment of the body of Alexander by Chaldean and Egyptian specialists: Curt.10.10.9-13.

mummy of the Macedonian hero and gave him honours by placing a golden crown on the mummy and scattering flowers on it.[338]

Embalming the dead was the most important part of the peristolē stage. The mummification process was also accompanied with ritualistic and magical spells. A further consequence of the rites of mummification was the awakening or animating of the *ba* of the deceased,[339] which is referred to as εἴδωλον on Greek mummy labels.[340] The so-called Ritual of Embalming, which is preserved in two Theban Hieratic and Demotic papyri (P.Boulaq III and P.Louvre 5.158) of the first century AD, constitutes eleven operations to be performed on the corpse at the embalmers' workshop.[341] These operations included anointing and wrapping various parts of the corpse, where prayers and apotropaic formulae were recited in conjunction with the ritual acts. These rituals were recited by the master of secrets, the lector priest, the seal-bearer, and the embalmers, who represented the gods who anointed the body of Osiris and wrapped him in linen bandages, to assist the passage of the deceased into the netherworld.[342] In a similar way, modern Egyptians recite verses from the Quran on the corpse to help the soul of the deceased leave the house in which the person died.[343] The funerary lamentations and glorifications texts (*s3ḥw*) were also performed on the mummy in the Graeco-Roman period. In lamentation texts, weeping women representing Isis and Nephthys mourn and praise the deceased, while glorification texts enable successful transition of the dead person to a transfigured state of being.[344]

The embalming process is conceived not just as a preservation of the corpse, but rather as its transfiguration to a new body. The Egyptian word for mummy, *sch*, also means 'nobility' and 'dignity', denoting the elevated sphere of existence to which the deceased has been transferred and initiated in the course of the process of embalment.[345] Since human access to the hereafter came through Osiris, prayers were repeated over the deceased to help bring about his/her gradual union with Osiris. For the same purpose, the body was decorated with a gold leaf to transform the desiccated skin into the golden flesh of a god. The decoration of the body's external wrappings also emphasised the identification of the deceased with Osiris. Images reproduced on mummy coverings often included the celestial boat of Osiris, which carried the dead across the heavens.[346] After death, the dead person was given the appellation of an Osiris, indicating that the deceased was going through the same triumphant reassertion of self as the dead king.[347]

Death is profane insomuch as it is related to the earthly mortal body of a dead person. Death is also sacred as far as it is associated with the immortal soul. The house also had this double symbolic connotation. The front door of the house, for example, was a private and semi-public space. It is a transitional physical and spatial element of the house, but also an indispensible part of the street structure.[348] The ekphora and apostolē processions started from the house. The profane and sacred meanings of the house and death should not be conceived as two oppositions. By contrast, they complement each other. The dead body moves from one house, the temporary abode of the living, to another though everlasting house, the tomb.[349] Modern Egyptians call this earthly life *Dar El-Fana* or 'the house of evanescence'. As opposed to this life, there are two *Dars* or houses. There is *Dar El-Maut*, which means 'the house of the dead', in reference to the tomb in which dead people wait until the day of resurrection. Secondly, there is *Dar El-Akhira* or 'the otherworldly housee', which is also described as *Dar El-Baqa* or 'the everlasting house'.[350] Unfortunately, nothing is recorded about the role of the house of the living while the body was kept at the embalming workshop. Presumably, it continued to serve as a mourning arena for visiting relatives and friends, wishing to offer condolence to the bereaved family. Close-kin relatives were expected to observe the same taboos on dress, food, and means of luxury and entertainment during the peristolē.

VII.2.3.3. The Kēdeia

The kēdeia came after the body was embalmed for seventy days and was returned home.[351] Although the word kēdeia often comes before the term peristolē in Greek papyri,[352] it probably encompassed all the rituals that followed the mummification process, including those performed at the house or in the necropolis. That is, the kēdeia seems to describe what happened to the mummified body after it received its peristolē and was returned to the relatives. It is usually translated as 'funeral', though this has slightly wrong connotations. It may cover the whole package of ritual obsequies: the viewing of the mummy by friends and relatives, mourning rituals, the domestic cult of the dead, the despatch of the body to the necropolis, and the funerary banquet.[353] A fully prepared mummy being despatched for burial is described as kekēdeumenos.[354]

---

[338] Suet. *Aug.* 18.
[339] Smith 2009a, 4.
[340] Quaegebeur 1978, 253-4.
[341] Mariette 1871; Sauneron 1952; Smith 2009a, 215-44.
[342] Riggs 2010, 2.
[343] El-Aswad 1987, 217.
[344] Faulkner 1936; Bleeker 1958; Riggs 2010, 2.
[345] Assmann 1989, 137-8.
[346] Montserrat 2004, 475.

[347] Griffith 1909, 16, 55; Otto 1905, 98.
[348] Abdelwahed 2015, 83-91.
[349] Cf. Dio. Sic. 1.51
[350] El-Aswad 1987, 209-10.
[351] Dio. Sic. 1.91.6.
[352] *Stud.Pal.* XXII.56.1; *P.Oxy.* IX.1218.7.
[353] Montserrat 1997, 34.
[354] *P.Paris* 18.2.234.

After the mummification process, the embalmers directly handed over mummies to families.³⁵⁵ The mummy was brought back to the house of the living so that family members, relatives, and friends could see the deceased before his/her final departure to the necropolis. Papyri and mummy labels confirm long delay between death and burial.³⁵⁶ The absence of family members could be a reason for such a delay. In such case, the embalmed bodies were kept at home in the care of relatives or friends until their associates could come and arrange their funerals. In the second or third century AD, Besas, a goldsmith, writes to his friend Eidos to 'fetch the body of my father and keep it safe until, god willing, I am able to sail up for his despatch. You will make a gift in friendly fashion. You are not again neglectful of the property. The body would be given a funeral another time'.³⁵⁷ Similarly, the mummy label of Takhenmet daughter of Petarsomtheus records that she died in year 9, month 3 of spring, day 10 of an unnamed emperor; she was not buried at Thebes until year 11, month 1 of inundation, day 19, that is, a year and four months after her death.³⁵⁸ The mummy of Takhenmet probably remained in the possession of the family at home.

Some mummies were kept unburied for a time while they received a domestic cult from their relatives. Houses were dwelling places not only for living members of the family and their consecrated animals,³⁵⁹ but also for family members who had passed away. This practice is confirmed by textual sources and apparently also by archaeological finds. Mummies were kept in houses for some time before their interment in the necropolis. Several classical writers affirm that the Egyptians kept their embalmed dead in their houses. Cicero states that 'the Egyptians embalm their dead and keep them in the house'.³⁶⁰ Sextus Empiricus also confirms this custom, 'the Egyptians take out their entrails and embalm them and keep them above ground with themselves'.³⁶¹ Pomponius Mela equally reports that the Egyptians 'act in a very different way from the rest of the people of this land. They lament the dead with mud; they neither burn nor bury the dead, but embalm them and place them between the chambers', apparently somewhere in houses.³⁶² Herodotus similarly affirms the Egyptian practice of keeping mummies in houses: 'They [the embalmers] give back the dead man to his friends. These make a hollow wooden figure like a man, in which they enclose the corpse, shut it up, and preserve it safe in a coffin-chamber, placed erect against a wall'.³⁶³ Diodorus similarly writes, 'Those who have private tombs lay the body in a box [coffin] reserved for it [in the tomb], but those who possess none construct a new chamber in their own house (κατὰ τὴν ἰδίαν οἰκίαν) and stand the coffin upright against the firmest wall'.³⁶⁴

Diodorus attributes this practice to financial reasons alone. Well-off Egyptians, in his view, would have the mean to construct private tombs due to their financial abilities, whereas the poor built a chamber in their house to receive the dead. It is, however, misleading to follow Diodorus and think that only the houses of the poor served a mortuary role as temporary sepulchres. To Greek and Roman writers writing from an outsider's perspective, this alien practice is an expression of the cultural distinctiveness of the Egyptians. Yet Roman citizens in Egypt identified by their *tria nomina* were embalmed and buried in an Egyptian manner.³⁶⁵ Diodorus's explanation that the dead were kept in houses for financial reasons alone is mistaken for several reasons. First, even the construction of a new room to receive the deceased would require a significant financial outlay. Second, the provision of a coffin, set 'upright in the firmest wall', could also be expensive. Third, it is clear that what would be placed in the coffin is the mummy. It is known that mummification was a costly practice.³⁶⁶ Any person who could afford the construction of a chamber in his/her house, the provision of a coffin for the deceased, and the embalming of his/her dead relative must have been wealthy enough to offer at least a small private tomb. Equally, wealthy Egyptians in Roman Thebes, who held important priestly titles and presumably could afford a private tomb, consciously avoided new tomb construction in favour of reusing earlier Pharaonic graves and pits.³⁶⁷

In the light of all these indications, a different reason for preserving mummies within houses should be sought. Since keeping mummies in houses was an Egyptian practice, the reason for its emergence needs to be looked for within ancient Egyptian religion. For Barbara Borg, the practice of keeping mummies in houses was derived from ancient Egyptian ancestral cult as part of the domestic cult of the dead. Although the Romans did have cult associated with their ancestors, there is no evidence in Greek and Roman cultures for a domestic cult of the dead.³⁶⁸ In contrast, a domestic cult for the deceased in the house of the relatives already existed in Pharaonic Egypt. The so-called $3ḥ iḳr n=R^c$ stelae (figure 51) indicate that a domestic cult of the dead was known

---

³⁵⁵ Dio. Sic. 1.91.6.
³⁵⁶ Although Tutankhamen died in the late summer, it is clear from botanical evidence in his tomb that his burial took place in spring (Bryce 1990).
³⁵⁷ *P.Princ*. III.166.
³⁵⁸ D'Aura et al 1988, 229.
³⁵⁹ Hdt. 2.36.
³⁶⁰ Cic. *Tusc*. 1.45.108: *Condiunt Aegyptii mortuos et eos servant domi*.
³⁶¹ Sext. Emp. *Pyr* 3.226: καὶ σὺν ἑαυτοῖς ὑπὲρ γῆς ἔχουσιν.
³⁶² Pompon. *De Chorographia* 1.48: Cultores regionem multo aliter a ceteris agunt. Mortuos limo obliti plangunt; nec cremare aut fodere fos putant, verum arte medicatos inter penetralia conlocant.

³⁶³ Hdt. 2.68.
³⁶⁴ Dio. Sic. 1.92.6.
³⁶⁵ Riggs 2005, 21-2.
³⁶⁶ On the costs of funerals: Montserrat 1997, 40-41.
³⁶⁷ For wealthy Egyptian priests buried in earlier structures: Montserrat and Meskell 1997.
³⁶⁸ Borg 1997, 28-9. On ancestral cult in Roman culture: Toynbee 1971.

FIGURE 51. AN *3ḥ iḳr n=Rᶜ* STELA.

FIGURE 52. AN ANTHROPOMORPHIC BUST BELONGING TO A DOMESTIC CULT OF THE DEAD.

FIGURE 53. A STELA FROM ABYDOS SHOWING A WOMAN INVOLVED IN WORSHIPPING AN ANCESTRAL BUST.

in the Pharaonic period at least since the Eighteenth and Twentieth Dynasties.[369] These stelae came mainly from Deir el-Medina, Abydos, and Thebes. Those uncovered in Deir el-Medina were all found in the living quarters of the town in different rooms of houses. The inscriptions on the stelae often state that they were dedicated to the deceased by his/her family members. Such stelae were a suitable means whereby the relatives could engage with the dead and offer them sacrifices.[370]

Equally important is a group of anthropomorphic busts belonging to a domestic cult of the dead (figure 52).[371] These busts represent images of dead persons to whom the living paid honour and offered sacrifices. A domestic cult of the dead is also confirmed by a group of stelae uncovered from Abydos, showing individuals involved in worshipping ancestral busts (figure 53).[372]

Ancestral cult continued as an important feature of ancient Egyptian religion under Roman times.[373] By contrast, Roman ancestor masks (*imagines*) of family members who held high offices, which were kept in houses and were indeed a vital part of Roman culture, were not used for a domestic cult of the dead. The Roman *imagines* were not related to beliefs about life after death, though they were used in funerary processions.[374] Since

---

[369] Demarée 1983.
[370] Borg 1997, 28.
[371] Kaizer 1990, 269-85.
[372] Borg 1997, 29.
[373] Fitzentreiter 1994.

[374] Flower 1996, 209-11. On the use of *imagines* in funerary processions of Roman office-holders: Flower 1996, 91-106.

the Egyptians used to honour their parents and ancestors after their death, it follows that mummies were kept in houses as part of an ancestral cult.[375] This practice allowed the deceased to participate in family life and even in the meals of the living. Some literary statements affirm that the Egyptians used to dine in the presence of the dead. Herodotus states that wooden images of corpses placed in coffins were brought out at banquets.[376] Silius Italicus affirms the same custom: 'The Egyptians enclose their dead after the funeral, standing in an upright position, in a coffin of stone, and worship it; and they admit a bloodless specter to their banquets'.[377] The heavy weight of mummies, sometimes over a hundred kilograms,[378] necessitated that comparatively light wooden images of the dead were made and brought into symposia.

In addition to literary sources, archaeology supports the existence of mummies in houses in Graeco-Roman Egypt. The practice of keeping the corpse at home for some time before burial explains the poor state of coffins, mummies, and mummy portraits, which Petrie observed at Hawara:

Many of them had been much injured by exposure during a long period before burial. The gilt-bust mummies had often been knocked about, the stucco chipped off, sometimes the nose bashed in by a fall, the gilding dirtied, fly-marked, caked with dust which was bound on by rain. The portraits show the same exposure…on the feet of one mummy the wrapping had been used by children, who scribbled caricature upon it…thus every sign shows that the mummies, both with and without portraits, has stood exposed for a long time before burial.[379]

In addition to rain, women cleaning houses and sprinkling water might have been a reason for dirtying coffins standing upright. Many mummies at Hawara had vertical piles of bird droppings on their shoulders, showing that they had once been placed upright,[380] the same position confirmed by Herodotus, Diodorus, and Silius Italicus.[381] Equally, the discovery of framed panel portraits at Hawara[382] and at Karanis in a domestic context[383] confirms that mummy portraits were hung in houses.[384]

The presence of the so-called mummy cupboards, inside which mummies were kept, offers archaeological support for the theory of keeping mummies in the house before burial. Numerous examples of these wooden cupboards

FIGURE 54. THE FIRST CENTURY AD MUMMY-CUPBOARD OF PADIKHONS FROM ABUSIR EL-MELEK.

have come to light from Abusir el-Melek, near the Fayum, like that of Padikhons of the first century AD (figure 54).[385] It is likely that mummy cupboards were kept in houses; however, their exact location within houses remains obscure. Diodorus's statement that the Egyptians used to 'stand the coffin upright in the firmest wall' of their houses suggests that mummy cupboards were probably placed against the strongest and thickest wall of the house, possibly one of those shared with neighbours. Given the heavy weight of mummies,

---

[375] Dio. Sic. 1.93.1.
[376] Hdt. 2.78.
[377] Sil. *Pun.* 13.474-6: Aegyptia tellus claudit odorato post funus stantia saxo corpora et a mensis exsanguem haud separat umbram.
[378] Petrie 1911, 16.
[379] Petrie 1911, 2.
[380] Montserrat 1997, 38.
[381] Hdt. 2.86; Dio. Sic. 1.92.6; Sil. *Pun.* 13.474-6.
[382] Petrie 1889, 10 and pl. 12.
[383] Root 1980, 7.
[384] Corcoran 1997, 48.

[385] Willeitner 2004, 319. The mummy cupboard of Padikhons is in the Ägyptisches Museum, Berlin, 17039.

mummy cupboards were probably positioned against the strongest wall of the house to bear the heavy weight of the cupboard and its content. Mummy cupboards have double doors, which could be easily opened whenever grieving relatives or friends wanted to see the mummy kept in its cupboard. Taken together, the dead received a domestic cult in the house before its final despatch to the necropolis, the apostolē.

VII.2.3.4. The Apostolē and Beyond

At the end of the kēdeia period, the relatives and friends gathered once again to arrange for the final despatch of the body from the house to the necropolis.[386] The day of burial marked the transition of the deceased from the world of the living to that of the dead. The carrying forth of the mummy in a spectacular procession to the necropolis is called in Greek papyri the apostolē or sending-off.[387] The starting point for the funeral procession from the realm of the living to the necropolis was the house of the deceased. In the Old Kingdom tomb of Ankhma-Hor at Saqqara, the funeral procession is described as 'Going out from the house of the estate to the beautiful west'.[388] Depending on the location of the tomb, the apostolē might have involved a voyage across the Nile on funeral barges.[389] Like the ekphora-procession, women are expected to show the utmost distress of mourning gestures during the apostolē-procession.

The funeral procession to the necropolis was probably used as a marker of social status. Entries in household accounts of the first century AD from Oxyrhynchus record four obols spent on incense for the sending-off of the daughter of Phna, and one drachma on incense at the funeral of the daughter of Pasis.[390] The torches, masks, mourners, garlands, and fare of the donkey on boat, which are mentioned in an account of funeral expenses, were almost certainly associated with the funeral procession to the necropolis.[391] For members of the elite, the route and activities of the funeral procession in the Roman Forum was similarly used to display their importance in the society.[392] Polybius specifically cited the wearing of ancestral masks and giving eulogies at funeral processions as evidence of Roman elite superiority.[393]

Greek and Demotic rules governing guilds, whether trade or religious, specify the behaviour of their members at this part of the funeral ritual. The Tiberian examples lay down that whichever of the guild members 'has taken no part in the funeral and has not placed a wreath on the tomb shall be fined four drachmas'.[394] The colleagues of the deceased were also obliged to throw dust, presumably on their heads, in the funeral and lay a wreath (στεφανικωόν) at the tomb.[395] While 12 obols were spent on the wreaths,[396] the expenses for the wreaths sometimes amounted to 16 obols.[397] In some guilds there was a funeral allowance (τὸ ταφικόν) paid to the family of the dead colleague.[398]

Since the Old Kingdom, the chief celebrants of the funeral procession are the seal-bearer of the god and chief embalmer, the lector priest, the embalmer of Anubis, and finally the weeping women.[399] Together funeral processions on tomb walls of the Graeco-Roman period and Greek papyri indicate a remarkable continuity of this earlier funerary custom. The funeral processions in the fourth century BC tomb of Petosiris at Tuna el-Gebel and the nearby first century AD tomb of Ta-shery[...] represent *sem*-priests and lector priests.[400] In the Dakhla oasis, the first century AD tomb of Petubastis depicts an extensive burial procession, where an array of deities carrying funerary goods.[401] Papyri similarly affirm that the embalmer wearing the mask of Anubis participated in the funeral procession to the necropolis. In *Stud.Pal.* XXII.56, the eight drachmas 'for the dog' probably refers to the embalmer of Anubis, who, since the New Kingdom, wore the mask of the god.[402] In *P.Ashm* I.17 the embalmer who was designated 'the man of Anubis' perhaps participated in the funeral procession to the necropolis.[403] The 'dog-headed one' associated with the public procession of the god Serapis at Oxyrhynchus[404] was 'the official who took the part of Anubis in the festival'.[405]

The participation of female weepers (θρηνήτριαι) in the funeral procession is a continuation of an earlier Egyptian custom confirmed in Pharaonic tomb paintings.[406] However, men (θρηνηταί) could fill this office by the second century AD.[407] Female mourners were hired to perform lamentations during the funerary procession. The wailing women presumably occupied a fixed place in the funerary procession, in front of and behind the coffin, and were identified as Isis and Nephthys, the most famous female weepers of ancient Egyptian

---

[386] *P.Oxy.* IX.1218; *P.Princ.* III.166.6.
[387] Montserrat 1997, 40.
[388] Wilson 1944, 203.
[389] Cf. Dio. Sic. 1.92.1.
[390] *P.Oxy.* IV.736-13-14, 84.
[391] *Stud.Pal.* XXII.56.
[392] Favro and Johanson 2010.
[393] Polyb. 6.52-54.
[394] Greek: *P.Mich.Inv.* 243. Demotic: de Cenival 1972, 7-10, 47-8, 75-6.
[395] *P.Mich* V.243.9; *P.Mich* V.244.6-18.
[396] *P.Fay.* 103.4.
[397] *Stud.Pal.* XXII.56.25.
[398] *P.Enteux.* 20, 21.
[399] Wilson 1944, 203-5.
[400] Petosiris: Lefebvre 1924; House No. 21: Gabra 1941, 39-50; Riggs 2005, 129-39.
[401] Fakhry and Osing 1982, 70-81.
[402] *Stud.Pal.* XXII.56.22.
[403] *P.Ashm* I.17.1.
[404] *SB* IV.7336.42.
[405] Wormald 1929, 242.
[406] *SEG* VIII.621.17-18; Wilson 1944.
[407] *Stud.Pal.* XXII.56.27; *BGU* I.34.ii.20, iv.4.

religion.⁴⁰⁸ Isis and Nephthys often stand at both ends of the funerary bier or beside the head of the deceased, both in the texts and in the monuments.⁴⁰⁹ They were the two chief mourners (djerty), first of Osiris, and then of gods associated with him. Later on, they became mourners of all the dead, who were identified and honoured as Osiris. They had certain lamentations and incantations to perform during the funeral.⁴¹⁰ Two early Ptolemaic papyri with litanies from the cult of Osiris have been published under the titles: 'The Songs of Isis and Nephthys' (The Bremner-Rhind Papyrus, British Museum No. 10188) and 'The Lamentations of Isis and Nephthys' (P.Berlin 3008).⁴¹¹ As the two women assume the role of Isis and Nephthys and recite the hymns in the Osirian mysteries of Khoiak, the human representatives of the two goddesses similarly intone laments for the departed person at the funeral procession.

VII.2.3.5. The Tribunal

When the mummy is ready to be buried 'the family announces the day of interment to the judges and to the relatives and friends of the deceased, and solemnly affirms that he who had just passed away –giving his name- is about to cross the lake'.⁴¹² Once the funeral procession reach the necropolis, the coffin containing the body was placed outside the tomb and, as customs prescribed, a tribunal was held to judge his/her deeds on the earth.⁴¹³ The forty-two juries symbolised the judges of Egyptian nomes, who appear with Osiris in the Hall of the Two Truths. Since the First Intermediate Period, the judgment of the dead was crucial to the possibility of an Osirian afterlife beyond the tomb for all individuals.⁴¹⁴

In search for justification, and in the presence of Osiris and the nome judges in the judgement hall, the deceased advocates his/her innocence by uttering the Negative Confession, swearing not to have committed forty-two sins.⁴¹⁵ For Diodorus, those who had accusations brought against them or their bodies have been made security for a loan 'are forbidden burial and their bodies were kept in their own homes as a punishment. If sometimes happens that their sons' sons have become prosperous and paid off the debt or cleared them of the charges, give them later a magnificent funeral'.⁴¹⁶ Although Herodotus equally mentioned that the Egyptians pawn the mummies of their fathers, this extraordinary custom is not confirmed in Greek papyri.⁴¹⁷ Yet there is evidence that the choachytes (χοαχύτης), the pourer of water, who took care of the dead in the Theban necropolis on behalf of the family, could borrow money on dead bodies in the Graeco-Roman period.⁴¹⁸

VII.2.3.6. The Opening of the Mouth Ritual

Having been declared innocent by the tribunal, other ceremonies were performed at the preparation of the mummy and the provisioning of the deceased: the Opening of the Mouth Ritual and the Funerary Banquet. One section of a late Ptolemaic papyrus in Demotic (P.BM 10507) is entitled, 'The book which was made in exact accordance with his desire for Hor, the son of Petemin, to cause it to be recited as an Opening of the Mouth document in his presence on the night of his burial feast'.⁴¹⁹ This text indicates the continuity of the Pharaonic Opening of the Mouth ritual performed on the mummy on the day of burial. Tomb walls indicate that this ritual is always performed by the *sem*-priest outside the tomb. Female weepers are sometimes shown mourning before the mummy, which is supported by a man wearing the mask of Anubis (figure 55).⁴²⁰ This visualises the female weepers and the dog-masked priest of Anubis who appear in papyri.

The Opening of the Mouth ceremony was performed to symbolically bring the dead back to life so that it could reunite with the soul, the *ba*.⁴²¹ A Demotic text, Papyrus Harkness of the first century AD, includes a section headed, 'The chapters of awakening the *ba* which they will recite on the night of burial', suggesting the time and place of the ritual performance.⁴²² The 'awakening the *ba*' is another function ascribed to funerary rituals like the glorification texts.⁴²³ Once the Opening of the Mouth ritual has been finished, the mummy was finally placed in its resting place. In Papyrus Harkness, one also reads, 'It is the great gods of your town who have freed your brick', presumably a reference to the mud brick placed under the head of the deceased.⁴²⁴ This position reminds of the Greek term used to describe the burial place as κοιμητήριον, which means the 'sleeping-room'.⁴²⁵ In modern Egypt, the undertakers used to put a mud brick under the corpse's head to elevate it in such a way that the deceased seems as if he/she were sleeping.⁴²⁶

VII.2.3.7. The Funerary Banquet

The interment of the body was also marked with a funerary banquet, which was held on the day of burial and on other feast days. As in Rome, visits to the dead usually took place on the birthday of the deceased or the anniversary

---

⁴⁰⁸ Bleeker 1958.
⁴⁰⁹ Texts: Smith 2009a. Tombs: Venit 2002; Riggs 2005.
⁴¹⁰ D'Aura et al 1988, 97.
⁴¹¹ Faulkner 1933, 1936.
⁴¹² Dio. Sic. 1.92.1.
⁴¹³ Dio. Sic. 1.72.2-5.
⁴¹⁴ O'Neill 2015.
⁴¹⁵ Budge 1967.
⁴¹⁶ Dio. Sic. 1.92.6.
⁴¹⁷ Hdt. 2.136.
⁴¹⁸ *UPZ* II.157.34; *P.Lond*. I.1.1; Vleeming 1995.
⁴¹⁹ Smith 1987.
⁴²⁰ Taylor 2010, 8.
⁴²¹ Lichtheim 1976.
⁴²² Smith 2005.
⁴²³ Riggs 2010, 3.
⁴²⁴ Smith 2009a, 278.
⁴²⁵ *IG* III.2545; *IG* VII.235.43.
⁴²⁶ El-Aswad 1987, 221.

Figure 55. The Opening of the Mouth ritual on the papyrus of Nesitanebisheru, the daughter of Pinedjem II, who died around 930 BC. © Trustees of the British Museum

of death when offerings were made.[427] Early Christians similarly refer to the day of one's death as the day of one's birth (*natus*) or birthday (*dies natalis*).[428] Thus, Tertullian writes, 'on the anniversary of their death we make ritual offerings to the dead in celebration of their birth'.[429] The funeral feast is frequently depicted in New Kingdom tombs, where the relatives and friends wear holiday garb, eat and drink, watch the dancing women, and listen to the song of the harper.[430] Banqueting and sacrifices in the company of the dead occurred in the offering place of the tomb accessible to living visitors.[431] As a time-honoured part of Egyptian funerary practices, dining with the dead in the tomb or necropolis survived into the Graeco-Roman period.[432] The sacrifice for the deceased was integral to the sustenance of his/her body and soul.[433] In an account of funeral costs, 12 obols were spent on the grain porridge (ἀθήριον), probably for the funerary banquet.[434] Numerous papyri refer to this funerary custom, apparently called the 'banquet of Anubis'. The kline of Anubis at Oxyrhynchus was probably a funerary feast 'in the oikos of the Serapeum' in the presence of a statue of the god.[435]

Professional guilds stipulate that living members should contribute to the burial and funeral feast of their dead colleagues. One such agreement specifies that the association will sponsor 'two days of drinking at the pr-nfr',[436] perhaps a funerary chapel with associated dining area near the tomb,[437] like those excavated at Deir el-Medina or Marina el-Alamein.[438] The triclinium at Kom el-Shoqafa is an archaeological evidence for banqueting with the dead in Roman Alexandria.[439] In the chora, the relatives and friends of the deceased could dine near the tomb in the necropolis, as in Tune el-Gebel.[440] The offerings presented to the dead included garlands and hair. Garlands frequently appear in papyri in association with the funeral.[441] The excavations of the necropolis of Doush in the Kharga oasis have yielded hair or shaving hair among the offerings deposited in the tombs.[442] As previously mentioned, hair was closely associated with Osiris and Isis. The Egyptians also make vows to certain gods on behalf of their children who have been delivered from an illness, in which case they shave off their hair and weigh it against silver or gold, and then give the money to the attendants of sacred animals.[443]

---

[427] Rome: *CIL* VI.10248; Hopkins 1983, 226-34; Carroll 2006, 180-6. Egypt: *P.Oxy.* III.494.22-5 (AD 165).
[428] Shaw 1996.
[429] Tert. *De Corona* 3: oblationes pro defunctis pro nataliciis annua die facimus.
[430] Erman 1907, 138.
[431] Wente 1982, 18.
[432] Montserrat 2004, 475
[433] Meskell 1999.
[434] *Stud.Pal.* XXII.56.29.
[435] *SB* XX.14503; Montserrat 1992.

[436] *P.Berlin* 3115 = de Cenival 1972, 189. Also, Smith 1987, 22-4.
[437] Frandsen 1992.
[438] Meskell 1999; Daszewski 1997, 2008.
[439] Venit 2002, 124-45.
[440] Montserrat 1992, 304. Cf. *P.Oxy.* III.494.24.
[441] *Stud.Pal.* XXII.56.26; *P.Mich.Inv.* 243.
[442] Wagner et al 1985, 88.
[443] Dio. Sic. 1.83.2. Cf. Hdt. 2.65.

VII.3. Conclusion

A synthesis of different types of documents allows better understanding of the role of dogs in Graeco-Roman Egypt. Literary sources highlight dogs' position in the myth of Isis and Osiris and their association with chthonic deities, which triggered canine reverence through Pharaonic and Graeco-Roman times. The goddess Isis asked the Egyptian priests and inhabitants to venerate animals and pay to them the same honour they gave to Osiris in lifetime and after death. The dog was primarily divinised because of its outstanding position in the Osirian legend, let alone other exceptional capabilities. The priests took charge of both sacred and votive dogs in temple precincts and hypogea, whereas the inhabitants were responsible for family dogs. Dogs' mummies not only perpetuated the role of the dog and Anubis in the Osirian myth, but also served as guardians and companions of the givers and dead in the journey to the underworld. The connection between the dog/the dog-headed Anubis and Osiris guaranteed the continuity of dog's symbolism in Graeco-Roman Egypt, where the 'dog-headed one' participated in funeral processions to the necropolis as well as public processions of the festivals of Isis and Serapis in Egypt and Rome. House occupants performed certain mourning rituals after the demise of their dogs, strongly matching those offered to Osiris by Isis and Anubis. Dead dogs were ultimately taken to be embalmed and buried in their final destination, the necropolis, where the god Anubis was the master.

The journey of the dead from the house, the earthly dwelling, to the tomb, the everlasting abode, encompassed different stages of rituals: the ekphora; the peristolē; the kēdeia, and the apostolē and beyond. These ritual processes mirror different episodes and symbolic acts, which found their root in the Osirian myth of death (dismemberment) and rebirth (mummification and ritual recitations). The primary mourning four-day period of the ekphora imitates the mourning period for Osiris, culminating with the discovery of the god's corpse ready then for embalmment by Anubis. The carrying forth of the corpse to the embalming workshop introduced the peristolē or mummification process, which normally lasted for seventy days, corresponding with the movement of the Dog Star Sirius. Sometimes it took up to seventy-two days, corresponding with the fellow conspirators of Seth who murdered Osiris. Through mummification, the peristolē was physically meant to preserve the corpse in an imitation of the first mummy of Osiris. Moreover, the lamentation and glorification texts recited over the departed body were originally designed for the benefit of Osiris. Once embalmed, mummies were kept in houses for some time before burial as part of a domestic cult of the dead during the kēdeia. In addition to the funerary procession, the apostolē is marked with the tribunal, the Opening of the Mouth ritual, and the funerary banquet. Only three domestic and funerary structures are involved in the processing of the dead: the house, the embalming workshop, and the tomb. The house was the bridge through which the embalming workshop and the grave were connected. From the house began the ekphora-procession of the corpse to the mummification workshop. Again, the house was the starting point for the apostolē-procession to the sepulchre. The house therefore served as the node of the different steps of the post-mortem journey of the deceased to the necropolis.

General conclusion

Although the Graeco-Roman period is characterised by the diversity of domestic properties, urban housing appears to have been more diverse than rural housing in Egypt. The bath-house, the oikia dipurgia, and the oikia tripurgia were closely associated with wealthy families, including magistrates. Houses were not only places of rest, safety, and privacy, but also arenas for different forms of ritual activities associated with Graeco-Roman and Egyptian cultural traditions and through which the occupants had the potential to express their personal and social identities. There was a close relationship between the house and its residents. Equally, there was a tendency to create an imposing house frontage, which asserted the resident's social status and marked the boundary between the private and public. The front door was a liminal zone between public and private space, and had some unclear religious significance. As a private and semi-public area, the space before the front door of houses served as a social and religious focus times of gatherings around certain rituals. On the 9th of Thoth and on the 15th of Pachon, the front door had incorporated the public space before it, forming together a spatial framework where the residents respectively sacrificed fish and pigs. By performing rituals related to their cultural and religious life, the house occupants asserted aspects of their personal and social identities within society. These rites probably enabled the participants to promote a sense of belonging to their local community in the domestic sphere.

On the 13th of Epeiph, the inhabitants burnt lamps in great quantity for the goddess Athena-Neith in Sais, Esna, and elsewhere in Egypt. Although the illumination of lamps was associated with Athena-Neith, it seems that the act of illumination commemorates the search for and discovery of the body of Osiris. References in the temple of Esna to rituals accompanied by the lighting of lamps in honour of Neith can be connected to similar references in the mythological episodes involving the death and resurrection of Osiris. People probably kindled lamps within and around houses to commemorate this part of the Osirian myth. The internal arrangement and mural decoration of houses explicitly confirm that the domestic space exceeded its basic function as an ephemeral abode of the living. The house had important economic, social, religious, and funerary functions. The central courtyard was a focus of domestic and other forms of ritual activities. Other forms of social ceremonies like birthdays, the mallokouria, the epikrisis, and wedding ceremonies were also celebrated within the house. The performance of these social practices enabled the hosts to express the wealth of their home and assert their social status and position within the local community to their guests. Although the precise location of such social activities within the house remains uncertain, the central light-courtyard or the domestic pylon could be easily used for such ceremonies, particularly given the presence of triclinia within the pylon and the spacious measurement and use of the courtyard as the kitchen of the house. The *kline* of Serapis is confirmed in the Serapeum and other temples as well as private houses; however, the difference between the *kline* in temples and houses is vague. The performance of domestic rituals is a manifestation of the family's social identity.

Inhabitants in Graeco-Roman Egypt experienced religion in all spheres of their life, including the domestic. Papyri, figurines made of terracotta, stone, and other material, and mural paintings on domestic shrines and elsewhere in the house confirm a domestic cult of Graeco-Roman and Egyptian deities in the house. The visual and physical presence of deities in the domestic property was an integral part of the Graeco-Romano-Egyptian culture. Archaeological and other material remains from houses cannot determine the ethnic and legal status of the residents, however. The occupants of many houses had a shared cultural heritage with Graeco-Roman and Egyptian traditions. The co-existence of Graeco-Egyptian religious themes and figures of Graeco-Roman and Egyptian deities in a number of houses indicates that the occupants of such houses had a mixture of differing cultural traditions. The shared cultural heritage is a prominent feature of Romano-Egyptian archaeology, and houses are no exception.

The house was not only a dwelling place of humans, but also an abode of animals held sacred through their association with traditional Egyptian deities. The demise of beloved animals such as dogs and cats stimulated the performance of certain rituals in the house. Family members who had passed away were kept in the house before their departure to the mummification workshop. After mummification, the embalmed corpse was given back to the family for the final preparation of burial. As part of the domestic cult of the dead, mummies were also kept in the house at least for some time before burial. The funeral procession began also from the house, through the village or town, until the interment of the corpse in the necropolis. In short, the house was the arena for different forms of social, religious, and funerary rites. Critical events in the inhabitants' lifecycle such as birth, adulthood, marriage, and death and their associated ceremonies all occurred largely within the house, which was the locus of different rites of passage of the people living in Graeco-Roman Egypt.

Appendix 1
Catalogue of Roman-period Houses

When compared to houses of the Roman period, Ptolemaic houses uncovered from Egypt are less documented. For a sample of houses of the Ptolemaic period, one can consult Husselman 1977. This catalogue will therefore focus on well-documented houses of Roman Egypt. It only draws on archaeological evidence from the Fayum and the Dakhla Oasis, both of which sites have produced the best documented evidence for houses in Roman Egypt. Domestic evidence in other sites, if any, is extremely fragmentary or not yet explored.

1. Houses in the Fayum, the Arsinoite:

1.1. A sample of houses at Karanis (Kom Aushim):

1.1.1. House C42
Location: Near granary C65.
Date: 2nd-3rd century.
Architecture: The house extends from street CS 23 on the east to a short passageway, CS 30, on the west. The entrance from CS 23 led into an open courtyard, which had a stone pavement and contained two stone milling and storage jars. The house measures 7 m from north to south and 4 m from west to east, with an added room, D, that measures 3×4 m on the west. Apart from the courtyard, the house consists of six rooms: two in the underground level, two on the ground floor and two in the second storey. The two basement rooms, F and G, had vaulted ceilings and windows in the walls. Room D has three windows and four cupboard niches in the walls. A door opened into a stairway, which leads into the large room C, which had two windows in its eastern wall and two in the northern wall, each window with a sloping sill and a cupboard niche below.
Finds: A stone milling jar and storage jar were found in the courtyard and 11 pieces of household glassware, 25 pieces of glass in two jars, terracotta lamps, glass beads and several carved bone amulets were found in the basement room F.
Bibliography: Harden 1936, 36-7; Husselman 1979, 67-8, plans 25-6.

1.1.2. House C43
Location: Near granary C65.
Date: 2nd-3rd century.
Architecture: The house originally overlooked three streets: CS 32 on the north; CS 31 on the west; and CS 48 on the south. It adjoined house C45 on the east. Like house C42, house C43 consists of underground rooms and two storeys. The ground level contains a courtyard, which had not direct entrance from a street, but could only be entered through room E on the north. It was divided into five bins and a long storage room M on the west. The two vaulted rooms in the basement, H and G, were constructed with stone slabs set in mud mortar, and were divided into bins by low mud-brick walls. A stairway around a rectangular pillar led from the underground level to the ground and second floors.
Finds: None.
Bibliography: Husselman 1979, 67-8, plans 27-8.

1.1.3. House C45
Location: East of House C43.
Date: 2nd-3rd century.
Architecture: The main part of house C45 consists of two underground rooms built of stone slabs and mud mortar, two on the ground floor and two in the second storey. To the south were three large courtyards. The courtyard C on the west was paved with slabs of limestone. The large courtyard on the east was shared with the neighbouring house C47. The main entrance to the house was from CS 32 on the north into room J. An interesting feature in the entrance doorway is the slot through which the bolt was drawn. It is framed by a carving in the form of an Egyptian temple doorway, the lintel of which is curved outward in imitation of the cavetto cornice and rests on jambs like square pilasters. There is a cupboard niche in room J, and a domestic shrine with an unidentified painting in room B.
Finds: A water jar stand was uncovered along the north wall next to the doorway from courtyard C into room J.
Bibliography: Husselman 1979, 41, 60, plans 20-30, pls. 25, 62b, 65a, 69a, 94b.

1.1.4. House C50/51
Location: Near granary C65.
Date: 2nd-3rd century.
Architecture: This house was bordered on the east by CS46 and on the south by CS52. The main part of house C50/51 measures 7.5 m square. House C50/51 provides a good example of the use of concave construction of outer walls. The foundation walls were made of limestone set in mud mortar. The outer entrance doorway had door bolts and a door bar. This house had two underground vaulted rooms which are divided into compartments by low walls of mud brick. These rooms had no windows, but only air vents in the floor of the two rooms above them. In addition to the basement rooms, the house had a ground floor, a first floor and a second floor. The walls of the large room C51 A were plastered and covered with a black wash. The room had a window in its north wall, beneath which there was a domestic shrine surmounted by a shell and flanked by two columns, the capitals of which had two helices set back to back.
Finds: A long storage jar was found in the domestic shrine.

Bibliography: Husselman 1979, 69-70, plans 31-7, pls. 13a, 42, 47a-b, 58, 62a, 66b, 67a, 73b, 80a; Davoli 1998, 82.

1.1.5. House C56
Location: Near granary C65.
Date: 2nd-3rd century.
Architecture: The foundation walls of house C56 were made of limestone set in mud mortar. The main entrance to house C56 was overlooking street CS52. Before this doorway there was a low wall, 1m high, which served as a windbreak. The house consisted of an underground floor and three stories above the street level. The main entrance led into a large room, G, from which a door led into the stairway passage H, which in turn led down to the underground rooms and up to the first and second floors. The courtyard is located in the rear part on the ground floor. It served as the kitchen of the house, where ovens and bins for grain storage are located. Under the courtyard there were four underground vaulted storage chambers.
Finds: None.
Bibliography: Husselman 1979, 71-2, plans 38-9, pl. 8b.

1.1.6. House C57
Location: Near granary C65.
Date: 2nd-3rd century.
Architecture: House C57 is located to the west of house C62. It overlooks street CS52 on the south and street CS46 on the west. It consists of an underground floor, a ground floor and either a flat roof or a second storey, which is now completely damaged. Like other houses in this area in Karanis, the foundation walls of house C57 were made of stone set in mud mortar. The underground floor is divided into a number of vaulted rooms for storage. The ground floor consisted of a courtyard, a large room, D, and the stairway passage. The stairway led down to the basement rooms and up either to a flat roof or a second storey. The underground room J is only reached by a trapdoor in the floor of room D above it. Entrance to room D is from the courtyard. In the east wall of room D there is a large domestic shrine, with engaged columns supporting a wooden architrave. It is flanked on either side by plain rectangular niches or openings for holding lamps.
Finds: Storage jars.
Bibliography: Husselman 1979, 72-3, plans 42-3, pl. 70a.

1.1.7. House C59
Location: Near granary C65.
Date: 2nd-3rd century.
Architecture: House C59 was closely connected with houses C56, C62 and C65 by the passageway C59S. The main entrance of the house is approached from street CS46. It led into the main part of the house, which consists of room M on the south and room C on the north, with the stairway unit and a small room. Beneath room C there were two under ground rooms, each reached by a trapdoor in the floor of room C. There is no evidence of a second storey. The stairway did not descend below the ground floor level. A doorway led from room M to the courtyard areas, K and L. In L there was a mill base and a grain bin, and in K an oven.
Finds: A mill base, a grain bin, and an oven.
Bibliography: Husselman 1979, 73, plans 44-5.

1.1.8. House C60
Location: Near granary C65.
Date: 2nd-3rd century.
Architecture: In the north wall to the left side of the doorway into room B in House C60, and on the same level as the lintel of the doorway, there is a rectangular domestic shrine, which has a frame of moulded mud plaster and is surmounted by a projecting cornice of plaster.
Finds: None.
Bibliography: Husselman 1979, 47.

1.1.9. House C62
Location: Near granary C65.
Date: 2nd-3rd century.
Architecture: The house consisted of an underground floor and two stories above the street level. Like many other houses in Karanis, the underground walls of house C62 were made largely of stone, except for the mud-brick south wall. The only entrance from street CS52 into house C62 was through a narrow passage on the west. The ground floor consisted of a large room, C, on the north with the stairway unit and a smaller room on the north. The courtyard was located in the rear part of the house on the east. The architectural arrangement of the second floor followed that of the ground floor, except that there was no courtyard on the second storey.
Finds: None.
Bibliography: Husselman 1979, 72, plans 40-1.

1.1.10. House C68
Location: Near granary C65.
Date: 2nd-3rd century.
Architecture: The lintel of the entrance-door of House C68 consists of four superimposed parts: a strip of wood projects slightly across the top of the lintel. Beneath this strip of wood is a heavy beam, which is curved to match the concave courses of bricks in the wall in which it was set and is held in place by means of tenons. Below this beam and supporting it on either side of the doorway is a series of smaller binding blocks with short facing strips of wood between them. Under these binding blocks, again on either side of the entrance doorway, is a long strip of wood supported by four blocks set horizontally into the wall. The doorway was locked by a wooden bolt, still *in situ*, set in a heavy case on the left side of the doorway.
Finds: None.
Bibliography: Husselman 1979, pl. 41.

1.1.11. House C71
Location: Near granary C65.
Date: 2nd-3rd century.
Architecture: At floor level in the south wall of House C71 in Karanisis a small domestic shrine, made of mud brick and plaster, taking the form of a portal. It rests on a rectangular base, measuring 41 cm in width, 39 cm in length and 20 cm in height. The shrine measures 36 cm in width and 43 cm in height; it consists of two pillars supporting a lintel, the top of which is moulded into a concave pattern in imitation of a cavetto cornice. At the front of each pillar is an attached column in relief.
Finds: None.
Bibliography: Husselman 1979, 47.

1.1.12. House C119
Location: Near granary C65.
Date: 2nd-3rd century.
Architecture: The back of the shell-niche of the domestic shrine of house C119 is curved and flanked by two engaged, fluted columns. The columns rest on high pedestals and support capitals with helices, beneath which are narrow bands moulded into a zigzag pattern. The helices look like those of Alexandrian capital Type II, where the helices set back to back and spring directly from the collar of acanthus leaves. However, the helices of this shrine are suspended from the arch and, extraordinarily, held upside down. The top of the curved shell-niche takes the shape of a shell surmounted by an arch, which consists of four decorated bands surmounted by a projecting arched course of bricks. Both the shell-niche and its surrounding frame are covered with a thin coat of white lime wash, and it measures about 1.5 m in width and 2.15 m in height. On either side of the niche is a small opening in the adjacent wall, possibly intended to hold brackets by which lamps for the domestic shrine could be clasped.
Finds: None.
Bibliography: Husselman 1979, 30, fig. 54.

1.2. Houses at Soknopaiou Nesos (Dimê):

The area excavated on the east side of the temple precinct of Soknopaiou Nesos contains four houses, II 201, II 202, II 203 and II 204, which formed an irregular block or *insula*. The east half of the *insula* is occupied by the large House II 201, while the west half contains the smaller Houses II 201, II 203, and II 204. The Roman coins which were found in the houses range from Augustus to Antoninus Pius. The earliest datable papyrus uncovered from the *insula* dates to Claudius and the latest to 215. Based on papyri and coins, the *insula* was occupied from Augustus to Caracalla. It was probably abandoned at some time between 215 and 250.

1.2.1. House II 201
Location: East Area.
Date: 1st-3rd century.
Measurements: It measures 18.80 m from north to south and 17.20 m from east to west.
Architecture: House II 201 is square in plan. The main, single entrance of the house opens directly into an anteroom, A, which gives access to rooms D and E. Room E leads into other rooms in this floor. The northeast room, H, served as a kitchen, with a storage bin and baking ovens. From the anteroom a stairway leads up to the upper floor or floors and down to the basement. The walls of the ground-floor rooms of the house were not preserved above the window sills, and its upper floor or floors had completely disappeared. The underground rooms had vaulted ceilings and measured 4 m high. They have windows with sloping sills in addition to air vents opening through the floors of the rooms above. There are two secret chambers in this house, one under the stairs leading from the antechamber to the underground floor, and the other under the passage between rooms D and F. The first is entered through a trap door concealed in the stairway, while the second is approached via a trapdoor set in the passage above. This house had been stripped of its furnishings and decorations in antiquity.
Finds: None.
Bibliography: Boak 1932, 522-3; Boak 1935, 6-14, figs. 4-7; Davoli 1998, 46-7, fig. 7.

1.2.2. Houses II 202, II 203 and II 204
Location: East Area.
Date: 1st-3rd century, based on datable papyri and coins.
Architecture: Only the underground floors of Houses II 202, II 203, and II 204 are intact, but these and the adjacent courtyards yielded a considerable amount of pottery, furniture, coins, and papyri. Apart from the stone pavements of some rooms, there is little worthy of note in their layout or construction. Like those of Karanis, the courtyards of houses at Dimê served as both stables and kitchens, where storage bins and baking ovens are found.
Wall-paintings: Fragmentary wall paintings were found only in Houses II 202 and II 204. The painting in House II 202 was on the east wall of the southeast room D. Only the forepart of a horse and a rider are still visible. It was probably a representation of the Thracian rider-god Heron, of whom a representation was preserved in House B50 at Karanis. In House II 204, the representation was painted on the white plaster, which originally covered the north wall of the narrow passage D, which had a domestic shrine. On the back wall of the niche was a group of two standing figures, a male on the right and a female on the left, facing outward. To the left of each figure was a small horned incense altar, over which each extended the left hand, while the right hand was folded across the chest. Due to their bad state of preservations, the scenes of the side walls of the niche could not be interpreted. Parts of the scenes on the walls to the right and left of the niche, however, could still be identified. To the right of the niche was the lower part of an incense altar. Next to the altar a tall palm branch was depicted on a pot. Still farther to the right stood the crocodile healed-god Sobek or Soknopaios, who is shown holding a palm branch in his upraised left hand and facing toward the niche. Above Soknopaios are the remains of a chariot, a bull, and

an unidentified object. To the left of the niche are parts of an incense altar, a palm branch, a bird, and a bull.
Finds: Papyri, coins, storage jars, baking ovens, and stone mortars.
Bibliography: Boak 1932, 523; Boak 1935, 6-14, figs 4-7; Davoli 1998, 46-7, fig. 11.

1.2.3. Houses on the West Area
Location: West Area.
Date: 1st-3rd century.
Architecture: The area excavated on the west side of the temple precinct revealed four distinct levels, each representing a different occupation period. The top level corresponded in date to the complex cleared on the east area. It contained the underground floors of 13 houses bounded by streets on the north, east and south and on the west by the town limit, which was formed by the doorless outer walls of houses and brick walls closing the ends of streets.
Finds: Coins, papyri, ostraca, pottery and household utensils.
Bibliography: Boak 1932, 523; Davoli 1998, 46-7, fig. 10.

1.3. Houses at Bacchias (Kom Umm el-Atl):

In 1993, the mission of the Universities of Bologna and Lecce excavated the northeast side of the town, where six structures numbered as I, II, II, IV, V, and VI were brought to light. Only structures I, III, and V have been identified as houses.
Location: Northeast of Bacchias.
Date: 3rd-4th century, based on datable pottery sherds.
Architecture: The houses of Bacchias are built in mud-brick. Stratigraphical evidence confirms that House I was constructed at different times and was occupied on two levels. The lowest phase preceded structure II, which appears to be an entrance gate to the town from the north, and the highest phase was probably contemporaneous with it. The house has an external court served as a kitchen, with a fireplace and many pottery fragments datable to the Roman period. To the south of House I is structure III, which has been identified as a tower-house. House III consists of two external stairs, one internal stair constructed in two flights, a large room and two smaller rooms. At the rear of House III is a small courtyard, where a large jar containing cereals was inserted into the floor. House V has not yet been excavated.
Finds: Too damaged coins, fragments of pottery, glass and faience.
Bibliography: Piacentini 1996, 57-60, fig. 1; Davoli 1998, 121-22, figs. 47-9, 53.

1.4. Houses at Philadelphia (Kom el-Kharab el-Kebir):

Location: *Insula* D 6.
Date: 1st-4th century.
Architecture: In *insula* D 6 at Philadelphia, one of the houses has been roughly dated to the Roman period. The house is square in plan, and consists of an entrance leading to a court, around which a number of rooms are built. The walls of this house are painted so as to reproduce coloured marbles. Inside one of the niches, the underside of a representation with tendrils and part of a human figure had been preserved. A picture painted on a wooden panel of the same type as those which adorned the mummies from Roman times, still with its frame, is also found in this house. This was possibly hanging from one of the walls.
Finds: A wooden panel.
Bibliography: Davoli 1998, 12, fig. 62.

1.5. Houses at Tebtunis (Kom Umm el-Boreigat):

1.5.1. House No. 1100
Location: East of the temple of Soknebtunis.
Date: 1st-2nd centuries, based on datable Greek and demotic papyri.
Architecture: House No. 1100 is rectangular in plan, measuring 9.80 × 8.40 m; it consists of four rooms separated by a long corridor leading to a courtyard on the north side. The brick walls of the house were plastered and still retain fragments of frescoes with unidentified themes inside the domestic shrines, while those in stone were coated with stucco, with decorative mouldings still partially preserved.
Finds: Terracotta figurines, lamps and various Greek and demotic papyri.
Bibliography: Davoli 1998, 188-9, fig. 88.

1.5.2. House No. 3000
Location: East of the temple of Soknebtunis.
Date: 1st-2nd centuries.
Architecture: It measures 6.60 × 6.80 m, and consists of two large rooms, one of which has wall niches whose interpretation remains uncertain. Two small cellars are located below this room. The house had two periods of occupation: first, the Ptolemaic period (first century BC), in which the cellars were in use; and the second, the Roman period (first-second century), when the cellars fell out of use.
Finds: None.
Bibliography: Davoli 1998, 187, fig. 87.

1.5.3. House No. 3200
Location: East of the temple of Soknebtunis.
Date: 1st-2nd centuries, based on Greek and Demotic papyri.
Architecture: House No. 3200 is located in the northeast corner of the insula. The house underwent a first phase of construction during the Ptolemaic period. It was re-inhabited from the second half of the first century until the beginning of the third century. It is square in plan; the main entrance of the house is located on the north and is approached by a stone staircase.
Finds: None.
Bibliography: Davoli 1998, 190, fig. 94a.

1.6. Houses at Kom Medinet Ghoran:

Location: Kom Medinet Ghoran.
Date: Roman.
Architecture: House A in Kom A is square in plan and consists of 9 rooms, two of which, according to the interpretation of Pierre Jouguet, were open; a flight of stairs leads to a terrace or maybe to a second floor. A room (G) has been recognized as a kitchen for the presence of a domestic oven in one of the corners and ashes on the floor, while another (B) was used as a bathroom where it has a bath carved in stone. Two interior doors and windows, in Egyptian style, were made of stone and decorated with a cavetto cornice and a torus moulding.
Finds: None.
Bibliography: Jouguet 1901, 380-411; Davoli 1998, 218, fig. 100.

1.7. Houses at Narmuthis (Kom Medinet Maadi):

Location: East of the dromos of the temple of Narmuthis.
Date: Roman.
Architecture: Ten structures have been excavated along the east side of the dromos of the temple of Narmuthis. Based on stylistic grounds, some of these buildings have been identified as houses. These houses are generally in a poor state of preservation; they are all built in mud-brick with abundant use of wood and stone, particularly for stairs and windows. They form a single block of houses, and are intersected by narrow alleys. Like other houses in the Fayum and countrywide, the houses at Narmuthis usually had a central courtyard, which was probably used as a kitchen, a number of rooms on the ground floor and underground vaulted cellars.
Finds: None.
Bibliography: Davoli 1998, 234-5, fig. 113.

1.8. Houses at Theadelphia (Kharabit Ihrit):

Location: Southwest of Theadelphia.
Date: Roman.
Architecture: The houses were preserved to a height of about 5 m and had been buried by desert sand, which is accumulated by the action of wind. At the time of their excavations, all houses were empty and all household goods had been removed. The walls, the thickness of which is 50-80 cm, were built with mud mixed with a high proportion of straw and wooden beams, which were inserted horizontally and gave them more stability. The use of wooden beams set vertically in the corner is observed in only one house. Stone elements are rarely used in houses. For example, a door lintel carved in limestone is used in a partially destroyed house. In other houses, it was found that the stone was used in the bases and capitals of columns and brick pillars that decorated the niches inside the houses, and rarely in the threshold of the door. One of the houses is preserved to a height of 4 m, and has an L-shape. It is divided into four rooms, with a central courtyard. It has an internal staircase leading upstairs. The staircase consists of three unequal mud-brick steps built around a central pillar of mud-brick reinforced with wood. Under the staircase there is a small room that was probably used as a cellar. Another house, larger and more elaborated, has been interpreted due to its decorative details as the residence of an important person, perhaps an officer, if not as a real public office. The entrance had been destroyed by illegal excavations, but the other rooms, seven in total, had not been touched. Near the entrance there is a ladder-like structure in a worse state of preservation. At the centre of the building there was a big rectangular room, interpreted as a courtyard, which gives access to the other rooms and from which the house was lighted. The room more interesting is square, 6 × 5 m, and lies in the south-east side, opening onto the courtyard with three gates that were originally meant to be closed with wooden doors. In the walls there is a series of three rectangular niches, with half-pillars decorated with brick bases and capitals in limestone. These are decorated with carved and painted motifs like vines, grapes, and acanthus leaves.
Finds: None.
Bibliography: Rubensohn 1905, 1-25; Davoli 1998, 281-2, fig. 136.

1.9. Houses at Euhemeria (Qasr el-Banat):

Location: Southeast of Euhemeria.
Date: 1st-3rd century AD.
Architecture: The houses are partially destroyed. Like those of Theadelphia, they were built of mud-brick with the rare use of stone structural and decorative elements. There are very few stone columns and jambs of doors. Rooms were rarely used as cellars. One of the houses still retained part of the plaster on which was painted a series of figures, of which only the lower part is still recognizable. Papyri dating from 1st to 3rd century AD were found in some houses, while in a domestic oven of a house more than seventy *ostraca* are found.
Finds: Papyri and *ostraca*.
Bibliography: Grenfell, Hunt and Hogarth 1900, 47-50; Davoli 1998, 281-2, fig. 136.

1.10. Houses at Dionysias (Qasr Qarun):

Location: East of Dionysias.
Date: 1st-4th century, based on coins found in the houses.
Architecture: To the east of Dionysias, a small house with an adjoining public bathroom was excavated. The house was built out of mud-brick, but the main entrance, located on the west side, had limestone door jambs. There was a second door on the east side, which connects the house with the bathroom. The largest house at Qasr Qarun was composed of 10 rooms, being divided into two groups by a central corridor. The main entrance is located on the south side of the corridor. There was a

staircase leading once to the upper storey, the first three steps of the staircase were made of limestone and the other steps were made of mud-brick reinforced with wood. The coins found in the houses of Qasr Qarun date to the Roman period, including Constantine.

Wall-paintings: In one of the rooms of the largest house, a fresco was partially preserved. It depicts three male figures in frontal view. One of the figures wears red tunic with an armour lace. This fresco was the subject of a long iconographical analysis; however its subject-matter cannot be identified. It has been suggested that the fresco depicts a religious theme, in which the central figure was identified as the god Heron, though this has not been confirmed.

Finds: Coins.

Bibliography: Schwartz and Wild 1950, 51-62; Davoli 1998, 305-06, figs. 150-2.

2. Houses in the Dakhla Oasis, the Thebaid:

2.1. Houses at Kellis (Ismant El-Kharab):

During its recent excavations at Kellis, the Dakhleh Oasis Project of Columbia University has focused on houses. However, the site is still under excavations and any investigations are preliminary.

2.1.1. Houses Nos. 1, 2, and 3

Location: Kellis.

Date: 4th century, based on papyri and coins.

Architecture: The three houses form a single block; they are rectangular is shape and have different layouts. The internal arrangement of houses 1 and 2 is simple. None of the two houses has an *aithrion*; however, both houses had an *aule*. House 1 consists of an *aule* which gives access to a long corridor, around which eleven unequal rooms are clustered. House 2 consists of an *aule* and 9 rooms. The layout of House 3 is more complicated. It consists of an entrance hall, which leads into a passageway, which leads into two successive courts. The court nearer the entrance served as an *aithrion*, around which the other rooms were clustered. It was here that hundreds of fragments of papyri and wooden boards and a small number of coins were found. The *aithrion* gave access to eight rooms, although only six rooms had direct access to the court. The rear court functioned as an *aule*, where animal pins and evidence of food preparation have come to light.

Finds: Papyri and coins.

Bibliography: Hope 1988, 160-78; Gardner and Lieu 1996; Knudstad and Frey1999, 189-214; Alston 2002, 105-7, figs. 3.15-16.

2.1.2. House No. B/3/1

Location: Area B.

Date: 2nd-3rd century, based on wall-paintings.

Architecture: It is a mud-brick structure, measuring 28 m from north to south and 24 m from east to west. It was entered from the north through a 14 × 14.8 m open area. The entrance room leads into a square (10.6 × 10.8 m) room (1b), in which stand the lower parts of four substantial columns, which have two torus mouldings at their bases. To the south of room 1b lies a slightly smaller (9.8 × 7 m) room (1a). To the west of room 1b lies a rectangular (7.2 × 5.6 m) space, which has two rooms (4-5) to the south, one (7) to the north and two rooms (9-10) to the east. To the west of room 1a are 2 rooms (2-3). To the east of room 1a lie three rooms, one (12) has a large semi-circular niche at its south side and two (13-14) have painted decoration.

Wall-paintings: In the five rooms examined, Hope and Whitehouse, the excavators, have identified six different decorative schemes, which were employed in the house; two variations on panelled décor; 'wallpaper'; and three designs incorporating columns. At the northern end of room 1a, the main zone of the wall is divided into large panels with a motif at the centre of each. The details of the motifs are difficult to identify. The majority show a bird, apparently a cockerel. The panel nearer the door shows a female face in frontal view. At the southern end of room 1a, the main zone is decorated with a 'wallpaper' pattern of intersecting circles. The dado is decorated with oblong panels framed by black and yellow bands. The ceiling fragments show parts of a geometric scheme with golden-yellow busts of Isis and Serapis-Helios. The goddess Isis is shown with her characteristic headdress, consisting of two bovine horns and a solar disc and two plumes in between. The god Serapis-Helios is depicted with a thick beard and a modius upon his head. As in room 3, Corinthian capitals of Alexandrian Type 1 are depicted atop the columns painted on the north wall.

Finds: None.

Bibliography: Hope and Whitehouse 2006, 312-28.

2.2. Houses at Trimithis (Amheida):

The excavations at Trimithis so far have focused on three areas of this large site: a centrally located upper-class fourth-century house with wall paintings, an adjoining school and underlying remains of a Roman bath complex; a more modest house of the third century; and the temple hill with remains of the Temple of Thoth built in the first century and of earlier structures. Architectural conservation has protected and partly restored two standing funerary monuments, a mud-brick pyramid and a tower tomb, both date to the Roman period.

2.2.1. The House of Serenos

Location: Area 2.

Date: 4th century AD, based on coins and ostraca.

Architecture: The House of Serenos consists of a central courtyard with decorated rooms to the west and south, utilitarian rooms to the north and additional undecorated rooms to the east. The material culture found in the mud-brick house suggest that the major period of occupation was sometime between the late third through the middle of the fourth century. The latest datable coins and ostraca date to the reign of Constantius II, which gives a *terminus ante quem* for the occupation of the house and the execution of the wall paintings.

Wall-paintings: The representational media in the painted room of this house commemorate Greek and Roman heritage through mythology. The visible wall paintings depict several Greek myths, predominantly from Homer. To the left of door of the painted room leading into the courtyard, Perseus is shown holding the head of Medusa, while he rescues Andromeda from a sea monster. To the right of door leading into the courtyard, Eurycleia is depicted washing Odysseus' feet while he reclines on an elevated stool covered in sheepskin. A noble woman, presumably Penelope, sits to the right of these figures and looks off into the distance rather than at Odysseus. The eastern wall of the same room is divided into two horizontal registers containing smaller painted figures. Only the lower portion of the upper register and the geometric zone survive *in situ*. A possible temple is represented on the left with four columns and an architrave and the city walls below. To the right of the temple, a woman labelled as Polis, gestures toward the temple with her right hand and holds a golden sceptre in her left. To the right of Polis, the eastern wall depicts Aphrodite and Ares caught in the act of adultery. Hephaestus uses an invisible net of chains to hold them while a group of inquisitive male gods steals a look as the drama unfolds. The west wall of the room is only partially preserved. The figured scene portrays a family at dinner. Three adult males and a woman recline on a couch and listen to a musician to their left. A male child stands next to the musician. The south wall of the room is the most poorly preserved wall of the painted room. It contained a large niche, to the right of which only a horse's head above a reclining woman wearing a turban remain *in situ*.

Finds: Coins and *ostraca*.

Bibliography: Mills 1980, 1993, 1998; Boozer 2005; Walter 2005; Whitehouse 2005.

2.2.2. The House of Area 1

Location: Area 1.

Date: 2nd century.

Architecture: This house is located at Area 1 in the northern side of the site. It is smaller than Serenos' house and follows a square plan. It consists of an entrance, leading onto a central courtyard, around which a number of rooms were arranged. The building itself is considerably damaged by the strong sand-laden wind. The material culture and botanical remains were preserved to a higher degree than the house in Area 2. This house used slightly different building methods than the House of Serenos, where brick-laying are similar to those used in the Fayum region. Ceramics and associated demotic texts suggest that this house might be slightly earlier date than the house in Area 2. Soil samples taken from this second house have better preserved botanical remains than elsewhere at Trimithis. High concentrations of desiccated rodent remains have been found in and around intact vessels on the floor of one room. A piece of a Djed-pillar amulet was also found in the house.

Finds: Ceramics, botanical remains, ceramics with demotic texts, and a Djed-pillar amulet.

Bibliography: Boozer 2005, 20-1.

Bibliography

Abbas, E. S. 2010. *The Lake of Knives and the Lake of Fire: Studies in the Topography of Passage in Ancient Egyptian Religious Literature*, BAR International Series 2144, Oxford.

Abbas, E. and Abdelwahed, Y. 2014. 'The Domestic Pylon in the Light of Greek Papyri', *Rosetta* 15, 1-27.

Abdelwahed, Y. 2015. *Egyptian Cultural Identity in the Architecture of Roman Egypt (30 BC-AD 325)*, Archaeopress Roman Archaeology 6, Oxford.

Abdelwahed, Y. 2016. 'Two Festivals of the God Serapis in Greek Papyri', *Rosetta* 18, 1-15.

Abu-Loughd, L. 1993. 'Islam and the Gendered Discourses of Death', *IJMES* 25:2, 187-205.

Allen, T. G. 1974. *The Book of the Dead or Going Forth by Day*, Chicago.

Allen, M. L. 1985. *The Terracotta Figurines from Karanis: A Study of Technique, Style and Chronology of Fayoumic Coroplastics 1-2*, Ann Arbour.

Alliot, M. 1949. *Le culte d'Horus à Edfou au temps des Ptolémées* I, Bd'É 20, Cairo.

Allison, P. 2001. 'Using the Material and written Sources: Turn of the Millennium Approaches to Roman Domestic Space' *AJA* 105:2, 181-208.

Alston, R. 1995. *Soldier and Society in Roman Egypt: A Social History*, London and New York.

Alston, R. 1996. 'Conquest by Text: Juvenal and Plutarch on Egypt', in J. Webster and N. J. Cooper (eds.), *Roman Imperialism: Post-Colonial Perspectives*, Proceedings of a Symposium held at Leicester University in November 1994, 99-109.

Alston, R. 1997a. 'Ritual and Power in the Romano-Egyptian City', in H. M. Parkins (ed.), *Roman Urbanism: Beyond the Consumer City*, London and New York, 147-72.

Alston, R. 1997b. 'Changing Ethnicity: from the Egyptian to the Roman City', in T. Cornell and K. Lomas (eds.), *Gender and ethnicity in Ancient Italy*, London, 83-96.

Alston, R. 1997c. 'Houses and Household in Roman Egypt', in R. Laurence and A. Wallace-Hadrill (eds.), *Domestic Space in the Roman World: Pompeii and Beyond. JRA* Suppl. 22, Portsmouth, 25-39.

Alston, R. 2001. *The City in Roman and Byzantine Egypt*, London.

Alston, R. 2002. 'Reading Augustan Alexandria', *Ancient West & East* 1, 141-61.

Alston, R. and Alston, R. D. 1997. 'Urbanism and the Urban Community in Roman Egypt', *JEA* 83, 199-216.

Ammerman, R. M. 1991. 'The Naked Standing Goddess: A Group of Archaic Terracotta Figurines from Paestum', *AJA* 95:2, 203-30.

Andrews, C. 1994. *Amulets of Ancient Egypt*, London.

Anselmino, L. Bouchenaki, M. and Carandini, A. 1989. *Il castellum del Nador: Storia di una fattoria tra Tipasa e Caesarea, I-VI sec. d.C.*, Rome.

Anthes, R. 1928. *Die Felsinschriften von Hatnub*, UGAÄ 9, Leipzig.

Anti, C. 1931. 'Gli scavi della Missione archeologica italiana a Umm el Breighât (Tebtunis)', *Aegyptus* 11:3, 389-91.

Aravecchia, N., Dupras, T. L., Dzierzbicka, D., and Williams, L. 2015. 'The church at Amheida (ancient Trimithis) in the Dakhleh Oasis, Egypt: A bioarchaeological perspective on an Early Christian mortuary complex', *Bioarchaeology of the Near East* 9, 21-43.

Arnold, D. 1995. *An Egyptian Bestiary*, The Metropolitan Museum of Fine Art Bulletin, New York.

Arnold, D. 1999. *Temples of the Last Pharaohs*, Oxford.

Assmann, J. 1977. 'Die Verborgenheit des Mythos in Ägypten', *GM* 25, 7-43.

Assmann, J. 1989. 'Death and Initiation in the Funerary Religion of Ancient Egypt', in W. K. Simpson (ed.), *Religion and Philosophy in Ancient Egypt*, Yale Egyptological Studies 3, 135-59.

Assmann, J. 1995. *Egyptian Solar Religion in the New Kingdom: Re, Amun and the Crisis of Polytheism*, London and New York.

Assmann, J. 2001.*The Search for God in Ancient Egypt*, Ithaca.

Assmann, J. 2002. *Altägyptische Totenliturgien* I: *Totenlitugien in den Sargtexten des Mittleren Reiches*, Heidelberg.

Assmann, J. 2005. *Death and Salvation in Ancient Egypt*, Ithaca and London.

Assmann, J., Allen, J. P., Lloyd, A. B., Ritner, R. K., and Silverman, D. P. 1989. *Religion and Philosophy in Ancient Egypt*, New Haven.

Aufderheide, A. C., Zlonis, M., Cartmell, L. L., Zimmerman, M. R., Sheldrick, P., Cook, M. and Molto, J. E. 1999. 'Human Mummification Practices at Ismant el-Kharab', *JEA* 85, 197-210.

Aune, D. E. 1997. 'Amulets', in E. M. Meyers (ed.), *The Oxford Encyclopedia of Archaeology in the Near East*, Oxford, 113-15.

Badawy, A. 1966. *A History of Egyptian Architecture* II, Berkeley and Los Angeles.

Bagnall, R. S. and Frier, B. W. 1994. *The Demography of Roman Egypt*, Cambridge.

Bagnall, R. S. and Rathbone, D. W. 2004. *Egypt from Alexander to the Early Christians*, Los Angeles.

Bagnall, R., Davoli, P., Kaper, O. E., and Whitehouse, H. 2006. 'Roman Amheida: Excavating a Town in Egypt's Dakhla Oasis', Minerva 2006, 26-9.

Bailey, D. M. 2001. 'Lamps from the Sacred Animal Necropolis, North Saqqara and the Monastery of Apa Antinos', *JEA* 87, 119-33.

Baines, J. 1995. 'Origins of Egyptian Kingship', in D. O'Connor and P. Silverman (eds.), *Ancient Egyptian Kingship*, Leiden, New York, Köln, 95-156.

Barsh, R. L., Jones, J. M., and Suttles, W. 2006. 'History, Ethnography, and Archaeology of the Coast Salish Woolley-Dog', in L. M. Snyder and E. A. Moore (eds.), *Dogs and People in Social, Working, Economic or Symbolic Interaction*, Oxford, 1-11.

Beard, M. 2008. *Pompeii: The Life of a Roman Town*, London.

Beck, W. 1991. 'Dogs, Dwellings, and Masters: Ensemble and Symbol in the Odyssey', *Hermes* 119:2, 158-67.

Beinlich, H. 2006. 'Zwischen Tod und Grab: Tutanchamun und das Begräbnisritual', *SAK* 34, 17-31.

Bell, C. 1992. *Ritual Theory, Ritual Practice*, New York and Oxford.

Bell, H. I. 1940. 'Antinoopolis: A Hadrianic Foundation in Egypt', *JRS* 30 (2), 136-47.

Bell, H. I. 1942. 'P. Giss. 40 and the Constitutio Antoniniana', *JEA* 28, 39-49.

Bell, H. I. 1948. 'Popular Religion in Graeco-Roman Egypt I: The Pagan Period', *JEA* 34, 82-97.

Bell, H. I., Nock, A. D., and Thompson, H. 1933. *Magical Texts from a Bilingual Papyrus*, Oxford.

Belova, G. A. 2016. http://news.nationalgeographic.com.au/news/2008/01/080130-egypt-mummies.html (accessed on 20/32/2016) and http://news.softpedia.com/news/The-First-Dog-Mummies-Ever-Found-in-Egypt-77591.shtml (accessed on 20/03/2016).

Benaissa, A. 2010. 'The Onomastic Evidence for the God Hermanubis', *Proceedings of the Twenty-Fifth International Congress of Papyrology*, Ann Arbor, 67-76.

Bernal, M. G. 2006. *Black Athena: The Afroasiatic Roots of Classical Civilization III: The Linguistic Evidence*, New Jersey.

Bernand, É. 1969. *Inscriptions métriques de l'Égypte gréco-romaine: Recherches sur la poésie épigrammatique des Grecs en Égypte*, Paris.

Betz, H. D. 1986. *The Greek Magical Papyri in Translation, including the Demotic Spells*, Chicago.

Bierbrier, M. L. 1997. *Portraits and Masks: Burial Customs in Roman Egypt*, London.

Blackman, A. M. 1915. *Les Temples immergés de la Nubie: The Temple of Bigeh*, Cairo.

Blackman, A. M. and Fairman, 1942. 'The Myth of Horus at Edfu II.C: The Triumph of Horus over His Enemies: A Sacred Drama', *JEA* 28, 32-8.

Blackwood, R., Crossett, J., and Long, H. 1962. 'Gorgias 482b', *The Classical Journal* 57:7, 318-19.

Bleeker, C. J. 1958. 'Isis and Nephthys as Wailing Women', *Numen* 5:1, 1-17.

Boak, A. E. R. 1926. 'The University of Michigan's Excavations at Karanis: 1924-5', *JEA* 12, 19-21.

Boak, A. E. R. 1932. 'Archaeological Discussions: Dimê', *AJA* 36, 522-3.

Boak, A. E. R. 1935. *Soknopaiou Nesos: The University of Michigan Excavations at Dimê in 1931-32*, Ann Arbor.

Boak, A. E. R. 1937. 'The Organisation of Gilds in Graeco-Roman Egypt', *TAPA* 68, 212-20.

Boak, A. E. R. 1955. 'The Population of Roman and Early Byzantine Karanis', *Historia* 4, 157-62.

Boak, A. E. R. and Peterson, E. E. 1931. *Karanis: Topographical and Architectural Report of Excavations during the Seasons of 1924-8*, Ann Arbor.

Boddens-Hosang, L. 1985. 'The Birthday of Pharaoh', *Wepwawet* 1, 22-3.

Bonneau, D. 1991. 'Le sacrifice du porc et Liloïtion en Pachôn', *CdE* LXVI, 330-40.

Bonnet, H. 1952. *Reallexikon der ägyptischen Religionsgeschichte*, Berlin.

Booth, C. 2005. 'A Ptolemaic Terracotta Head in the Petrie Museum', *JEA* 91, 197-200.

Boozer, A. L. 2005. 'In Search of Lost Memories: Domestic Spheres and Identities in Roman Amheida, Egypt', *ISERP* Working Paper 05-07, New York, 1-36.

Boozer, A. L. 2015. *Amheida II: A Late Romano-Egyptian House in the Dakhla Oasis: Amheida House B2*, New Digital Publication from ISAW, New York.

Borchardt, L. 1897. *Die aegyptische Pflanzensäule: Ein Kapitel zur Geschichte des Pflanzenornaments*, Berlin.

Borg, B. 1997. 'The Dead as a Guest at Table? Continuity and Change in the Egyptian Cult of the Dead', in M. L. Bierbrier (ed.), *Portraits and Mask: Burial Customs in Roman Egypt*, London, 26-32.

Borg, B., Herberg, H., and Linfert, A. 2005. *Die antiken Skulpturen in Castle Howard*. Monumenta Artis Romanae xxxi, Wiesbaden.

Bourdieu, P. 1973. 'The Berber House', in M. Douglas (ed.), *Rules and Meanings: The Anthropology of Everyday Knowledge*, London, 98-110.

Bourdieu, P. 1977. *Outline of a Theory of Practice*, Cambridge.

Bourdieu, P. 1990. *The Logic of Practice*, translated by R. Nice, California.

Bowman, A. K. 1986. *Egypt after the Pharaohs (332 BC-AD 642) from Alexander to the Arab Conquest*, London.

Bowman, A. K. 1995. 'Public Buildings in Roman Egypt', *JRA* 5, 495-503.

Bowman, A. K. 2000. 'Urbanization in Roman Egypt', in E. Fentress (ed.), *Romanization and the City: Creation, Transformations, and Failures*, Portsmouth, 173-187.

Bowman, A. K. and Rathbone, D. 1992. 'Cities and Administration in Roman Egypt', *JRS* 82, 107-27.

Brewer, D., Clark, T., and Phillips, A. 2001. *Dogs in Antiquity. Anubis to Cerberus: The Origins of the Domestic Dog*, Waminster.

Bryce, T. R. 1990. 'The Death of Niphururiya and Its Aftermath', *JEA* 76, 97-105.

Budge, E. A. W. 1909. *The Book of the Dead*, London.

Budge, E. A. W. 1967. *The Egyptian Book of the Dead: (The Papyrus of Ani) Egyptian Text Transliteration and Translation*, New York.

Bunson, M. R. 2002. *Encyclopedia of Ancient Egypt*, New York.

Burkhalter, F. 1992. 'Le gymnase d'Alexandrie: centre administrative de la province romaine d'Égypte', *BCH* 116, 345-73.

Burr, D. 1933. 'The Terracotta Figurines', *Hesperia* 2:2, 184-94.

Burriss, E. E. 1935. 'The Place of the Dog in Superstition as Revealed in Latin Literature', *Classical Philology* 30:1, 32-42.

Budge, E. A. W. 1898. *The Chapters of Coming Forth by Day*, London.

Cadbury, A. 1990. 'Taken by Haros: Death in a Cycladic Village', *The Georgia Review* 44:3, 413-20.

Camp, J. M. 1980. *Gods and Heroes in the Athenian Agora*, Princeton.

Cannata, M. 2007. 'Social Identity at the Anubieion: A Reanalysis', *AJA* 111:2, 223-40.

Cannuyer, C. 2001. *Coptic Egypt: The Christians of the Nile*, New York.

Carroll, M. 2006. *Spirits of the Dead: Roman Funerary Commemoration in Western Europe*, Oxford.

Cartwright, C., Spaabaek, L. R., and Svoboda, M. 2011. 'Portrait Mummies from Roman Egypt: Ongoing Collaborative Research on Wood Identification', *The British Museum Technical Research Bulletin* 5, 49-58.

Cary, E. 1961. *The Roman Antiquities of Dionysus of Halicanassus* II, the Loeb Classical Library, Cambridge, Mass.

Chantraine, P. 1964. 'Grec ΑΙΘΡΙΟΝ', *Recherches de Papyrologie* 3, 7-15.

Chantraine, P. 1973. 'Grec ΠΥΛΩΝ et français Pylône', *Classica et Mediaevalia Dissertations* IX, 659-64.

Chapman, G. 2001. *Homer's Batrachomyomachia, Hymns and Epigrams*, Adamant Media Corporation.

Chapple, E. D. and Coon, C. S. 1942. *Principles of Anthropology*, New York.

Chassinat, É. 1934. *Le temple d'Edfou* XIII, Cairo.

Chassinat, É 1966. *Le mystère d'Osiris au mois de Khoiak*, Cairo.

Ciałowicz, K. M. 1992. 'La composition, le sens et la symbolique des scènes zoomorphes prédynastiques en relief. Les manches de couteaux', in R. Friedman and B. Adams (eds.), *The Followers of Horus. Studies dedicated to Michael Allen Hoffman*, Oxford, 247-58.

Clark, A. J. 2007. *Divine Qualities: Cult and Community in Republican Rome*, Oxford.

Clarke, J. R. 1991. *The Houses of Roman Italy 100 BC-AD 250: Ritual, Space, and Decoration*, Berkeley, Los Angeles, and Oxford.

Corcoran, L. H. 1997. 'Mysticism and the Mummy Portraits', in M. L. Bierbrier (ed.), *Portaits and Masks: Ritual Customs in Roman Egypt*, London, 45-53.

Cornelius, I., Swanepoel, L. C., du Plessis, A., and Slabbert, R. 2012. 'Looking inside Votive Creatures: Computed Tomography (ct) Scanning of Ancient Egyptian Mummified Animals in Iziko Museums of South Africa: A Preliminary Report', *Akroterion* 57, 29-148.

Counts, D. B. 1996. 'Regum Externorum Consuetudine: The Nature and Function of Embalming in Rome', *Classical Antiquity* 15:2, 189-202.

Crouch, D. 1998. 'The Street in the Making of Popular Geographical Knowledge', in N. R. Fyfe (ed.), *Images of the Street: Planning, Identity and Control in Public Space*, London and New York, 160-75.

Crum, W. E. 1930. *A Coptic Dictionary*, Oxford.

Daszewski, W. A. 1997. 'Mummy Portraits from Northern Egypt: The Necropolis in Marina el-Alamein', in M. L. Bierbrier (ed.), *Portraits and Masks: Burial Customs in Roman Egypt*, London, 59-65.

Daszewski, W. A. 2008. 'Graeco-Roman Town and Necropolis in Marina el-Alamein, *PAM* 20, 421-56.

David, D. 2007. 'Ancient Egypt', in Hinnells, J. R. (ed), *A Handbook of Ancient Religions*, Cambridge, 46-104.

Davies, D. 2008. 'Cultural Intensification: A Theory for Religion', in A. Day (ed.), *Religion and the Individual: Belief, Practice, Identity*, Ashgate Press, 7-18.

Davies, N. de G. 1903. *The Rock Tombs of El Amarna: The Tomb of Meryra*, London.

Davies, N. de G. 1924. 'A Peculiar Form of New Kingdom Lamp', *JEA* 40 (1), 9-14.

Davies, N. de G. 1927. *Two Ramesside Tombs at Thebes*, New York.

Davies, N. de G. 1929. 'The Town House in Ancient Egypt', *Metropolitan Museum Studies* 1 (2), 233-55.

Davoli, P. 1998. *L'archeologia urbana nel Fayyum di età ellenistica e romana*, Bologna.

Davoli, P. and Kaper, O. 2006. 'A New Temple for Thoth in the Dakhleh Oasis', *Egyptian Archaeology* 28, 12-14.

D'Aura, S., Lacovara, P. and Roehrig, C. 1988. *Mummies and Magic: The Funerary Arts of Ancient Egypt*, Boston.

Dawson, W. R. 1928. 'References to Mummification by Greek and Latin Authors', *Aegyptus* 9:1/2, 106-112.

De Buck, A. 1935. *The Egyptian Coffin Texts* 1, Chicago.

De Cenival, F. 1972. *Les associations religieuses en Égypte d'après les documents démotiques*, Cairo.

De Grossi Mazzorin, J. and Minniti, C. 2006. 'Dog Sacrifice in the Ancient World: A Ritual Passage', in L. M. Snyder and E. A. Moore (eds.), *Dogs and*

People in Social, Working, Economic or Symbolic Interaction, Oxford, 62-6.
Delia, D. 1991. *Alexandrian Citizenship during the Roman Principate*, Atlanta.
Delorme, J. 1960. *Gymnasion: Étudesur les Monuments consecré à l'Éducation en Grèce*, Paris.
Demarée, R. J. 1983. *The #X iQr n Ra-Stelae. On Ancestor Worship in Ancient Egypt*, Leiden.
De Vaux, R. 1966. *The Bible and the Ancient Near East*, London.
Dieleman, J. 2005. *Priests, Tongues, and Rites: The London-Leiden Magical Manuscripts and Translation in Egyptian Ritual (100-300 CE)*, Leiden.
Dillon, J. 1989. 'Plutarch and Second Century Platonism', in A. H. Armstrong (ed.), *Classical Mediterranean Spirituality*, London, 214-29.
Dixon, D. M. 1989. 'A Note on Some Scavengers of Ancient Egypt', *World Archaeology* 21:2, 193-7.
Dodson, A. 2009. 'Rituals Related to Animal Cults', in J. Dieleman and W. Wendrich (eds.), *UCLA Encyclopedia of Egyptology*, Los Angeles, 1-8. http://digital2.library.ucla.edu/viewItem.do?ark=21198/zz001nf7d0. Last accessed (14/3/2016).
Dombart, T. 1933. 'Zweitürmige Tempel-Pylon altaegyptischer Baukunst und seine religiöse Symbolik', *Egyptian Religion* 1, 87-98.
Donadoni, S. 1980. 'Karanis', in *LÄ* III, 327-8.
Donalson, M. D. 2003. *The Cult of Isis in the Roman Empire: Isis Invicta*, New York.
Douglas, N. 1928. *Birds and Beasts of the Greek Anthology*, London.
Doxey, D. M. 2001. 'Anubis', in D. B. Redford (ed.), *The Oxford Encyclopaedia of Ancient Egypt* I, Oxford, 97-8.
Dreyer, G., Engel, E.-M., Hartung, U., Hikade, T., Köhler, E. C., and Pumpenmeier, F. 1996. 'Umm el-Qaab: Nachuntersuchungen im frühzeitlichen Königsfriedhof: Vorbericht. 7/8', *MDAIK* 52, 11-81.
Drexhage, H.-J. 1991. *Preise, Mieten/Pachten, Kosten und Löhne im römischen Ägypten bis zum Regierungsantritt Diokletians*, St Katherinen.
DuQuesne, T., El-Sadeek, W., Razek, S.A., Hawass, Z.A. and Fatah, M.A. 2007. *Anubis, Upwawet and Other Deities: Personal Worship and Official Religion in Ancient Egypt*, Cairo.
Dunand, F. 1976. 'Lanternes gréco-romaines d'Égypte', *Dialogues d'histoire ancienne* 2, 71-97.
Dunand, F. 1979. *Religion populaire en Égypte romaine*, Leiden.
Dunand, F. and Lichtenberg, R. 2005. 'Des chiens momifiés à El-Deir Oasis de Kharga', *BIFAO* 105, 75-87.
Durdin-Robertson, L. 1982. *Juno Covella: Perpetual Calendar of the Fellowship of Isis,* Ireland.
Dwyer, E. 1991. 'The Pompeian Atrium House in Theory and Practice', in E. K. Gazda (ed.), *Roman Art in the Private Sphere: New Perspectives on the Architecture and Decor of the Domus, Villa, and Insula*, Ann Arbor, 25-48.

Edgar, M. C. C. 1905. *Catalogue Général des Antiquités Égyptiennes du Musée du Caire: Graeco-Egyptian Coffins, Masks and Portrait*, Cairo.
El-Abbadi, M. A. H. 1962. 'The Alexandrian Citizenship', *JEA* 48, 106-23.
El-Aswad, E. 1987. 'Death Rituals in Rural Egyptian Society: A Symbolic Study', *Urban Anthropology and Studies of Cultural Systems and World Economic Development* 16:2, 207.
El-Khadragy, M. 2006. 'The Northern Soldiers-Tomb at Asyut', *SAK* 35, 147-64.
Ellis, S. P. 1991. 'Power, Architecture, and Decor: How the Late Roman Aristocrat Appeared to His Guests', in E. K. Gazda (ed.), *Roman Art in the 25 Private Sphere: New Perspectives on the Architecture and Decor of the Domus, Villa, and Insula*, Ann Arbour, 117-134.
Ellis, S. P. 1997. 'Late-Antique Dining: Architecture, Furnishings and Behaviour', in R. Laurence and Wallace-Hadrill (eds.), *Domestic Space in the Roman World: Pompeii and Beyond*, JRA Suppl. 22, Portsmouth, 41-51.
Elmendorf, W. W. 1992. *The Structure of Twana Culture: With Comparative Notes on the Structure of Yurok Culture*, Washington.
El-Sawy, A. and Bouzek, J. 1979. 'Clay Lamps From the Terenouthis Cemetery in Egypt', *Folia Philologica* 2 (3), 128-132.
El-Sayed, R. 1982. *La déesse Neith de Saïs*, Cairo.
Endruweit, A. 2004.'Houses, Cities, and Palaces-Ancient Egyptian Lifestyles', in R. Schulz and M. Seidel (eds.), *Egypt the World of the Pharaohs*, Könemann, 386-97.
Engelbach, R. 1931. 'Four Models of Houses from the Graeco-Roman Period', *ASAE* 31, 129-31.
Engelmann, W. 1929. *New Guide to Pompeii*, second edition, Leipzig.
Erichsen, W. 1954. *Demotisches Glossar*, Copenhagen.
Erman, A. 1907. *A Handbook of Egyptian Religion*, London.
Erman, A. 1915. 'Zwei Grabsteine griechischer Zeit', in G. Weil (ed.), *Festschrift Eduard Sachau zum Siebzigsten Geburtstage gewidmet von Freunden und Schülern*, Berlin, 103-12.
Erman, A. and Grapow, H. 1926. *Wörterbuch der Aegyptischen Sprache* I, Leipzig.
Erskine, A. 2002. 'Life after Death: Alexandria and the Body of Alexander', *Greece & Rome* 49:2, 163-79.
Fakhry, A. and Osing, J. 1982. *Denkmäler der Oase Dachla aus dem Nachlass von Ahmed Fakhry*. Archäologische Veröffentlichungen 28, Mainz am Rhein.
Fairman, H. W. 1954. 'Worship and Festivals in an Egyptian Temple', *BJRL* 37, 165-203.
Favro, D. and Johanson, C. 2010. 'Death in Motion: Funeral Processions in the Roman Forum', *JSAH* 69:1, 12-37.
Faulkner, R. O. 1933. The Papyrus Bremner-Rhind (Brit. Mus. No. 10188), Bibliotheca Aegyptiaca III, Brussels.

Faulkner, R. O. 1936. 'The Bremner-Rhind Papyrus: I. A. The Songs of Isis and Nephthys', *JEA* 22:2, 121-40.

Faulkner, R. O. 1972. *The Book of the Dead*, New York.

Faulkner, R. O. 1988. *A Concise Dictionary of Middle Egyptian*, Oxford.

Feder, F. 2003. 'Der ägyptische Tierkult nach den griechischen und römischen Autoren', in M. Fitzenreiter (ed.), *Tierkulte im pharaonischen Ägypten und im Kulturvergleich*, Berlin, 159-66.

Finnestad, F. B. 1997. 'Temples of the Ptolemaic and Roman Periods: Ancient Traditions in New Contexts', in B. E. Shafer (ed.), *Temples of Ancient Egypt*, New York, 185-237.

Fischer, H. G. 1961. 'A Supplement to Janssen's List of Dogs' Names', *JEA* 47, 152-3.

Fischer, H. G. 1978. 'More Ancient Egyptian Names of Dogs and Other Animals', *The Metropolitan Museum of Art* 12, 173-8.

Fitzentreiter, M. 1994. 'Zum Ahnenkult in Ägypten', *GM* 143, 52-72.

Flower, H. I. 1996. *Ancestor Masks and Aristocratic Power in Roman Culture*, Oxford.

Forster, E. S. 1941. 'Dogs in Ancient Warfare', *Greece & Rome* 10:30, 114-7.

Fowden, G 1986. *The Egyptian Hermes: A Historical Approach to the Late Pagan Mind*, Cambridge.

Frandsen, P. J. 1992. 'On the root *nfr* and a clever remark of embalming', in J. Osing and E. K. Nielsen (eds.), *The Heritage of Ancient Egypt: Studies in Honour of Erik Iversen*, Copenhagen, 49-62.

Frandsen, P. J. 2008. 'Aspects of Kingship in Ancient Egypt', in Brisch, N. (ed.), *Man and Power: Divine Kingship in the Ancient World and Beyond*, Chicago, 47-73.

Frankfort, H. and Pendlebury, J. D. S. 1933. *The City of Akhenaten* II. *The North Suburb and the Desert Altars*, London.

Frankfurter, R. 1998. *Religion in Roman Egypt: Assimilation and Resistance*, Princeton.

Froidefond, C. 1972. 'Notes critiques sur quelques passages du de Iside et Osiride de Plutarque', *REG* 85, 63-71.

Froidefond, C. 1978. 'Études critiques sur le traité Isis et Osiris de Plutarque I', *REG* 91, 340-357.

Froidefond, C.1979. 'Études critiques sur le traité Isis et Osiris de Plutarque II', *REG* 92, 99-111.

Froidefond, C. 1987. 'Plutarque et le Platonism', *ANRW* 2.36.1, 184-233.

Fyfe, N. R. 1998. 'Introduction: Reading the Street', in N. R. Fyfe (ed.), *Images of the Street: Planning, Identity and Control in Public Space*, London and New York, 1-10.

Gaballa, G. A. and Kitchen, K. A. 1969. 'The Festival of Sokar', *Orientalia* 38, 1-76.

Gabra, S. 1941. *Rapport sur les fouilles d'Hermoupolis ouest (Touna el-Gebel)*, Cairo.

Gallo, P. 1997. 'Lucerna osiriforme', in E. Arslan (ed.), *Iside: il mito, il mistero, la magia*, Milan, 500.

Gallo, P. 1998. 'Lucerne osiriformi d'epoca romana', in J.-Y Empereur (ed.), *Alexandrina* 1, Études alexandrines 1, Cairo, 149-55.

Gamal, M. 1937. 'Essai d'observations sur les rites funéraires en Égypte actuelle relevées dans certains regions campagnardes', *Revue des Études Islamique Année 1937, Cahiers II-III*, 135-292.

Game, A. 1995. 'Time, space, memory, with reference to Bachelard', in M. Featherstone, S. Lash and R. Robertson (eds.), Global Modernities, London, 192-208.

Gardiner, A. H. 1957. *Egyptian Grammar: Being an Introduction to the Study of Hieroglyphs*, Oxford.

Gardiner, A. H. and Sethe, K. 1928. *Egyptian Letters to the Dead*, London.

Gardner, I. M. F. and Lieu, S. N. C. 1996. 'From Narmuthis (Medinet Madi) to Kellis (Ismant El-Kharab): Manichean Documents from Roman Egypt', *JRS* 86, 146-69.

Gauthier, H. 1925. *Dictionnaire des noms géographiques contenus dans les textes* hiéroglyphiques I, Cairo.

Gauthier, A. 2007. 'Review', *JAR* 63:2, 277-9.

Gazda, E. K. 1983. *Karanis: An Egyptian Town in Roman Times, Discoveries of the University of Michigan Expedition to Egypt (1924-1935)*, Ann Arbor.

Gazda, E. K. 1991. *Roman Art in the Private Sphere: New Perspectives on the Architecture and Decor of the Domus, Villa, and Insula*, Ann Arbor.

Gazda, E. K., Hessenbruch, C., Allen, M. L., and Hutchinson, V. 1978. *Guardians of the Nile: Sculptures from Karanis in the Fayoum (c. 250 BC - AD 450)*, Ann Arbor.

George, G. 1997a. 'Repopulating the Roman House', in B. Rawson and P. Weaver (eds.), *The Roman Family in Italy: Status, Sentiment and Space*, Oxford, 297-319.

George, G. 1997b. 'Servus and Domus: the Slave in the Roman House', in R. Laurence and A. Wallace-Hadrill (eds.), *Domestic Space in the Roman World: Pompeii and Beyond. JRA* Suppl. 22, Portsmouth, 15-24.

George, G. 2004. 'Domestic Architecture and Household Relations: Pompeii and Roman Ephesos', *JSNT* 27.1, 7-25.

Georgiadou, A. and Larmour, D. H. J. 1998. *Lucian's Science Fiction Novel/True Historie: Interpretation and Commentary*, Brill.

Germer, P. 2004. 'Mummification', in R, Schulz and M. Seidel (eds.), *Egypt the World of the Pharaohs*, Könemann, 458-69.

Gilliam, J. F. 1978. 'Some Roman Elements in Roman Egypt', *Illinois Classical Studies* 3, 115-31.

Godley, A. D. 1920. *Herodotus*, Cambridge.

Görg, M. 2004. 'Gods and Deities', in R, Schulz and M. Seidel (eds.), *Egypt the World of the Pharaohs*, Könemann, 433-43.

Gourevitch, D. 1968. 'Le chien, de la therapeutique populaire aux cultes sanitaires', *Mélanges d'Archéologie et d'Histoire* 801, 247-81.

Graefe, E. 1983. 'Der Sonnenaufgangzwischen den Pylontürmen', *OLP* 14, 55-75.

Grahame, M. 1998. 'Material Culture and Roman Identity: The Spatial Layout of Pompeian Houses and the Problem of Ethnicity', in R. Laurence and J. Berry (eds.), *Cultural Identity in the Roman Empire*, London, 157- 175.

Gransard-Desmond, J.-O. 2004. *Étude sur les canidae des temps pré-pharaoniques en Égypte et au Soudan*, BAR International Series 1260, Oxford.

Grenfell, B. P. and Hunt, A. S. 1906. *The Hibeh Papyri* I, London.

Grenfell, B. P., Hunt, A. S., and Hogarth, D. G. 1900. *Fayûm Towns and their Papyri*, London.

Grießler, M. T. J. 1991. 'The Last Dynastic Funeral: Ritual Sequence at the Demise of the Empress Dowager Cixi', *Oriens Extremus* 34:1/2, 7-35.

Griffith, F. L. 1909. *Catalogue of the Demotic Papyri in the John Rylands Library* III: *Key-list, Translations, Commentaries and Indices*, Manchester.

Griffiths, J. G. 1958. 'The Horus-Seth Motif in the Daily Temple Liturgy', *Aegyptus* 38 (1/2), 3-10.

Griffiths, J. G. 1970. *Plutarch's De Iside et Osiride*, Cambridge.

Griffiths, J. G. 1975. *Apuleius of Madauros: The Isis Book (Metamorphoses, Book XI)*, Brill.

Griffiths, J. G. 2001. 'Plutarch', in D. B. Redford (ed.), *The Oxford Encyclopedia of Ancient Egypt* III, Oxford, 54-5.

Griffiths, J. G. and Barb, A. A. 1959. 'Seth or Anubis?', *Journal of the Warburg and Courtauld Institutes* 22:3/4, 367-71.

Gros, P. 1996. *L'Architecture romaine du début du IIIe siècle av. J.-C. à la fin du Haut-Empire* II, Paris.

Haatvedt, R. E. and Peterson, E. E. 1964. *Coins from Karanis*, Ann Arbor.

Hales, S. 2003. *The Roman House and Social Identity*, Cambridge.

Hani, J. 1976. *La Religion Égyptienne dans la pensée de Plutarque*, Paris.

Hanson, A. E. 1992. 'Egyptians, Greeks, Romans, *Arabes*, and *Ioudaioi* in the First Century A.D. Tax Archive from Philadelphia: P. Mich. Inv. 880 Recto and P. Princ. III 152 Revised', in J. H. Johnson (ed.), *Life in a Multi-cultural Society: Egypt from Cambyses to Constantine and Beyond*, Chicago, 133-45.

Harden, D. B. 1936. *Roman Glass from Karanis found by the University of Michigan Expedition in Egypt, 1924-29*, Ann Arbor.

Harding, M. E. 1971. *Woman's Mysteries: Ancient and Modern*, Boston.

Hart, G. 2005. *The Routledge Dictionary of Egyptian Gods and Goddesses*, New York and London.

Hartley, M., Buck, A. and Binder, S. 2011. 'Canine Interments in the Teti Cemetery North at Saqqara during the Graeco-Roman Period', in M. Bárta, F. Coppens, and J. Krejčí (eds.), *Abusir and Saqqara in the Year 2011/1*, Prague, 17-29.

Hecker, H. M. 1982. 'A Zooarchaeological Inquiry into Pork Consumption in Egypt from Prehistoric to New Kingdom Times', *JARCE* XIX, 59-71.

Heidegger, M. 1975. 'Building Dwelling Thinking', in *Poetry, Language, Thought*, translated by A. Hofstadter, New York and London, 145-61.

Helck, H. W. 1984. 'Schwein', in *LÄ* V, Wiesbaden, 764.

Hellmann, M.-C. 1992. *Recherches sur le Vocabulaire de l'Architecture Grecque d'Après les Inscriptions de Dèlos*, Paris.

Heyob, S. K. 1975. *The Cult of Isis among Women in the Graeco-Roman World*, Leiden.

Hobson, D. W. 1985. 'House and Household in Roman Egypt', *YCS* 28, 211-29.

Hodder, I. 1994. 'Architecture and Meaning: The Examples of Neolithic Houses and Tomb', in M. P. Pearson and C. Richards (eds.), *Architecture and Order: Approaches to Social Space*, London and New York, 73-86.

Hoerber, R. G. 1963. 'The Socratic Oath "By the Dog"', *The Classical Journal* 58:6, 268-9.

Hondius-Crone, A. 1955. *The Temple of Nehallenia at Domburg*, Amsterdam.

Hoogendijk, F. A. J. and van Minnen, P. 1987. 'Drei Kaiserbriefe Gordians III. an die Bürger von Antinoo*polis*. P. Vindob. G25945', *Tyche* 2, 71-4.

Hope, C. A. 1988. 'Three Seasons of Excavation at Ismant el-Gharab in Dakhleh Oasis, Egypt', *Mediterranean Archaeology* 1, 160-78.

Hope, C. A. and Whitehouse, H. 2006. 'A Painted Residence at Ismant el-Kharab (Kellis) in the Dakhla Oasis', *JRA* 19, 312-28.

Hopkins, K. 1983. *Death and Renewal*, Cambridge, 226-34.

Hornung, E. 1983. 'Vom Sinn der Mumifizierung', *Die Welt des Orients* 14, 167-75.

Houlihan, P. F. 1996. *The Animal World of the Pharaohs*, Cairo.

Houlihan, P. F. 2001. 'Pigs', in D. B. Redford (ed.), *The Oxford Encyclopedia of Ancient Egypt* III, Oxford, 47-8.

Hubbell, H. M. 1935. 'Ptolemy's Zoo', *The Classical Journal* 31:2, 68-76.

Humphrey, J. H. 1986. *Roman Circuses: Arenas for Chariot Racing*, London.

Husselman, E. M. 1971. *Papyri from Karanis: Third Series (Michigan Papyri IX)*, Ann Arbor.

Husselman, E. M. 1979. *Karanis: Topography and Architecture*, Ann Arbor.

Husson, G. 1981. 'Traditions pharoniques attestees dans l'Architecture domestique de l'Egypte grecque, romaine et byzantine', *Proceedings of the XVI International Congress of Papyrology*, Chicago, 519-26.

Husson, G. 1983. *Oikia. Le vocabulaire de la maison privée en Égypte d'après les papyrus grecs*, Paris.

Husson, G. 1990. 'Houses in Syene in the Patermouthis Archive', *BASP* 27, 123-37.

Ikram, S. M. 2005. *Divine Creatures: Animal Mummies in Ancient Egypt*, Cairo.

Ikram, S. M. 2007a. 'Animals in the Ritual Landscape at Abydos: A Synopsis', in Z. Hawas and J. Richards (eds.), *The Archaeology and Art of Ancient Egypt* I, Cairo, 417-32.

Ikram, S. M. 2007b. 'Mummified Menageries: Ancient Egyptian Animal Mummies', *British Institute of Radiology News* 2007, 12-13.

Ikram, S. 2008. 'Egypt's Frontier Oasis', *Archaeology* 61:6, 36-41.

Ikram, S. M. 2013, 'Man's Best Friend for Eternity: Dog and Human Burials in Ancient Egypt', *Anthropozoologica* 48:2, 299-307.

Ikram, S., Nickolson, P., Bertini, L., and Hurley, D. 2013. 'Killing Man's Best Friend?', *Archaeological Review from Cambridge* 28:2, 48-66.

Ischlondsky, N. D. 1966. 'A Peculiar Representation of the Jackal-God Anubis', *JNES* 25: 1, 17-26.

Janssen, J. J. and Janssen, R. M. 1990. *Growing up in Ancient Egypt, London.*

Janseen, J. J. and Pestman, P. W. 1968. 'Burial and Inheritance in the Community of the Necropolis Workmen at Thebes (Pap. Bulaq X and O. Petrie 16)', *JESHO* 11:2, 137-70.

Janssen, J. M. A. 1958. 'Über Hundenamen im pharaonischen Ägypten', *MDAIK* 16, 176-82.

Janssen, R. M. 1996. 'Soft Toys from Egypt', in D. M. Bailey (ed.), *Archaeological Research in Roman Egypt*, Proceedings of the Seventeenth Classical Colloquium of the Department of Greek and Roman Antiquities, British Museum, Held on 1-4 December, 1993, Ann Arbor, 231-9.

Jaritz, H. and Rodziewicz, M. 1994. 'Syene- Review of the Urban Remains and its Pottery', *MDAIK* 50, 115-41.

Jaros-Deckert, B. 1982. 'Pylon', in W. Helck and E. Otto (eds.), *LÄ* IV, Wiesbaden, 1202-5.

Jeffreys, G. and Smith, H. S. 1988. *The Anubieion at Saqqara* I: *The Settlement and the Temple Precinct*, London.

Johnson, K. 2004. 'Textile and Papyrus Figurines from Karanis', *Bulletin of the University of Michigan Museums of Art and Archaeology* 15, Ann Arbor, 49-64.

Johnson, J. de M. 1914. 'Antinoe and its Papyri', *JEA* 1, 168-81.

Johnston, S. 2012. 'Animals in War: Commemoration, Patriotism, Death', *Political Research Quarterly* 65:2, 359-71.

Jones, A. H. M. 1974. *The Roman Economy: Studies in Ancient Economic and Administrative History*, Oxford.

Jones, C. P. 1966a. 'Towards a Chronology of Plutarch's Works', *JRS* 56, 61-74.

Jones, C. P. 1966b. 'The Teacher of Plutarch', *HSCP* 71, 205-13.

Jones, M. 1990. 'The Temple of Apis in Memphis', *JEA* 76, 141-7.

Jouguet, P. 1901. 'Rapport sur les fouilles de Médinet-Mâ'di et Médinet-Ghôran', *BCH* 25, 380-411.

Junker, H. 1912. 'Der Bericht Strabos über den heiligen Falken von Philae im Lichte der ägyptischen Quellen', *WZKM* 26, 42- 62.

Kahl, J. 2007. *Ancient Asyut: The First Synthesis after 300 Years of Research*, Wiesbaden.

Kahl, J. 2012. 'Asyut and The Asyut Project', in J. Kahl, M. El-Khadragy, U. Verhoeven and A. Kilian (eds.), *Seven Seasons at Asyut: First Results of the Egyptian-German Cooperation in Archaeological Fieldwork, The Asyut Project 2*, Wiesbaden 1-30.

Kahl, J., El-Khadragy, M., Verhoeven, U., El-Khatib, A., and Kitagawa, C. 2009. 'The Asyut Project: Sixth Season of Fieldwork', *SAK* 38, 113-30.

Kaibel, G. 1878. *Epigrammata Graeca ex Lapidibus Conlecta*, Berlin.

Kaizer, W. 1990. 'Zur Büste als einer Darstellungsform ägyptischer Rundplastik', *MDAIK* 46, 269-85.

Karouzou, S. 1972. 'An Underworld Scene on a Black-figured Lekythos', *JHS* 92, 64-73.

Kemp, B. J. 1989. *Ancient Egypt: Anatomy of a Civilization*, London and New York.

Kessler, D. 1986. 'Tierkult', in W. Helck and E. Otto (eds.), *LÄ* VI, Wiesbaden, 571-87.

Kessler, D. 1989. *Die heiligen Tiere und der König* I: *Beiträge zu Organisation, Kult und Theologie der spätzeitlichen Tierfriedhöfe*, ÄAT 16, Wiesbaden.

Kessler, D. 2003. '*Tierische Missverständnisse*: Grundsätzliches zu Fragen des Tierkultes', in M. Fitzenreiter (ed.), *Tierkulte im pharaonischen Ägypten und im Kulturvergleich*, Berlin, 33-67.

Kessler, D. and Nur el-Din, A. H. 2005. 'Tuna al-Gebel: Millions of Ibises and Other Animals', in S. Ikram (ed.) *Divine Creatures: Animal Mummies in Ancient Egypt*, Cairo, 120-63.

Knight, M. 2001. 'Curing Cut or Ritual Mutilation?: Some Remarks on the Practice of Female and Male Circumcision in Graeco-Roman Egypt', *Isis* 92 (2), 317-38.

Knudstad, J. E. and Frey, R. A. 1999. 'Kellis: The Architectural Survey of the Romano-Byzantine Town at Ismant el-Kharab', in C. S. Churcher and A. J. Mills (eds.), *Reports from the Survey of the Dakhleh Oasis Western Desert of Egypt 1977-87*, Oxford, 189-214.

Koenen, L. 1967. 'Eine Einladung zur Kline des Serapis (P.Colon.Inv. 2555)', *ZPE* 1, 121-6.

Koenigsberger, O. 1936. *Die Konstruktion der Ägyptischen Tür*, Glückstadt.

Krüger, J. 1990. *Oxyrhynchos in der Kaiserzeit: Studien zur Topographie und Literaturrezeption*, Frankfurt.

Kühn, E. 1913. *Antinoopolis: Ein Beitrag zur Geschichte des Hellenismus im römischen Ägypten*, Göttingen.

Lacovara, P. and Trope-Teasley, B. 2001. *The Realm of Osiris: Mummies, Coffins, and Ancient Egyptian Funerary Art in the Michael C Carlos Museum*, Atlanta.

Laflı, E., Buora, M., and Mastrocinque, A. 2012. 'A New Osiriform Lamp from Antioch in the Hatay Archaeological Museum', *Greek, Roman, and Byzantine Studies* 52, 421-39.

Larmour, D. H. J. and Spencer, D. 2007. *The Sites of Rome: Time, Space, Memory*, Oxford.

Lauer, J. P. 1976. *Saqqara: The Royal Cemetery of Memphis*, Chicago.

Laurence, R. 2007. *Roman Pompeii: Space and Society*, London and New York.

Laurence, R. and Wallace-Hadrill, A. 1997. *Domestic Space in the Roman World: Pompeii and Beyond*, *JRA* Suppl. 22, Portsmouth.

Lauter, H. 1986. *Die Architektur des Hellenismus*, Darmstadt.

Lazenby, F. D. 1949. 'Greek and Roman Household Pets', *The Classical Journal* 44, 245-52.

Leahy, A. 1981. 'Saite Lamp Donations', *GM* 49, 37-46.

Leahy, A. 1988. 'The Earliest Dated Monument of Amasis and the End of the Reign of Apries Author', *JEA* 74, 183-99.

Lefebvre, G. 1924. *Le Tombeau de Petosiris* I-III, Cairo.

Legras, B. 1993. 'Mallocouria et mallocourètes. Un rite de passage dans l'Egypte romaine', *Cahier Centre G. Glotz* 4, 113-27.

Lesko, B. S. 1999. *The Great Goddesses of Egypt*, Oklahoma.

Lewis, N. 1983. *Life in Egypt under Roman Rule*, Oxford.

Lichtheim, M. 1976. *Ancient Egyptian Literature* II, London.

Lindsay, J. 1963. *Daily Life in Roman Egypt*, London.

Liszka, K. 2012. 'Esna/Latopolis', in R. Bagnall, K. Brodersen, C. Champion, A. Erskine, and S. Huebner (eds.), *The Encyclopaedia of Ancient History*, London, 2501.

Llewellyn, S. 1994. 'The εἰς τὴν οἰκίαν formula and the delivery of letters to third persons or to their property', *ZPE* 101, 71-87.

Lloyd, A. B. 1976. *Herodotus, Book II: Commentary 1-98*, Leiden.

Lloyd, A. B. 2007. 'Herodotus Book II', in D. Asheri, A. Lloyd, A. Corcella, O. Murray and A. Moreno (eds.), *A Commentary on Herodotus Books I-IV*, Oxford.

Lohmann, K. 1998. 'Das Gespräch eines Mannes mit seinem Ba', *SAK* 25, 207-36.

Luckhard, F. 1914. *Das Privathaus im ptolemäischen und römischen Ägypten*, Giessen.

Maehler, H. 1983. 'Häuser und ihre Bewohner im Fayûm in der Kaiserzeit', in G. Grimm, H. Heinen, and E Winter (eds.), *Das Römsich-Byzantinsiche Ägypten*, Mainz am Rhein, 119-37.

Malouta, M. 2009. 'Antinoite Citizenship under Hadrian and Antoninus Pius: A Prosopographical Study of the First Thirty Years of Antinoo*polis*', *BASP* 46, 81-96.

Malouta, M. 2012. 'Families, Children, and Household', in C. Riggs (ed.), *The Oxford Handbook of Roman Egypt*, Oxford, 288-304.

Mangold, B. 1973. 'Birdstone or Dog Effigy?', *Central States Archaeological Journal* 20:4, 146-9.

Manniche, L. 1985. 'The Beginning of the Festival Calendar in the Tomb of Neferhotep (No. 50) at Thebes', *BdÉ* 97 (2), 105-8.

Mark, R. 2004. 'Caring for the Dead', *Archaeology* 57:2, 30-35.

Mariette, A. 1871. *Les papyrus égyptiens du Musée du Boulaq* I, Paris.

Mastrocinque, A. 2008. 'Riletture del mito di Osiris e Seth nella magia del Vicino Oriente', in S. Pernigotti and M. Zecchi (eds.), *Sacerdozio e società civile nell'Egitto antico*, Imola, 237-45.

Mattha, G. 1975. *The Demotic Legal Code of Hermopolis West*, Cairo.

McFadden, S. 2014. 'Art on the Edge: The Late Roman Wall Painting of Amheida, Egypt', in Akten des XI. Internationalen Kolloquiums der AIPMA, *Archäologische Forschungen* 23, 359-70.

McKenzie J. 2007. *The Architecture of Alexandria and Roman Egypt (c. 300 BC to AD 700)*, London.

Meeks, D. 1979. 'Les donations aux temples dans l'Égypte du Ier millénaire avant J.-C.', in E. Lipinfiski (ed.), *State and Temple Economy in the Ancient Near East* II, OLA 6, Leuven, 605-87.

Merkelbach, R. 1993. 'Diodor über das Totengericht der Ägypter', *ZÄS* 120, 71-84.

Meskell, L. 1999. 'Archaeologies of Life and Death', *AJA* 103:2, 181-99.

Meskell, L. 2000. 'Cycles of Life and Death: Narrative Homology and Archaeological Realities', *World Archaeology* 31:3, 423-41.

Mettinger, T. N. D. 1988. *In Search of God: The Meaning and Message of the Everlasting Names*, Philadelphia.

Millard, D. B. 1987. 'St. Christopher and the Lunar Disc of Anubis', *JEA* 73, 237-8.

Millet, M. 2007. 'Urban Topography and Social Identity in the Tiber Valley', in R. Roth and J. Keller (eds.), *Roman by Integration: Dimensions of Group Identity in Material Culture and Text*. JRA Supplementary Series 66, Portsmouth, 71-82.

Mills, A. J. 1980. 'Lively Paintings: Roman Frescoes in the Dakhleh Oasis', *Rotunda* 13:2, 18-25.

Mills, A. J. 1993. 'The Dakhleh Oasis Columbarium Farmhouse', *BSAA* 45, 192-8.

Mills, A. J. 1998. 'Recent Work of the Dakhleh Oasis Project', *ASAE* 73, 84-91.

Millward, E. 2013. 'Mourning of the Deceased: An Overview of Current Research into the Gestures and Attitudes of Grief in Ancient Egypt', *Rosetta* 12.5: 43-50.

Mills, A. J. 1980. 'Lively Paintings: Roman Frescoes in the Dakhleh Oasis', *Rotunda* 13 (2), 18-25.

Mills, A. J. 1993. 'The Dakhleh Oasis Columbarium Farmhouse', *BSAA* 45, 192-8.

Mills, A. J. 1998. 'Recent Work of the Dakhleh Oasis Project', *ASAE* 73, 84-91.

Milne, J. G. 1925. 'The Kline of Serapis', *JEA* 11, 6-9.

Montserrat, D. 1990. 'P.Lond.Inv. 3078 Reappraised', *JEA* 76, 206-7.

Montserrat, D. 1991. 'Mallocouria and Therapeuteria: Rituals of Transition in a Mixed Society?', *BASP* 28 (1/2), 43-9.

Montserrat, D. 1992. 'The Kilne of Serapis', *JEA* 78, 301-7.

Montserrat, D. 1996. *Sex and Society in Graeco-Roman Egypt*, London and New York.

Montserrat, D. 1997. 'Death and Funerals in the Roman Fayum', in M. L. Bierbrier (ed.), *Portraits and Masks: Burial Customs in Roman Egypt*, London, 33-44.

Montserrat, D. 2004. 'Death, the Afterlife, and Other Last Things: Egypt', in S. I. Johnston (ed.), *Religions of the Ancient World*, Harvard University Press, 471-77.

Montserrat, D. and Meskell, L. 1997. 'Mortuary Archaeology and Religious Landscape at Graeco-Roman Deir el-Medina', *JEA* 83, 179-97.

Montevecchi, O. 1941. 'Ricerche di sociologia nei documenti dell'Egitto gréco-romano', *Aegyptus* 21, 93-151.

Morenz, S. 1975. 'Anubis mit dem Schlüssel', in E. Blumenthal and S. Hermann (eds.), *Religion und Geschichte des alten Ägyptens*, Cologne, 510-20.

Morgan, C. 1991. 'Ethnicity and Early Greek States: Historical and Material Perspectives', *PCPS* 37, 131-63.

Morgan, L. W. and McGovern-Huffman, S. 2008. 'Noninvasive Radiographic Analysis of an Egyptian Falcon Mummy from the Late Period 664-332 BC', *JAB* 39:5, 584-7.

Moyer, I. S. 2011a. *Egypt and the Limits of Hellenism*, Cambridge; New York.

Moyer, I. S. 2011b. 'Court, Chora, and Culture in Late Ptolemaic Egypt', *AJP* 132 (1), 15-44.

Neils, N. 1992. 'The Panathenaea: An Introduction', in J. Neils (ed.), *Goddess and Polis: The Panthenaic Festival in Ancient Athens*, Princeton, 13-28.

Nelson, C. A. 1979. *Status Declarations in Roman Egypt*, Amsterdam.

Nevett, L. 1994. 'Separation or seclusion? Towards an Archaeological Approach to investigating Women in the Greek Household from the fifth to third centuries BC', in M. P. Pearson and C. Richards (eds.), *Architecture and Order: Approaches to Social Space*, London, 98-112.

Nevett, L. 1995. 'The Organisation of Space in Classical and Hellenistic Houses from Mainland Greece and the Western Colonies', in N. Spencer (ed.), *Time, Tradition and Society in Greek Archaeology: Bridging the Great Divide*, London & New York, 89-108.

Nevett, L. 2005. *Ancient Greek Houses and Household: Chronological, Regional, and Social Diversity*, Philadelphia.

Newberry, P. E. 1928. 'The Pig and the Cult-Animal of Set', *JEA* 14, 211-25.

Newberry, P. E. and Griffth, F. L. 1893. *El-Bersheh* II: *Detailed Description of the Other Tombs*, London.

Nims, C. F. 1965. *Thebes of the Pharaohs: Pattern for Every City*, London.

Nock, A. D. 1932. 'Cremation and Burial in the Roman Empire', *The Harvard Theological Review* 25:4, 321-59.

Nowicka, M. 1972. 'À propos des tours-πύργοι dans les papyrus grecs', *Archaeologia* 21, 53-62.

Nowicka, M. 1973. 'À propos d'ΟΙΚΙΑ ΔΙΠΥΡΓΙΑ dans le monde grec', *Archaeologia Polona* 14, 175-8.

Nur el Din, A. 1992. 'Report on New Demotic Texts from Tuna-El-Gebel', in J. H. Johnson (ed.), *Life in a Multi-cultural Society: Egypt from Cambyses to Constantine and Beyond*, Chicago, 253-4.

O'Neill, B. 2015. *Setting the Scene: The deceased and Regenerative Cult within Offering Table Imagery of the Egyptian Old to Middle Kingdoms (c. 2686-c. 1650 BC)*, Oxford.

Osing, J., Moursi, M., Arnold, Do., Neugebauer, O., Parker, R. A., Pingree, D., Nur-el-Din, M. A. 1982. *Denkmäler der Oase Dachla aus dem Nachlass von Ahmed Fakhry*, Mainz.

Oslon, B. 1927. 'Sprachliche Bemerkungen zu eineigen Papyrusstellen', *Aegyptus* 7, 111-12.

Otto, W. 1905. *Priester und Tempel im hellenistischen Ägypten: Ein Beitrag zur Kultureheschichte des Hellenismus* I, Leipzig.

Pantalacci, L. and Denoix, S. 2009. 'Travaux de l'Institut Français d'Archéologie Orientale en 2008-2009', *BIFAO* 109, 599-604.

Parlebas, J. 1977. 'Les Égyptiens et la ville d'après les sources littéraires et archéologiques', *Ktema* 2, 49-57.

Parsons, P. 2007. *City of the Sharp-Nosed Fish: Greek Lives in Roman Egypt*, London.

Pedding, R. W. 1991. 'The Role of the Pig in the Subsistence System of Ancient Egypt: A Parable on the Potential of Faunal Data', in P. J. Crabtree and K. Ryan (eds.), *Animal Use and Cultural Change*, Philadelphia, 20-30.

Peet, T. E. 1914. *The Cemeteries of Abydos* II, Egypt Exploration Fund 34, London.

Pepper, T. W. 2010. 'A Patron and a Companion: Two Animal Epitaphs for Zenon of Caunos (P.Cair.Zen. IV 59532 = SH 977)', Proceedings of the Twenty-Fifth International Congress of Papyrology, Ann Arbor 2007, ASP 2010, Ann Arbor, 605-22.

Perdrizet, P. 1921. *Les Terres cuites grecques d'Égypte de la collection Fouquet*, Nancy, Paris, and Strasbourg.

Perlzweig, J. 1963. *Lamps from the Athenian Agora*, Princeton.

Perpillou-Thomas, F. 1993 : *Fêtes d'Égypte ptolémaique et romaine d'àpres la documentation papyrologique grecque*, Studia Hellenistica 31, Leuven.

Perrot, G. and Chipiez, C. 1882. *Histoire de l'Art dans l'Antiquite: L'Egypte*, Paris.

Perry, M. A. 2002. 'Life and Death in Nabataea: The North Ridge Tombs and Nabataean Burial Practices', *Near Eastern Archaeology* 65:4, 265-70.

Pestman, P. W. 1961. *Marriage and Matrimonial Property in Ancient Egypt*, London.

Petrie, W.M.F. 1889. *Hawara, Biahmu, and Arsione*, London.

Petrie, W. M. F. 1902. *Abydos* I, Egypt Exploration Fund 22, London.

Petrie, W. M. F. 1911. *Mummy Portraits and Memphis* IV, London.

Phillips, D. W. 1948. *Ancient Egyptian Animals*, The Metropolitan Museum of Art, New York.

Piacentini, P. 1996. 'Excavating Bakchias', in D. M. Bailey (ed.), *Archaeological Research in Roman Egypt. The Proceedings of the Seventh Classical Colloquium of the Department of Greek and Roman Antiquities, British Museum, held on 1-4 December 1993*, JRA Suppl. 19, Ann Arbor, 57-60.

Pisani, M. 2006. 'The Collection of Terracotta Figurines in the British School at Athens', *ABSA* 101, 269-368.

Platvoet, J. 1995. 'Ritual in Plural and Pluralist Societies', in J. Platvoet and K. van der Toorn (eds.), *Pluralism and Identity: Studies in Social Behaviour*, Leiden, New York, and Köln, 25-51.

Preisigke, F. 1919. 'Die Begriffe ΠΥΡΓΟΣ und ΣΤΕΓΗ bei der Hausanlage', *Hermes* 54, 424-32.

Priese, K.-H. 1991. *Ägyptisches Museum*, Mainz.

Purola, T. 1994. 'P. Cair. Zen. 4.59532 - Two Epitaphs for a Hunting Dog Called Tauron', *Arctos* 28, 55-62.

Raffaele, F. 2010. 'Animal Rows and Ceremonial Processions in Late Predynastic Egypt', in F. Raffaele, M. Nuzzolo and I. Incordino (eds.), *Recent Discoveries and Latest Researches in Egyptology. Proceedings of the First Neapolitan Congress of Egyptology, Naples, June 18th-20th 2008*, Wiesbaden, 245-85.

Ray, J. 1976. *The Archive of Hor*, London.

Rea, J. R. 1986. 'A Letter of Condolence: CPR VI 81 Revised', *ZPE* 62, 75-78.

Reisner, G. A. 1938. 'Ancient King Gives Dog A Royal Burial', *The American Kennel Gazette* 55:5, 7-12.

Richter, D. S. 2001. 'Plutarch on Isis and Osiris: Text, Cult, and Cultural Appropriation', *TAPA* 131, 191-216.

Riccobono, S. 1950. *Il Gnomon dell'Idios Logos*, Palermo.

Riggs, C. 2005. *The Beautiful Burial of Roman Egypt: Art, Identity, and Funerary Religion*, Oxford.

Riggs, C. 2010. 'Funerary Rituals (Ptolemaic and Roman Periods)', in J. Dieleman and W. Wendrich (eds.) *UCLA Encyclopedia of Egyptology*, Los Angeles, 1-7.

Rigsby, K. J. 1977. 'Sacred Ephebic Games at Oxyrhynchus', *CdÉ* 62, 147-55.

Ritner, R. K. 1985. 'Anubis and the Lunar Disc', *JEA* 71, 149-55.

Robins, F. W. 1939. 'Graeco-Roman Lamps from Egypt', *JEA* 25 (1), 48-51.

Robins, G. 1999. 'Hair and the Construction of Identity in Ancient Egypt, c. 1480-1350 B.C.', *JARCE* 36, 55-69.

Robinson, D. M. and Graham, J. W. 1938. *Excavations at Olynthus* VIII: *The Hellenic House*, Baltimore.

Rondot, V. 2004. *Tebtynis* II: *Le Temple de Soknebtynis et son dromos*, Cairo.

Root, M. C. 1980. *Faces of Immortality: Egyptian Mummy Masks, Painted Portraits, and Canopic Jars in the Kelsey Museum of Archaeology*, Ann Arbor.

Rouse, W. H. D. 1902. *Greek Votive Offerings*, Cambridge.

Routledge, C. 2004. 'Review', *JARCE* 41, 191-2.

Rubensohn, O. 1905. 'Aus griechisch-römischen Funde in Ägypten', *JDAI* 17, 1-25.

Rutherford, I. C. 2005. 'Down-Stream to the Cat-Goddess: Herodotus on Egyptian Pilgrimage', in J. Elsner and I. Rutherford (eds.), *Pilgrimage in Graeco-Roman & Early Christian Antiquity: Seeing the Gods*, Oxford, 131-50.

Quaegebeur, J. 1978. 'Mummy Labels: An Orientation', in E. Boswinkel and P. Pestman (eds.), *Textes grecs, démotiques et bilingues*, Leiden, 232-59.

Quaegebeur, J. 1983. 'Cultes égyptiens et grecs en Egypte hellénistique. L'exploitations des sources', in E. *Van't Dack*, P. van Dessel, and W van Gucht (eds.), *Egypt and the Hellenistic World*, Leuven, 303-24.

Quaegebeur, J., Clarysse, W. and Van Maele, B. 1985. 'Athêna, Nêith and Thoêris in Greek Documents', *ZPE* 60, 217-32.

Quibell, J. E. 1898. 'Slate Palette from Hieraconpolis', *ZÄS* 36, 81-4.

Sacks, D. 2005. *Encyclopedia of the Ancient Greek World*, London.

Salem, M. S. 1937. 'The Lychnapsia Philocaliana and the Birthday of Isis', *JRS* 27:2, 165-7.

Salter, W. J. 1991. *Dining in a Classical Context*, Ann Arbor.

Sauneron, S. 1952. *Rituel de l'embaumement*, Cairo.

Sauneron, S. 1962. *Les Fêtes religieuses d'Esna: Aux Derniers Siècles du Paganisme* V, Cairo.

Sayce, A. H. 1903. *The Religions of Ancient Egypt and Babylonia*, Edinburgh.

Scalf, F. D. 2014. *Passports to Eternity: Formulaic Demotic Funerary Texts and the Final Phase of Egyptian Funerary Literature in Roman Egypt*, Unpublished PhD Thesis, Department of Near Eastern Languages and Civilizations, Chicago.

Scholz, H. 1937. *Der Hund in griechisch-römischen Magie und Religion*, Berlin.

Schulz, D. 2010. 'De Villa van Serenus – een reconstructie', *Monumenten* 31:6.

Schulz, D. 2011. 'Die neue Villa des Serenus: Rekonstruktionsarbeiten in der Wüste', *Antike Welt* 2, 20-23.

Schulz, D. 2015. 'Colours in the oasis: the Villa of Serenos', *Egyptian Archaeology* 46, 23-6.

Schwartz, J. and Wild, H. 1950. *Fouilles franco-suisses. Rapports I Qasr-Qârûn/Dionysias 1948*, Cairo.

Scott, J. A. 1921. 'The Goose and the Dog in Homer', *The Classical Journal* 16:9, 556-7.

Scott, J. A. 1948. 'Dogs in Homer', *The Classical Weekly* 41:15, 226-8.

Scott-Moncrieff, P. D. 1909. 'De Iside et Osiride', *JHS* 29, 79-90.

Sear, F. 1982. *Roman Architecture*, London.

Sergis, M. G. 2010. 'Dog Sacrifice in Ancient and Modern Greece: from the Sacrifice Ritual to Dog Torture (*kynomartyrion*), *Folklore* 45, 61-88.

Sethe, K. 1933. *Die Bau- und Denkmalsteine der alten Ägypter und ihre Namen*, Berlin.

Sewell, W. H. 1999. 'The Concept(s) of Culture', in V. E. Bonnell and L. Hunt (eds.), *Beyond the Cultural Turn: New Directions in the Study of Society and Culture*, California, 35-61.

Shaw, B. D. 1992. 'Explaining Incest: Brother-Sister Marriage in Graeco-Roman Egypt', *Man* 27:2, 267-99.

Shaw, B. D. 1996. 'Seasons of Death: Aspects of Mortality in Imperial Rome', *JRS* 86, 100-38.

Shaw, I and Nicholson, P. 1995. *The British Museum Dictionary of Ancient Egypt*, London.

Shelmerdine, S. C. 2000. *The Homeric Hymns*, Focus Classical Library, London.

Shore, A. F. 1992. 'Human and Divine Mummification', in A. B. Lloyd (ed.), *Studies in Pharaonic Religion and Society in Honour of J. Gwyn Griffiths*, London, 226-35.

Shubert, S. B. 1981. 'Studies on the Egyptian Pylon', *JSSEA* 11, 135-64.

Simpson, W. K. 1977. 'An Additional Dog's Name from a Giza Mastaba', *JEA* 63, 175.

Sijpesteijn, P. J. 1969. 'A New Document concerning Hadrian's Visit to Egypt', *Historia* XVIII (1), 109-18.

Skeat, T. C. 1975. 'Another dinner invitation from Oxyrhynchus (P. Lond. Inv. 3078)', *JEA* 61, 251-4.

Smelik, K. A. D and Hemelrijk, E. A. 1984. 'Who knows not what monsters demented Egypt worships? Opinions on Egyptian Animal Worship in Antiquity as Part of the Ancient Conception of Egypt', *ANRW* II.17.4, 1852-2000, 2337-2357.

Smith, E. B. 1968. *Egyptian Architecture as Cultural Expression*, New York and London.

Smith, G. E. 1906. 'A Contribution to the Study of Mummification in Egypt', *MIE* 5:1, 3-53.

Smith, M. 1987. *The Mortuary Texts of Papyrus BM 10507*: Catalogue of Demotic Papyri in the British Museum 3, London.

Smith, M. 2005. *Papyrus Harkness (MMA 31.9.7)*, Oxford.

Smith, M. 2009a. *Traversing Eternity: Books for the Afterlife from Ptolemaic and Roman Egypt*, Oxford.

Smith, M. 2009b. 'Resurrection and the Body in Graeco-Roman Egypt', in F. V. Reiterer, P. C. Beentjes, N. Calduch-Benages, and B. G. Wright (eds.), *Deuterocanonical and Cognate Literature Yearbook*, Berlin, 27-42.

Smith, H. S. and Jeffreys, D. G. 1981. 'The Anubieion, North Saqqâra: Preliminary Report, 1979-80', *JEA* 67, 21-3.

Spencer, P. 1984. *The Egyptian Temple: A Lexicographical Study*, London.

Strauss-Seeber, C. 2004. 'Gifts of the Nile- The Agriculture of a River Oasis', in R. Schulz and M. Seidel (eds.), *Egypt the World of the Pharaohs*, Könemann, 376-85.

Swain, S. 1991. 'Plutarch, Hadrian, and Delphi', *Historia* 40 (3), 318-30.

Taubenschlag, R. 1927. 'Das Recht auf εἴσοδος und ἔξοδος in den Papyri', *ZPE* 8, 25-33.

Taylor, J. H. 2010. *Journey through the Afterlife: Ancient Egyptian Book of the Dead*, London.

Taylor, T. 1820. *The Commentaries of Proclus on the Timaeus of Plato*, London.

Te Velde, H. 1980. 'A Few Remarks upon the Religious Significance of Animals in Ancient Egypt', *Numen* 27:1, 76-82.

Thébert, Y. 1987. 'Private Life and Domestic Architecture in Roman North Africa', in P. Veyne (ed.), *A History of Private Life* I: *From Pagan Rome to Byzantium*, Cambridge, 313-409.

Thomas, E. V. 2007. *Monumentality and the Roman Empire: The Architecture of the Antonine Age*, Oxford.

Thomas, R. 2015a. 'Lamps in Terracotta and Bronze', in A. Villing, M. Bergeron, G. Bourogiannis, A. Johnston, F. Leclère, A. Masson, and R. Thomas (eds.), *Naukratis: Greeks in Egypt*, London, 1-18.

Thomas, R. 2015b. 'Lamps in Terracotta and Bronze', in A. Villing, M. Bergeron, G. Bourogiannis, A. Johnston, F. Leclère, A. Masson, and R. Thomas (eds.), *Naukratis: Greeks in Egypt*, London, 1-20.

Thompson, D. J. 1988. *Memphis under the Ptolemies*, Princeton.

Tooley, A. M. J. 1988. 'Coffin of a Dog from Beni Hasan', *JEA* 74, 207-11.

Török, L. 1995. *Hellenistic and Roman Terracottas from Egypt*, Rome, 132-3.

Toynbee, J. M. C. 1948. 'Beasts and Their Names in the Roman Empire', *PBSR* 16, 24-37.

Toynbee, J. M. C. 1971. *Death and Burial in the Roman World*, London.

Trench, R. C. 1873. *Plutarch: His Life, His Lives and His Morals*, London.

Turner, E. G. 1952. 'Oxyrhynchus and its Papyri', *Greece & Rome* 21:63, 127-37.

Turner, E. G. 1957. *The Oxyrhynchus Papyri* XXIV, Egypt Exploration Society, London, 142-5.

Vandoni, M. 1964. *Feste pubbliche e private nei documenti greci*, Milano.

Van Minnen, P. 1994. '*House-to-house enquiries*: An interdisciplinary approach to Roman Karanis', *ZPE* 100, 227-51.

Van Straten, F.T. 1981. 'Gifts for the Gods', in H.S. Versnel (ed.), *Faith, Hope, and Worship*, Leiden, 65-104.

Venit, M. S. 2002. *The Monumental Tombs of Ancient Alexandria: The Theatre of the Dead*, New York.

Vilà, C. and Wayne, R. K. 1999. 'Hybridization between Wolves and Dogs', *Conservation Biology* 13:1, 195-8.

Vleeming, S. P. 1995. 'The Office of a Choachyte in the Theban Area', in S. P. Vleeming (ed.), *Hundred-Gated Thebes: Acts of a Colloquium on Thebes and the Theban Area in the Graeco-Roman Period*, Leiden, 241-55.

Vos, R. L. 1993. *The Apis embalming ritual: P. Vindob. 3873*, OLA 50, Leuven.

Ucko, P. J. 1965. 'Anthropomorphic Ivory Figurines from Egypt', *JRAIGBI* 95:2, 214-239.

Ulmer, R. 2010. 'The Egyptian Gods in Midrashic Texts', *The Harvard Theological Review* 103:2, 181-204.

Wagner, G., Barakat, H., Françoise, D., Henry, H. N., Roger, L. and Colette, R. 1985. 'Douch. Rapport préliminaire de la campagne de fouille 1982. 1. Apercu général. 2. Un exemple de tombe complexe. 3. Etude des momies. 4. Examen radiologique. 5. Archaeobotanical Samples. 6. Les papyrus grecs', *ASAE* 70, 175-202.

Wallace-Hadrill, A. 1988. 'The Social Structure of the Roman House', *PBSR* 56, 43-97.

Wallace-Hadrill, A. 1994. *Houses and Society in Pompeii and Herculaneum*, Princeton.

Wallace-Hadrill, A. 1997. 'Rethinking the Roman Atrium House', in R. Laurence and A. Wallace-Hadrill (eds.), *Domestic Space in the Roman World: Pompeii and Beyond*, JRA Suppl. 22, Portsmouth, 219-40.

Wallace-Hadrill, A. 2008. 'Housing the Dead: The Tomb as House in Roman Italy', in R. Saller, L. Brink, and D. Green (eds.), *Commemorating the Dead: Texts and Artifacts in Context. Studies of Roman, Jewish and Christian Burials*, Berlin and New York, 39-78.

Walter, J. 2005. 'Archaeobotany', in R. S. Bagnall (ed.), *Amheida Project Field Reports*, Columbia University. This document is available online at http://www.leran.columbia.edu/amheida/html/field_reoprts.html.

Ward-Perkins, J. B., Balance, M. H. and Reynolds, T. M. 1958. 'The Caesareum at Cyrene and the Basilica at Cremna', *BPSR* 26, 137-94.

Wendland, P. 1903. 'Die hellenistischen Zeugnisse über die ägyptische Beschneidung', *AfP* 2, 22-31.

Wente, E. F. 1982. 'Funerary Beliefs of the Ancient Egyptians: An Interpretation of the Burials and the Texts', *Expedition* 24:2, 17-26.

Whitehorne, J. E. G. 1995. 'The Pagan Cults of Roman Oxyrhynchus', *ANRW* II 18.5, 3050-91.

Whitehouse, H. 2005. 'Wall-paintings of Area 2.1, Room 1', in R. S. Bagnall (ed.), *Amheida Project Field Reports*, Columbia University. This document is available online at http://www.learn.columbia.edu/amheida/html/field_reports.html.

Whittemore, T. 1914. 'The Ibis Cemetery at Abydos: 1914', *JEA* 1:4, 248-9.

Willeitner, J. 2004. 'Tomb and Burial Customs after Alexander the Great', in R, Schulz and M. Seidel(eds.), *Egypt the World of the Pharaohs*, Könemann, 313-21.

Willems, H. 1988. *Chests of Life: A Study of the Typology and Conceptual Development of Middle Kingdom Standard Class Coffins*, Leiden.

Wilson, J. A. 1944. 'Funeral Services of the Egyptian Old Kingdom', *JNES* 3:4, 201-18.

Wilson, P. 1997. *A Ptolemaic Lexicon: A Lexicographical Study of the Texts in the Temple of Edfu*, OLA 78, Leuven.

Wilson, P. 2001. *Sais* I: *The Ramesside-Third Intermediate Period at Kom Rebwa*, Egypt Exploration Society, London.

Witt, R. E. 1971. *Isis in the Graeco-Roman World*, London.

Wolinski, A. 1987. 'Egyptian Masks: The Priest and His Role', *Archaeology* 40 (1), 22-9.

Wormald, F. 1929. 'A Fragment of Accounts Dealing with Religious Festivals', *JEA* 15, 239-242.

Youtie, H. C. 1948. 'The *Kline* of Sarapis', *HTR* 41, 9-29.

Youtie, H. E. 1976. 'P. Mich. Inv. 795 and 853: Notification of Death', *ZPE* 22, 56-9.

Zanker, P. 1987. *Pompeji: Stadtbilder als Spiegel von Gesellschaft und Herrschaftsform,* Mainz.